D1564029

# Religion and Violence

# Religion and Violence

A Dialectical Engagement through the Insights
of Bernard Lonergan

Dominic Arcamone

☙PICKWICK *Publications* • Eugene, Oregon

RELIGION AND VIOLENCE
A Dialectical Engagement through the Insights of Bernard Lonergan

Pickwick Publications
An Imprint of Wipf and Stock Publishers
199 W. 8th Ave., Suite 3
Eugene, OR 97401

www.wipfandstock.com

ISBN 13: 978-1-4982-0694-5

*Cataloguing-in-Publication Data*

Arcamone, Dominic

Religion and violence : a dialectical engagement through the thoughts of Bernard Lonergan / Dominic Arcamone.

xii + 282 p. ; 23 cm. Includes bibliographical references.

ISBN 13: 978-1-4982-0694-5

1. Violence—Religious aspects. 2. Religion. 3. Lonergan, Bernard J. F. I. Title.

BL65.V55 A78 2015

Manufactured in the U.S.A.                                        08/13/2015

# Contents

# Acknowledgments

I WOULD LIKE TO thank Professor Neil Ormerod, of the Australian Catholic University, Faculty of Theology and Philosophy, School of Theology (New South Wales), for his mentoring and unwavering commitment and patience toward me during my doctoral studies. I would also like to thank Dr. Joel Hodge, of the School of Theology (Victoria) of the same university faculty, for his assistance, especially in helping me to understand the work of René Girard. To my lovely wife, Anita, my heartfelt thanks: I owe her a debt of gratitude. Finally, I acknowledge and appreciate the professional editorial assistance provided by Christopher Brennan.

# Introduction

IN SOCIAL AND CULTURAL milieus across the globe, religion and violence are often linked dramatically by the actions of violent religious agents, and intellectually by academics, commentators, and authors who seek to understand these actions.[1] The link between violent struggle and the Koran has become commonplace in Western media since the events of September 11, 2001. More broadly, diverse groups and individuals across the religious spectrum have been involved in violent actions: so-called Christian groups blow up abortion clinics for the purpose of killing health professionals involved with acts of abortion; Jewish fundamentalist groups defend militarily their perceived religious right to the land of Israel; Islamic groups carry out suicide bombings, in the claim that they are doing the will of God. The aim of this book is specifically to understand the link between religion and violence by religious agents who are concerned to bring social and cultural change through violent struggle and usually with a political outcome in mind.

The link between religion and violence is also a common theme in the polemical narratives of current atheistic thinkers such as Richard Dawkins, Christopher Hitchens, and Sam Harris.[2] Visitors to their websites and readers of their books find them espousing religion as a detrimental influence on social progress; a cause of division, violence and hatred; and as intellectually deficient in the light of knowledge from the natural and human sciences.

Broadly reflecting on the experience of religion and violence, the International Theological Commission, a consultative body of the Catholic

---

1. See Bellinger, "Religion and Violence." Bellinger gives a long list of books on religion and violence written post September 11, 2001.

2. Hitchens, *God Is Not Great*; Dawkins, *God Delusion*; and Sam Harris, *End of Faith*, 26–30. Harris attributes the death of millions of people to religion and describes faith as the "mother of hatred."

Church, released a document in December 1999 titled *Memory and Reconciliation: The Church and the Faults of the Past.* The document was a response to earlier actions by Pope John Paul II, who had asked forgiveness for the past sins of the church, sinful actions supposedly in the service of truth. These actions included sins committed against: other Christian communities, Jews, the dignity of women, and the cultures and religions of other people.[3] The document exhorts the church to admit complicity with those who sinned through violence and to make reparation for its faults and errors from the period of the Crusades to the Holocaust. In effect, John Paul II—as pope, symbolizing unity and authority in the Catholic Church—was seeking forgiveness for violence perpetrated by Catholic Christians in the name of Christ. Through the commission's document, there was an invitation to a purification of memory. The call to purification highlighted that oppression can have a terrifying effect on victims and perpetrators to such a degree that societies develop the capacity to turn way from suffering, to forget witnessed horrors, and to suppress the memory of the past, thus affecting their identity and ability to grow. The way ahead requires a restructuring of memories and a remembering of the truth so that believers might be effective vehicles for liberation.

In seeking to understand more broadly the phenomenon of religiously motivated violence, we may ask: Is religion a force for healing in our world or is it a force for violence? Why do certain people religiously commit themselves to violent change? How and why is a distorted religious imagination joined to political goals by those who perpetrate violence? If violence is a mark of our not living as we should toward the other, can we construct an account of authentic living with the help of religion that may help us discern a path that goes beyond violence and that contributes to better human living?

I address these questions in this book, drawing upon the insights of the Canadian Catholic philosopher and theologian, Bernard Lonergan. In chapter 1, I will justify my choice of Lonergan for this task. Then in chapter 2, I will engage in a selective literature review around the link between religion and violence. This review will identify a number of key symbols by academics and commentators from the social and human sciences who are trying to demonstrate how religion and violence are intimately related. These key symbols are: cosmic war, martyrdom, demonization, and warrior empowerment. Through a dialectical engagement of these symbols, I

---

3. See John Paul II, Homily; Accattoli, *Pope Asks Forgiveness.* Accattoli documents the pope's sin apologies from the beginning of his pontificate to 1999.

will unpack the truthful and mistaken assertions around the link between religion, warfare, and social order.

In chapter 3, I will give an exposition of some of Lonergan's key theological and philosophical insights that will help us understand how religious aberration emerges and endures, and thus contributes to violence, and how authentic religion can yet be a source of healing for overcoming violence. An exploration of the four key symbols mentioned above will then be the subject of chapters 4 to 9, using the insights offered by Lonergan and by others as a way of critiquing the validity of certain claims.

Accordingly, in chapter 4, I will explore the term "cosmos" within the symbol of cosmic war. I will argue that a better way of understanding the violently motivated religious believer is through the dialectic of grace and sin. However, I will show that such a dialectic carries a number of dangers and that the practice of violence as a means to political and social change is fraught with error since it does not grasp the subtlety of human world processes. Using the distinction between the secular and the sacred, I will discuss how a secular order can be a combination of both culturally legitimate and illegitimate meanings and values, and I will explore how a sacred order can be a combination of both culturally legitimate and culturally illegitimate meanings and values.

In chapter 5, I will explore the term "warfare" within the symbol of cosmic war. The claim is made that religion and warfare work naturally together since both have the goal of establishing social order. I will argue that this is usually the outworking of distorted religious traditions, which can be a tool in the hands of those who would seek to justify warfare within both religious communities and secular societies, so as achieve certain political ends. In chapter 6, I will present a constructive view for approaching warfare drawing on the just war tradition, which has come out of the Christian tradition and privileges the demands of justice with love of God and neighbor. I will offer a dialectical engagement with the three major criteria that inform *ius ad bellum* or deliberations on whether to resort to warfare.

In chapter 7, I will dialectically engage with the symbol of martyrdom, which has become a key category used by militant Islamic groups to honor those motivated by religious violence. I will seek to give some normative understanding of martyrdom within both the Christian community and the Islamic community, exploring an authentic meaning of self-sacrifice as distinct from the self-immolation of suicide martyrdom. In chapter 8, I will dialectically engage with the symbol of demonization, arguing that there is a difference between demonizing the other and naming the demonic. Without an understanding of this difference, victims and perpetrators may never arrive at a place beyond violence. In chapter 9, I will engage with the symbol of warrior empowerment, arguing that the insight of warriors engaged in violence for the sake of feeling empowered is only a partial account of what is going on in the hearts and minds of warriors. Religious imagination carries the possibility of empowering warriors; however, I will argue that what matters is the kind of empowerment being enacted. I will argue that warrior empowerment can be both an authentic and an inauthentic development and that both occur in different religious and cultural contexts. Yet within religious traditions we can find an understanding of warrior empowerment consistent with authenticity. In chapter 10, I will state my conclusions, briefly summarizing the arguments of the previous chapters.

# 1

# Why Draw on the Insights of Bernard Lonergan?

AT THIS POINT, I want to present a justification for turning to the insights of the Catholic Canadian theologian and philosopher, Bernard Lonergan. While Lonergan's works do not specifically concern themselves with religiously motivated violence, his insights nevertheless address the problem of violence by examining the performance of the subject as subject and by providing a philosophical analysis of the self-transcending subject. Lonergan postulates a set of foundational categories for discerning how we come to have religious knowledge, an explanatory account of historical progress and breakdown in human history, and a way forward for recovery in history that is achieved through authentic religious living.

I have also chosen two other conversation partners, namely, René Girard and Charles Taylor, and I provide a selective exposition of their insights. In contrast to the other authors I have chosen in the literature review, I will not subject these writers to any extended critique. Though there are differences in their approaches from that of Lonergan, their insights nevertheless complement his. However, I will argue that Lonergan's insights provide a much more nuanced approach for understanding religion, and for understanding violence and the means to overcoming violence through authentic religion.

## A Common Ground

More than any other philosopher and theologian that I know of, Bernard Lonergan seeks "a common ground on which [people] of intelligence might

meet."[1] Lonergan states that "the plain fact is that the world is in pieces before [us] and pleads to be put together again, to be put together not as it
stood before on the careless foundation of assumptions that happened to
be unquestioned but on the strong possibility of questioning and with full
awareness of the range of possible answers."[2] Such a crisis of which Lonergan speaks is a crisis of meaning, and the common ground he proposes is
the possibility of questioning in a collaborative manner. In any intellectual
culture that is saturated with subjectivism, relativism, historicism, dogmatism, and skepticism, the possibility of a common ground is viewed negatively. But the common ground in Lonergan's work, *Insight*, emerges not as
a set philosophical worldview; rather, it is a method founded in a basic set
of invariant and normative operations in human consciousness, the transcultural norms of self-transcending inquiry that constitutes all people as
knowers and choosers within an explanatory account of insight.[3]

Lonergan's common ground shifts the debate concerning the possibility of objectivity from the priority of language or logic to the priority of
method, discovered in the concrete performance of the subject as subject.
He thus proposes that a generalized empirical method is able to provide a
foundation for intellectual and moral objectivity.[4] The foundation of epis-
temology is cognitional theory, while the foundation of cognitional theory
is the performance of the subject as subject. This foundation is not the same
as the foundationalism spoken against by many postmodern thinkers, nor
is it just one other method among many methods. Rather, it is the subject's
lifting of attention above specific principles and historical models to the
methodological criteria by which we judge what is real, choose what is better or worse, and act in love. Genuine objectivity is then the consequence of
authentic subjectivity.[5]

All knowledge, whether theological, religious, philosophical, scientific,
moral, or practical is grounded in insights or acts of understanding, so that
one's normative source of meaning is insight into insight. Robert Doran, in
his notes on Lonergan's major work, *Insight*, gives a summary of the multiplicity of insights that we could potentially recognize in our experience.[6]

---

1. Lonergan, *Insight*, 7.

2. Ibid., 552.

3. Lonergan, *Method*, 4. Lonergan states that a method "is a normative pattern of
recurrent and related operations yielding cumulative and progressive results."

4. Ibid., 3–25; Lonergan, *Third Collection*, 140–44.

5. Lonergan, *Method*, 265.

6. Doran, "Introductory Lecture," 3. Doran explains the difference in meaning and
the interrelationship between various kinds of insights that Lonergan identifies: direct
insights, inverse insights, identifying insights, reflective insights, introspective insights,

Lonergan states that "insight is the source not only of theoretical knowledge but also of all its practical implications, and indeed all its intelligent activity. Insight into insight will reveal what activity is intelligent, and insight into oversights will reveal what activity is unintelligent."[7]

Any historical moment within a community will contain both insight and oversight intertwined. While insight can promote progress, oversight grounded in bias engenders decline. When oversight occurs, Lonergan asserts that

> we reinforce our love of truth with a practicality that is equivalent to obscurantism. We correct old evils with a passion that mars the new good. We are not pure. We compromise. We hope to muddle through. But the very advance of knowledge brings a power over nature and over men too vast and terrifying to be entrusted to the good intentions of unconsciously biased minds. We have to learn to distinguish sharply between progress and decline, learn to encourage progress without putting premiums upon decline . . . learn to remove the tumor of a flight from understanding without destroying the organs of intelligence.[8]

## The Differentiation of Consciousness

In *Method in Theology* Lonergan explains acts of meaning and their relation to the various differentiations of human consciousness, concluding that each realm of meaning can mix, blend, and operate in different ways within the subject.[9] Lonergan's examination of the "unfolding of a single thrust, the eros of the human spirit" from undifferentiated to differentiated realms of consciousness reveals a movement of the human mind out of a world in which reality is known directly and immediately to a world in which reality is mediated by meaning.[10] I will give a full account of these realms in chapter 3.

Here, though, I particularly want to focus on an observation by Robert M. Doran, who has done much to expound Lonergan's insights, and who argues that the concrete experience of contemporary life is taking place in a social and cultural milieu permeated by a vast increase in knowledge. Many complex theories have emerged from diverse disciplines, including

philosophic insights, metaphysical insights, genetic insights, dialectical insights, practical insights, limit insights, religious insights and theological insights.

7. Lonergan, *Insight*, 7–8.

8. Ibid., 8.

9. Lonergan, *Method*, 81–86, 227.

10. Ibid., 13.

theology, psychology and sociology, as well as the natural sciences, but such a milieu moves toward greater and greater specialization so that only a small dimension of any one field of study can be mastered.[11] Doran therefore states that unless we find "a ground beyond theory—for it will not do just to fall back on common sense—our situation becomes one of hopeless relativism"; moreover, this "ground beyond theory (and common sense) lies in the self-appropriation of interiority."[12]

Therefore I argue that discovering a better understanding of reality and enacting practical solutions toward the kind of violence justified by a distorted religious imagination will require a shift to take place in the performing subject. It will require that we move to what Lonergan calls "the third stage of meaning," which takes its stand in interiority, and which shifts its concern from the content of meanings to acts of meaning, from products to sources of products, from objects to operations in consciousness.[13] Lonergan states that we must "discover mind" and be able to distinguish "feeling from doing, knowing from deciding."[14]

## The Task of Self-Appropriation

Lonergan's writings are not so much concerned to present us with the content of any particular theological topic in order that we might argue authoritatively that "these are Lonergan's ideas on this topic." Rather, his key philosophical and theological insights are more concerned to lead us into a process of self-appropriation: the self-discovery and self-awareness of our knowing, choosing, loving, and religious selves by helping us experience ourselves in the full register of consciousness. Lonergan says "understand understanding and you will understand much of what there is to be understood."[15] All human development begins in the act of wonder, the spontaneous desire to understand.[16] According to Jerome Miller, self-appropriation helps the inquirer discover wonder so that through the experience of wonder, the inquirer and chooser can work from the "heart," where "to be heart is to be precisely this vulnerability, this defenselessness, this being-broken-open to all that is beyond the given. Wonder is, indeed the principle, the arche, of all intentional operations; but far from providing

11. Doran, *Intentionality and Psyche*, 405.

12. Ibid.

13. Lonergan, *Method*, 85.

14. Ibid., 90.

15. Lonergan, *Insight*, xxviii.

16. Ibid., 173, 185, 330.

the heart with an undeconstructible foundation, wonder insures that the heart will be radically and irreparably affected by all that will happen to it by virtue of being caught in its throe."[17]

Any person can be held under the sway of a violent ideology, whether religious or secular. By contrast, self-appropriation is an important process for those wanting to judge what is real, to deliberate on what is valuable, and so to overcome violence, whether in practical living or as academics writing objectively on these matters.[18] This process is not meant to provide the inquirer with a passionless foundation or to lead the inquirer to some impersonal objectivity. Rather, this process helps the inquirer integrate feeling, thought, decision, and action.

## The Importance of Authenticity

I have chosen Lonergan's approach in my exploration of the link between religion and violence because I am convinced that his approach necessarily speaks to the drama of human existence as authentic and inauthentic. By authenticity, Lonergan does not mean some form of moral superiority or elitist authority over others. To live an authentic life is the vocation of all people in order to realize their humanity. Lonergan states that persons "achieve authenticity in self-transcendence," that is, one's authenticity as a person does not rely on following abstract propositions but on following the operations of consciousness, living in the concrete and specific circumstances of one's life, and seeking direction to life even as one comes up against the limits of death, suffering, guilt, and struggle.[19] Authenticity involves studying the data of consciousness and discovering the inbuilt precepts that draw us along the path to authenticity. Self-transcendence is always an ongoing activity through conversion in such a way that the subject is committed to the drama of making one's life a work of art while negotiating the gap between the self we are and the inbuilt dynamism of the spirit.[20]

---

17. Miller, "All Love Is Self-Surrender," 63–64.

18. In a 1942 book review, Lonergan linked the excesses of capitalism, communism, and Nazism, stating that "their consequences are not a matter of abstract deduction. The experiment has been performed and still is being performed *on the quivering body of humanity.* The results are not pleasant" (my italics). Lonergan was reviewing the book, *Is Modern Culture Doomed?* by Andrew Krzensinski (New York: Devin-Adair, 1942) in the *Canadian Register*, September 19, 1949, page 8. Lonergan was subsequently quoted by Lamb, "Social and Political Dimensions," 269–70.

19. Lonergan, *Method*, 104.

20. Ibid., 270.

This dynamism of authenticity contrasts then with the two kinds of inauthenticity that Lonergan identifies: minor and major.[21] Minor inauthenticity pertains to the subject's adhering to a received tradition that has already been distorted yet which is accepted in good faith. The hope is that persons more in tune with an authentic heritage may persuade those who have received a distorted heritage to change. Major inauthenticity pertains to subjects who deliberately distort a tradition and through their own biases suppress questions that might lead to renewal and development. In choosing violence as a response to situations, religious agents not only desire to bring about a pragmatic change to their environment through a destructive venting of anger but they also end up changing themselves into men and women of violence. This change can all too easily result in a distorted understanding of a tradition. It is Lonergan's contention that violence, though seemingly useful to some, curtails self-transcendence and so destroys cultural achievements, sets a civilization into decline, and mutilates societies by "increasing division, incomprehension, suspicion, distrust, hostility, hatred and [further] violence."[22]

To demonstrate how religion might help heal those engaged in violence, we must also understand the content of diverse religious traditions and the manner by which violent religious agents either follow the insights of a distorted tradition handed onto them or intentionally distort and depart from their authentic source tradition. Here again, we come up against the problem not only of a difference in content but in the degree of authenticity within a tradition and among the adherents of the tradition. Differences between the content of religious traditions are explored by both comparative religion scholars and historians of religion by addressing questions for understanding, thus interpreting the data empirically and critically. Yet at the same time, questions of authenticity and inauthenticity within a tradition cannot be put aside. When theologians and academics from other disciplines appropriate the data of religious traditions, their concern should not only be empirical and critical but also dialectical, thus shifting the concern to authentic human existence, values worth preserving, and commitment to the truth. Lonergan asserts the impossibility of grounding any religious argument without understanding the religious horizon of the subject, determining his or her existential stance, and assessing the difference between authentic and inauthentic stances that might ground incompatible horizons.

21. Ibid., 80.
22. Ibid., 244.

## The Nature of Religion

Many scholars have questioned the nature of religion. Some academics claim that there is no normative approach to any field of study, proposing a value-free approach to religious phenomena, and understanding religious performances solely from a rigorous historical and sociological narrative perspective. Such a critique yields examples of enormous sanctity within a religious community or, alternatively, examples of violence (persecutions, violent crusades, witch hunts, and ethnic cleansing), all under the banner of religion. These descriptive sociologies often identify religiously motivated violent acts without investigating the broader how and why of their emergence and survival, and without investigating the value-laden presuppositions operative in the mind of the researcher that affect his or her research. These issues raise questions as to the relationship between theology and the social and human sciences that are, however, beyond the scope of this work.[23]

From a descriptive point of view, nevertheless, one could state that there are many examples of religious agents who continue to use violence in dealing with other people or who turn to violent sacred texts to justify the religious claims of their actions. From a normative point of view, I will argue that genuine religion actively works to reduce violence in the world through self-giving love and service. Nor can social scientists simply accept evil as part of the way groups and societies function. Theology draws the problem of evil in both its social and cultural manifestations to the attention of the social and human scientist, and identifies a supernatural solution to evil that goes beyond the knowledge that these sciences can offer. This normative vision can be shown to be internally consistent with the claims of Christianity, Judaism, and Islam and ultimately must be radically contrasted to any violence-riddled descriptive account of religion.

With regard to the nature of religion, on one side of the debate, there are scholars such as William T. Cavanaugh who argue against substantive, essentialist, and functionalist understandings of religion, concluding that there is "no transhistorical or transcultural concept of religion" and that all religion must be assessed according to its historical particularity alone.[24] Cavanaugh rightly emphasizes the importance of historical data in any understanding of the link between religion and violence and warns us against totalizing discourses about religion founded in power relations, especially when the discourse is provided by the state.[25]

23. On this relationship, see Ormerod, "Dialectical Engagement"; Baum, "Remarks of a Theologian."

24. Cavanaugh, *Myth of Religious Violence*, 59, 101–18.

25. Ibid., 119–22.

Other scholars have taken an approach that looks for "family resemblances" or dimensions across a range of religious expressions, preferring to ask the question: What categories can be used to systematize our experience of religion across various traditions?[26] This phenomenological approach takes the empirical method of the sciences as its starting point. One example of the latter is the work of Ninian Smart. He examines religion through the lens of seven dimensions: the practical and ritual; the experiential and emotional; the narrative and mythic; the doctrinal and philosophical; the ethical and legal; the social and institutional; and the material.[27] Smart's approach insightfully draws attention to the full scope of these dimensions rather than focus simply on ritual, myths, and doctrines, as is usually the case. The oversight of his approach, however, is a decision not to prioritize the existential dimension that is concerned with religious commitment, thereby not allowing for the possibility of distinguishing authentic and inauthentic religious observance. The attempt to use the empirical methods of the natural sciences in the social and human sciences thus also overlooks the fact that in the human sciences the researcher studies subjects in such a way that meaning and value become operative in both the research and the researcher. As Johnston notes, Smart's scheme could be helped by the further dimension of wisdom, which favors the synthesis of all the dimensions and allows for a greater coherence among them.[28]

Lonergan, by contrast, has a distinctive approach to the nature of genuine religion. For him, authentic religion, which begins in God's love for us, and moves us to love God and others, becomes a God-given fulfillment to the thrust of human consciousness.[29] Lonergan comes from the horizon of a Catholic theologian and philosopher within a Western tradition concerned to explain the manner by which the doctrines of the Catholic Church actually shape both a search for God, values and truth, and pastoral actions for Christian people. Lonergan sees the shift from theology to religious studies as part of a general cultural shift from classicist culture to an historically minded culture; from the first enlightenment, where religion was judged to be superstitious, to the second enlightenment, where religion is purged of inauthenticity, so that subjects may be known not only abstractly by nature,

26. This phrase is used by Ludwig Wittgenstein. See his *Philosophical Investigations*, sections 66 and 67.

27. Smart, *World's Religions*, 10–25.

28. Johnston, "Whatever Happened to Doctrine?," 184.

29. Lonergan, *Method*, 244, and 338: "What sublates goes beyond what is sublated, introducing something new and distinct, yet so far from interfering with the sublated or destroying it, on the contrary needs it, preserves all its proper features and properties, and carries them forward to a fuller realisation within a richer context."

but also concretely by history, not only by what we are but also by what we do.[30] The nature of religion is therefore appropriated by a shift from the realm of theory to the realms of interiority and transcendence (discussed in greater detail in chapter 3) in such a way that the inquirer can distinguish between Cavanaugh's emphasis on the historical context, Smart's phenomenological approach to religion, and Lonergan's theological approach to religion. Within this shift, Lonergan's notion of religion, though coming out of the Catholic Christian tradition, is not explicitly or even necessarily Christian. His notion places the emphasis on religious self-transcendence, being in love in an unrestricted manner, the experience of religious faith, the importance of religious conversion, and the difference between religious faith and belief.

## Historicity and Dialectic

The notions of historicity and dialectic are crucial to Lonergan and these will be discussed in greater depth in chapter 3. However, for the moment, it is worth noting that any solution to religiously motivated violence demands that the inquirer analyze the historical context and identify the set of conditions that may have influenced the violent decisions of religious agents. History as the ongoing change in human affairs is central to Lonergan's approach since history is what we make of ourselves.[31] The historian's concern is "what was going forward," which may have been "development or . . . the handing on of development and each of these may be . . . complete or . . . incomplete."[32] Such events are the product of religious, personal, cultural, and social influences from the past impacting on the subject's horizon and setting about anticipations for the future. Lonergan is committed to exposing the flaws in an ahistorical orthodoxy within traditions, since the shapers of history must be men and women of authenticity and self-transcendence, whether through the cognitional performance of articulating theology or through the dramatic performance of living a good life.

Lonergan uses two notions of dialectic: the first concerns the historical interplay of drivers of development that underlie the actual moral growth of persons and communities, and the second, more analytic notion, brings out competing and divergent positions. Dialectic in the first sense notes that development is constituted by a tension between linked but opposed

---

30. Riley, "Theology and/or Religious Studies," 120; Lonergan, *Lonergan Reader*, 562–65.

31. Lonergan, *Third Collection*, 170.

32. Ibid., 180.

principles or drivers of development within persons, cultures, and communities.[33] As Dunne states, "a dialectical model of moral development will
anticipate that the community will be a moving, concrete resultant of the
mutual conditioning of these . . . drivers."[34] Yet given that any historical
community is a mixture of authenticity and inauthenticity, it is only through
a mutual disclosure of a person's feelings, questioning, thinking, and valuing
that conflicting differences between people can be identified. This process
is dialectic in the second sense, functioning to bring to light each person's
stance, seeking to articulate conflicts between contrary orientations. These
conflicts may be found in research, interpretations, histories, styles of
evaluation, and ultimately doctrines, systems, and policies within religious
traditions, as well as in conflicts between religious traditions and secular
traditions, and in what would constitute an authentic tradition of religious
and moral progress.[35]

It is also important to acknowledge a dialectical relation between
the mentality of the religious subject and the social and cultural values in
society, recognizing that individual development can condition social development, and historical development can condition individual development. Lonergan is committed to exploring historical consciousness and the
manner by which persons, cultures, and communities interrelate with one
another to provide a solution to the problems of human living.[36] Solutions
need to take account of the mutual conditioning between cultural and social
influences in such a way that cultures of integrity require a social infrastructure and, at the same time, social infrastructure requires cultural integrity.
There is a tension between the "microhorizon of the individual" and the
"macrohorizon of the community," and a tension within the community
itself between bonds of connection and practical intelligence.[37] Finally, the
subject's self-transcendence must negotiate not only a complicated set of
conditions within the human situation but also the human situation itself,
between finitude and the infinite.[38]

33. Lonergan, *Insight*, 242.

34. Dunne, *Doing Better*, 175.

35. Lonergan, *Method*, 235.

36. Lonergan, *Third Collection*, 169–83.

37. McPartland, *Philosophy of Historical Existence*, 56–64.

38. Ibid., 66.

## Dialectic and the Scale of Values

Lonergan asserts that our historical existence is founded on our natural duties to society and one another through a stance of mutual care guided by a hierarchy or scale of values. This hierarchy of values is the basis for a greater explanatory account of history through postulating the dialectic within the subject, culture, and community; the interrelationship between the various levels of the scale; and an acknowledgment of the two vectors, of creativity and of healing, in human history.[39] I will also explore this account of history in greater detail in chapter 3.

Dialectic represents the tension between limitation and transcendence within each level of the scale, where self-transcendence is an ongoing negotiation of this tension to a higher integration. When the tension is broken, the result is a failure to achieve self-transcendence. Robert Doran gives an explanatory account of humankind's making of history by providing a theological theory of history that helps identify progress, decline, and restoration in persons, cultures, and communities. Lonergan and Doran's notion of dialectic will be important to understanding the creative tensions within the dialectic of community, culture, and persons; how violence can give rise to a failure in integrity; and how integrity is restored to human communities through attending to the healing vector in the scale of values.[40]

## Conclusion

The insights adumbrated above form my justification for choosing Lonergan's thought to address the questions of how and why violence and religious imagination combine. In the next chapter, I will give a selective literature review that explores religiously motivated violence.

39. Lonergan, *Third Collection*, 100–9; Doran, "Suffering Servant"; Doran, "Analogy of Dialectics" ; Doran, *Dialectics of History*, 93–107; Lonergan, *Method*, 31–32.

40. Lonergan, *Insight*, 269.

# 2

# A Selective Literature Review

IN THIS CHAPTER I review selective literature dealing with religiously motivated violence. My choice of authors is based on a desire to listen to a
diverse range of representative voices who have written academically in the
field from various perspectives: cultural anthropological, philosophical and
theological, psychological, and sociological. These authors include René
Girard, Charles Taylor, James W. Jones, and Mark Juergensmeyer.

## René Girard: Cultural Anthropology and Mimetic Theory

In terms of a cultural anthropology, René Girard has extensively explored
the roots of violence and its relationship to religion, though it is difficult
to pinpoint his writings as belonging to any one body of literature since
he covers literary theory, cultural studies, anthropology, scriptural exegesis,
and psychology.[1] There is much debate as to whether his writings represent
a systematic theory or are simply a number of key guiding insights for understanding violence in our world.[2] His insights have influenced a number
of scholars, including Sebastian Moore, Gil Bailie, Robert Daly, Michael
Kirwan, and James Alison.[3] There are a further range of scholars who have
entered into dialogue with Girard's insights to clarify some of his central
notions.[4]

1. Kirwan, *Discovering Girard*, 91–93.

2. Kirwan, *Girard and Theology*, 6–9.

3. Moore, *Contagion of Jesus*; Bailie, *Violence Unveiled*; Daly, *Sacrifice Unveiled*;
Kirwan, *Discovering Girard*; Kirwan, *Girard and Theology*; Alison, *Knowing Jesus*; Alison, *Joy of Being Wrong*.

4. Ormerod, "Eucharist as Sacrifice" ; Doran, "Essays in Systematic Theology 24,"
1–42.

I will now explore some key Girardian insights in three sections: the mechanism of desire and how it functions in society, the scapegoat mechanism, and the Judeo-Christian revelation.

## The Mechanism of Desire

First, Girard's writings are concerned with the mechanism of desire and its relationship to society. Girard's mechanism could be summed up in this simple statement: *we desire according to the desire of another*.[5] As such, Girard departs from the Freudian notion that the desires of an individual subject wait to be triggered as soon as some enticing object crosses his or her path. In this way, Girard challenges the view that there is some inherent quality in any object that directly attracts us prior to the object's having some significance within a community. Rather, Girard asserts that subjects are constituted by desires mediated through others. Our subjectivity and our experience of desires are profoundly formed socially and relationally. Even our freedom depends on being constituted by the other.[6] This intersubjective dimension moves desires from an instinctual base to human interiority. The intrinsic goodness of mimetic desire indicates a structure that liberates humans from instinct. Mimetic desire is distinguished from instinct or "appetite" since, while instinct is biologically determined as sociality, sexuality, and self-preservation, desire is malleable and open to development through intersubjectivity.[7]

Desire as intersubjective can be said to be triangular: the subject of desire/"respondent", the model/"rival," and the desired object are the three points of the triangle.[8] Girard uses the term "mimetic" to describe the simulated and triangular nature of desire between the subject, the model, and the object. Mimesis means that our desire is evoked in us while those from whom we "borrow" our desires are our models, mentors, or mediators. Mimesis builds on the assumption that humans possess a remarkable capacity for imitation.[9] Indeed, we often imitate others without being fully aware that we are imitating them, which also helps explain why it is that rivalry is so common. The mimetic nature of desire emphasizes the appearance rather than the reality of spontaneity and therefore less autonomy. It

5. Girard, *Girard Reader*, 9–10.

6. Girard, *I See Satan Fall*, 137 n. 2.

7. Kirwan, *Girard and Theology*, 50.

8. Webb, *Self Between*, 92.

9. Alison, *Joy of Being* Wrong, 10.

further explains why people might find no significance in an object until it is appreciated by another, giving the object a new meaning for them.

Normally, the structure of mimetic desire can lead to good relationships and actions: unobstacled, pacific, or nonrivalistic desire.[10] However, when two persons desire the same object, rivalry ensues. Without rivalry, desire itself can languish. Girard states:

> Our first task is to define the rival's position within the system to which he belongs, in relation to both subject and object. The rival desires the same object as the subject and to assert the primacy of the rival can lead to just one conclusion. Rivalry does not arise because of the fortuitous convergence of two desires on a single object; rather the subject desires the object because the rival desires it. In desiring an object, the rival alerts the subject of the desirability of the object. The rival then serves as a model for the subject, not only in regard to such secondary matters as style and opinions but also, and more essentially, in regard to desires.[11]

When desire leads to rivalistic action, Girard distinguishes between internal mediation, external mediation, and double mediation.[12] In rivalistic action characterized by internal mediation, the subject and the model become competitors within the same field of action, often due to their proximity to one another. With external mediation, the subject and the model are less likely to be rivals, since they are not in proximity and the object is outside their field of action.

Robert Doran, commenting on Girard's insight concerning internal mediation, concludes: "While all mimetic desire runs the risk of impairing the victim's perceptions of reality, since the desirability of the object stems not from its own merits but from its designation by the mediator, in internal mediation the result is always conflict, even hatred. That is not the case in external mediation. In internal mediation the rivals can come to resemble each other through the identity of their desires, so that finally they are no more than each other's doubles. The actual source of any desire is so obscured that the subject may even reverse the logical and chronological order of desires in order to hide his or her imitation."[13]

With double mediation, the subject who supposedly desires what the model desires finds the model imitating the desires of the subject in a

10. Ibid., 13; Girard, *I See Satan Fall*, 13. For example, Jesus invites us to imitate his desire for the Father. There is a difference between ordinary imitation and discipleship.

11. Girard, *Violence and the Sacred*, 145.

12. Girard, *Girard Reader*, 33–44.

13. Doran, "Mimesis," 156.

feedback process.[14] The distance or proximity between the model and the subject in each of these mediations is spiritual and psychological rather than only physical.[15]

According to Girard, rivalry can escalate to the point of violence through scandal. The model becomes both guide and obstacle to the attaining of a desire. The desire of the model increases and intensifies as he or she notices the desire of the subject/respondent. This intensification reaches such a level that the originally desired object loses much of its attraction and assumes secondary importance. This intense and preconscious rivalry adversely affects the ability of the subject to understand and make proper judgements. What becomes primary is that the rivals become more and more fascinated with each other as rivals. The desire of the respondent, first focused toward the object, shifts toward the model that inspired or evoked desire in the object. The model arrives at a situation of a double bind: imitate me and do not imitate me.[16] The model is both model/rival and model/obstacle, and therefore a state of scandal arises.[17] The consequences are that rivals become locked in a gravitational field of attraction generated by their competition. Even if the respondent were to triumph over the rival/model, it would not be long before the new model would find another rival. The more these rivalries intensify, the more these roles of model and respondent become interchangeable at the heart of a conflict, so that each comes to possess equal amounts of envy, jealousy, and hatred.[18] Rivals are transformed into mimetic doubles, mirroring the other's emotions and actions. In the end, mimetic rivalry erases differences and the loss of differences fosters even more mimetic rivalry.

When rivalry reaches this point, desire is no longer fixated on what people do, or how they appear, or what object they seek, but on *the desire to be the other*. With the growth of rivalistic competition, the prestige of the model grows because possession of the object seems to have invested the model with self-sufficiency, or greater being, or some special quality that the imitating subject/respondent lacks or feels to be lacking and finds desirable. Mimetic desire now becomes the *desire to be another*,[19] which Girard

---

14. Webb, *Self Between*, 95.

15. Girard, *Deceit, Desire*, 9.

16. Girard, *Things Hidden*, 291.

17. Girard, *Violence and the Sacred*, 147, 161. For Girard, "scandal" means stumbling block.

18. Kirwan, *Discovering Girard*, 41.

19. Girard, *Deceit, Desire*, 282.

calls "metaphysical desire" or "primordial desire."[20] The model that evokes my desire possesses a fullness of being that I lack. Girard notes that the romantic cult of individuality or originality serves to make clear what really is at issue, namely, that through mimesis the subject does not seek an object of desire but the mode of existence of the model.

Eugene Webb makes a sober analysis of "metaphysical desire."[21] Metaphysical desire is the foundation for the desire of all other objects. The objects are a means to greater being and self-sufficiency. We want what people have because we feel it makes us into what they are. The object is a means to an end. Yet the simplest and most popular tactic for denying our desire to possess the being of another is to attribute the source of desire to the attractive power of objects. In this way, we can claim that the desire is our own and can discard it when we want to, without having to admit that dependency, envy, or imitation have anything to do with it, since to admit such dependency is to admit an inequality between ourselves and models.

Trying to assuage felt unfulfilled desire in us leads beyond the disappointment we feel in objects toward a felt sense of nothingness: emptiness, violence, and destruction. To flee from one's own emptiness into seeking the supposed being of another by desiring what they desire, one hurls oneself into darkness, sacrificing one's own life in the vain hope that by joining to another's life one's own will have a meaning.[22] The consequences for violence are clear: in the quest to join another with real power, one will seek out increasingly powerful figures to try to win the object from them that will fulfill desire, thus increasing violent conflict. There are only two options: either we let this false task go as something hopeless in life or we redouble our efforts and escalate the violence. The second of these alternatives means that the respondent engages in masochistic identification.[23] The respondent seeking the fullness of being in the model tries to gain it imaginatively by identifying with the power of the model and subordinating his or her vulnerable existence to the model.[24]

## Religion and the Scapegoat Mechanism

For Girard, there is a definite relationship between mimesis, violence, and religion. Girard's simple assertion is that violence is the heart and soul of the

20. Webb, *Worldviews and Mind*, 83.

21. Ibid., 79–82.

22. Webb, *Self Between*, 97–99.

23. Webb, *Worldviews and Mind*, 82.

24. Ibid., 81–84.

sacred in archaic societies. Religion presents the Divine, who is inaccessible and impenetrable.[25] Violent opposition toward others is the signifier of the desire for divine self-sufficiency. Religiously, even the desire for God can become a desire to acquire the object and the identity of the model. This desire emerges out of a sense of ontological incompleteness revealed in the dynamics of mimetic desire. Humans can model themselves on God so as to become like God in order to acquire what God has and is. One strives to have the power of the Divine since one is ashamed at one's lack of being. To desire or obey the Divine is to turn to the source of all power, the ultimate owner of all that is desirable. If all desire and desiring is primarily primordial desire, that is, seeking to overcome the felt lack of a fullness of being, religion could easily gravitate toward becoming masochistically structured.

Girard, influenced by Durkheimian sociology, postulates an interrelationship between religion and social order. This is the kind of religion that is unrelated to the genuine experience of the transcendent but rather comes about due to unconscious human processes. Religion is born in an effort to preserve the unity and peace brought about in society by the killing of the scapegoat. Indeed for Girard, an act of collective murder against the victim is foundational to all human culture.[26] Since mimetic desire becomes mimetic rivalry, a situation of all in rivalry against all ensues and becomes the formula for social disharmony and long-term breakdown.[27] Girard proposes that social chaos comes to an end when a victim(s) or scapegoat(s) is chosen by the larger group.[28] This choosing begins in an arbitrary gesture directed against the potential scapegoat, who is viewed as being responsible for the collapse of order. The situation is transformed from all against all to a state of all against one.[29] This process is called the "scapegoat mechanism" and religious expression has, in the past, been the caretaker of social harmony through the scapegoat mechanism.[30]

Since guilt and innocence are ambiguously present in each person, by choosing a scapegoat, the rivals now have a victim. The victim turned enemy can come from within or from without the society; if from within the society, the victim is expelled; if from outside society, a "holy war" is

---

25. Girard, *Violence and the Sacred*, 148.

26. Kirwan, *Discovering Girard*, 54.

27. Ibid., 44–46. According to Kirwan, Girard stands in direct contrast to Hobbes's theory of the social contract.

28. Girard, *I See Satan Fall*, 154–60.

29. Kirwan, *Discovering Girard*, 49.

30. Ibid., 49. Kirwan asserts that Girard uses the term "scapegoat" not in a religious sense but in an everyday sense, as an unconsciousness psychological mechanism.

declared.[31] The victim, chosen on the basis of not being able to retaliate or take vengeance on the rivals, is subsequently sacrificed and becomes the bringer of unity to the group. The mechanism of scapegoating is allowed to occur and recur only because the group represses this mechanism. Those who scapegoat never believe themselves to be murdering or expelling innocent victims.[32] Finally, the victim is pronounced by the perpetrators of violence as god-like since through these actions and the scapegoat's death, the group is united.[33]

This mechanism for generating order persists even in post-religious societies. Girard further explores the fundamental role of scapegoating in society and culture once religious rites and rituals are no longer widely accepted, as in secular agnostic societies. As long as rites are able to preserve the distinction between the "good" violence sanctioned by religion and the "bad" violence of a community engulfed in mimetic chaos, then the community remains relatively stable. But when the rituals and myths of a community begin to lose their effectiveness and no longer insulate the community from violence, the community descends into a "sacrificial crisis."[34] The erosion of the distinction between pure and impure violence means that purification is no longer possible, and impure, contagious, reciprocal violence spreads throughout the community. Whole groups turn on each other.[35] Girard asserts that inevitably "the eroding of the sacrificial system seems to result in the emergence of reciprocal violence. Neighbors who had previously discharged their mutual aggressions on a third party, joining together in the sacrifice of an 'outside' victim, now turn to sacrificing one another."[36]

## The Judeo-Christian Revelation

For Girard, there is only one way by which a society perceives that a culture is founded on a lie. It requires that a community give rise to a slow and long discovery that victims can be innocent.[37] According to Girard, the revela-

---

31. Ibid., 52.

32. Girard, *Girard Reader*, 97–117.

33. Kirwan, *Girard and Theology*, 26.

34. See also Girard, "Violence and Religion," 2–4. Girard alludes to this crisis, stating that the "disappearance of sacrificial limitations and religious prohibitions facilitates the unleashing of mimetic rivalries."

35. Kirwan, *Girard and Theology*, 22–23.

36. Girard, *Violence and the Sacred*, 43.

37. Girard, *I See Satan Fall*, xvii–xviii.

tion that God is on the side of the victim emerges in the Judeo-Christian tradition. In his later writings, Girard has gravitated more and more toward Christianity properly understood as the revelation of Jesus Christ.[38] Christ exposes the role that victimization and scapegoating play in society and he shows us a way of nonviolence. Little by little, Girard affirms the Judeo-Christian revelation of the Divine understood as God on the side of the victim and distinguished completely from the violence of the gods.[39] God reveals God's very being not only by revealing what we do when we sacralize violence but what God does in response to violence.[40] This revelation emerges as a new form of self-giving mimesis incarnated in Christ and passed on through the Spirit to the Christian community.

Girard thus presents a number of guiding insights on the relationship between religion and violence that will prove useful in the following discussion. Now I proceed to Charles Taylor, whose insights on violence and religion emerge from an examination of Western cultural traditions around the relationship between the sacred and the secular.

## Charles Taylor: Transcendence, Violence, and Western Cultural Traditions

The Canadian philosopher, Charles Taylor, also examines the conjunction between violence and religion. In his most recent monumental work, *A Secular Age*, Taylor turns his attention to asking: If in the year 1500 to believe in God was a natural part of living in society, from the perspective of the West, what has happened in the last five hundred years such that it is a widely accepted proposition that many do not believe in God and belief in God is just one of many accepted options? Further, how has this situation helped or hindered the rise of violence in our world?[41]

Taylor explores the relationship between religion and violence as a hallmark of the twentieth century and against the backdrop of the process of secularization in the West. What distinguishes this historical period in the West is the destructiveness of categorical violence, where whole categories of people are targeted at the one time.[42] Hence, the usual distinctions —between combatants and noncombatants; soldiers of the state and irregular fighters; physically capable men, and women with their children;

---

38. Ibid., xviii–xix.
39. Girard, "Violence and Religion," 8.
40. Girard, *Girard Reader*, 117–88.
41. Taylor, *Secular Age*, 26.
42. Taylor, "Sources of Violence," 15–16.

and the guilty and the innocent—break down. Within this form of violence, a number of elements stand out: it is frequently excessive, spreading beyond its original target to include other victims, and resulting in atrocities; it involves the language of purification, and leads to evil acts such as ethnic cleansing; and it can include ritual elements.[43] He argues that to lay all these elements at the feet of religion because religion has traditionally dealt with purification and ritual is quite false. The truth of the matter is that many atheistic groups have also used these elements in their violent acts. If this is so, what could be a more thorough analysis?

The persistence of violence and our desire to deal with it are not disconnected from the three-cornered cultural and social debate that has played a significant role in the West. This debate is represented by three competing and dominant traditions, each with its own understanding of human transcendence, human well-being, suffering, and evil. These traditions are: secular humanism, which Taylor names as the romantic set (a cluster of ideas and actions); immanent counter-Enlightenment humanism, which Taylor names as the tragic set; and Christian religious belief.[44] Each of these understandings of society and human living has a perspective on how to deal with violence and on how religions may or may not play a part in transforming the human condition.[45]

## Exclusive Secular Humanism

Taylor's analysis of the rise of secularity is extensive. Taylor puts forward a number of assertions about the manner by which secular Western society makes sense of human evil and violence. The secular attribution of evil to biological causes or physical/chemical mechanisms is, for Taylor, only a partial insight yet one that is broadly accepted by Western secular thinking and practice.[46] Similarly attributing aggressiveness to some evolutionary mechanism of self-protection, where humans as fundamentally physical, chemical, and biological beings are protecting the group by excluding the outsider is also only a partial insight. For Taylor, both partial insights negate what is central to the human person, their spiritual make-up, and the question of

43. Taylor, *Secular Age*, 658.

44. Ibid., 623, 624, 369–74. The expression "immanent counter-Enlightenment humanism" represents a body of philosophical thought that turns against the Enlightenment values of harmony and security, and is critical of established religion.

45. Ibid., 660.

46. Ibid., 658–59.

transcendence.[47] When it comes to the healing of categorical violence, "meta-biological" factors must play a vital role.[48] He asserts that "not only our struggles to control unchained sexual desire and violence need to be understood in meta-biological terms; these 'drives' themselves have to be grasped through the matrices of meaning which give them shape in our lives."[49]

Exclusive secular humanism, or the romantic set, is one matrix of meaning. It affirms the ordinary pleasures of life, with a focus on the fullness of flourishing in this world alone.[50] The romantic set gives a direct critique of religion, especially Christianity, asserting that it must not be allowed to induce a repulsion of earthly existence with its ordinary pleasures.[51] The romantic set is also a reaction against what has been seen to be an overly rational approach to organizing society, spearheaded by the success of the scientific revolution since the 1500s. It attempts not to lose sight of the importance of human feeling and sympathy, yet it is nevertheless committed to human reason as the criterion for making decisions. The sociopolitical idea of secular humanism is centered in human autonomy, a harmony of interest and the power of human fellow feeling or sympathy. Taylor sums up the humanist criticisms of religion by stating that "religion actuated by pride or fear, sets impossibly high goals for humans; of asceticism, or mortification, or renunciation of ordinary human ends. It invites us to 'transcending humanity' and this cannot but end up mutilating us; it leads us to despise and neglect the ordinary fulfilment and happiness which is within our reach."[52]

For secular humanists, violence is pathological, or a product of underdevelopment, to be eradicated through education or therapies, where the spiritual healer is replaced by the psychologically trained therapist.[53] Therapy, then, becomes a means to modify behavior so that the individual may become more functional within the group.[54] In this trend, moral impotence that gives rise to violence is labeled on a sliding scale between abnormal and normal depending on the sort of context in which such actions occur.

For the romantic set, the goal of living is to deal with others according to benevolence and justice, increasing life, relieving suffering, and fostering

47. Ibid., 620.
48. Ibid., 659.
49. Ibid., 660.
50. Ibid., 624.
51. Ibid., 632.
52. Ibid., 624.
53. Ibid., 632–33.
54. Ibid., 618–23.

prosperity.[55] The psychological becomes the interpretative frame through which to articulate the ethical. Toward these therapeutic approaches, Taylor critically asks: Is the destructive behavior of individuals the diseased product of a distorted community? Are we in danger of adapting to a social situation that will not lead to human flourishing? What is a functionality that is adequate for human living? Are the language and procedure of psychotherapy adequate, or do we need to address the matter of violence spiritually as well? Will the cultural constructs of our society allow us to name, understand, and take responsibility for the disease that erupts into violent behavior?

Secular humanism further offers a new social imagining through the political secular state, which, at times, uses violence to enforce conformity, especially as a last resort when the innocent victim's well-being is at stake.[56] However, even with the dominance of secularity in the West, Taylor is aware that the promise of mutual benefit has not eliminated all violence. Secularity suffers from a lack of solidarity since the minimalist rules presented by secular humanism are in the end "inherently morally unstable."[57] Taylor says that people may benefit from mutual self-interest, yet the benefits of such an approach require an allegiance to the common good, rather than an aggressive individualism—something the free market cannot deliver through codes.[58] Further, there exist forms of social identity that do not, in the long run, progress human living. There are forms of imposed secularity (Marxism and fascism) that produce a smug superiority. There are kinds of solidarity through common identity, especially in the form of nationalism, that are flawed and can degenerate to a justification for being hostile to diversity, mobilizing against the other, or even torturing others, based on a war on terrorism.[59] Experience shows that neither rational argument nor emotional shaming is sufficient to motivate people toward solidarity and a sense of sympathy with others. Such motivations are too thin to be a "moral source" for inspiring people to embrace a morality and strengthen a commitment.[60] People can too easily be manipulated if sympathy is the only moral source.[61] Alternatively, secularists can adopt the way of existentialists and claim that one's moral source is simply a kind of stoic dignity requiring giving without expecting anything in return, while in the same breath

55. Ibid., 690–91.

56. Ibid., 673.

57. Ibid., 691.

58. Ibid., 691–92.

59. Ibid., 692.

60. Ibid., 694.

61. Ibid., 699.

affirming the worthlessness of life.[62] The difficulty with such a stance is that mutual benefit and the bond of love require reciprocity—giving and receiving—while a stance of giving without receiving ends up being a "unilateral heroism" that is "self-enclosed."

## Immanent Counter-Enlightenment Humanism

Taylor also explores what he calls the "tragic set" or immanent counter-Enlightenment humanism. The tragic set seems to be a revolt from within unbelief and secularity to a stable life as well as a revolt against a Christian faith that promises prosperity. Taylor states that the "reproach is levelled that religion cannot face the real hard facts about nature and human life; that we are imperfect beings, the products of evolution, with a lot of aggression and conflict built into our natures; that there is also much that is horrible and terrible in human life which cannot just be washed away. Religion tends to *bowdlerize* reality."[63]

The tragic set draws from the narratives of Nietzsche, who rebelled against the idea that the highest purpose of life was to relieve suffering and increase stability.[64] In contrast, life for the tragic set leads to cruelty, domination, and exclusion. The highest ideal is that contained in the movement of life itself, since all these actions are expressions of the will to power.[65] Again Taylor asserts that the tragic set "chafes at the benevolence, the universalism, the harmony and the order. It wants to rehabilitate destruction and chaos, the infliction of suffering and exploitation, as part of the life to be affirmed. Life properly understood also affirms death and destruction. To pretend otherwise is to try to restrict it, tame it, hem it in and deprive it of its highest manifestations, precisely those manifestations that make it something you can say 'yes' to."[66]

Alternatively, the tragic set espouses the virtues of dedication, sacrifice, suffering, and even domination for the sake of the right cause. They dismiss the anesthetized life of secular modern existence, devoid of passion and extremes. The tragic set opposes a way of life that normalizes immanent stability and saps human living of the need for heroism, commitment, and challenge.[67] For the tragic set, untroubled happiness is a delusion. As

62. Ibid., 702.
63. Ibid., 624.
64. Ibid., 664.
65. Ibid., 634–35.
66. Taylor, "Spirituality of Life," 5.
67. Taylor, *Secular Age*, 635.

humans, we cannot "remove the tragedy, the wrenching choices between incompatibles, the dilemmas, which are inseparable from the human life" or the illusion "that all things come together effortlessly."[68] In some ways it resembles the eschatological perspective of Christianity, with its demands to lose one's life in order to gain it but in the case of the tragic set without an otherworldly perspective. However, Christianity in its Nietzschean misinterpretation is to be condemned for its fear, denial, and avoidance of the sensual pleasures of the body. Nietzsche saw himself trying to revive the darker side of life, holding up the pre-Christian warrior as the ideal human for whom the noble virtues of courage, elite excellence, and greatness were lost through the *ressentiment* of Christians. In Taylor's estimation, the insights of the tragic set have been appropriated in a politically distorted manner, giving rise to an age of categorical violence: the Gulags, terrorism, fascism, and bolshevism.[69] It has turned into a justification for the distorted use of power, with a fascination with the negation of life and an exaltation of death. Certainly, there is no transcendent good beyond earthly life.

In response, Taylor notes that the challenge of our age should not be to lower the bar of normality according to a functional and adaptive approach to living with others; nor should the challenge simply be one of creating communities of mutual benefit where the standard of benefit is simply increasing pleasure and avoiding pain (secular humanism). Nor should our direction be one of grasping power so as to control others, negating the understanding that power can be authentically or inauthentically exercised (immanent counter-Enlightenment humanism). Indeed, secular humanists must come to realize that we may have to agree to sacrifice some of this ordinary human flourishing to assure our highest goals. The challenge is to appropriate a spiritual and moral aspiration that shows a path to transformation while not mutilating or denying what is essentially human. Taylor names this aspiration the "maximal demand."[70]

## Christianity and Transcendence

In an affirmation of Christian religion, Taylor asks: Could it be that the only way to escape the draw to violence is somewhere in the turn to transcendence?[71] Against the romantic set, development cannot simply be founded in mutual benefit nor can it be simply this-worldly. Against the

---

68. Ibid., 635.
69. Ibid., 638.
70. Ibid., 640–42.
71. Ibid., 639.

tragic set, change cannot simply be a product of the will to power. There are also examples in both religious and secular traditions where violence is controlled by people becoming warriors of death. In some religious traditions, there is a danger in giving divine meaning to suffering and destruction. The warrior aligns his or her actions to God as God's punisher, perpetuating a mechanism of inclusion and exclusion and justifying actions by asserting a divine mandate and mission.[72] Taylor also takes issue with secular warrior cultures and claims that the warrior ethic is a product of a distorted appropriation of the experience of suffering. The warrior understands him- or herself as the "walking dead," so that death is not feared but overcome. The warrior transcends suffering. What was terrifying is now exhilarating and fascinating. This exhilaration is an emotive uplift for the warrior. The warrior identifies with death, renouncing what is destroyed, purifying him- or herself, and bringing some sort of meaning to destruction.

In contrast, Taylor can see that Christianity proposes a transcending of humanity, looking beyond a code of behavior to people who have lived saintly lives through faith.[73] The tough demands of love, the wounds of humiliation crying out for justice, and a range of sensual desires congruent with healthy relationships all need to be equally addressed. However, Christianity does not have some "blueprint" for life. It prefers to invite the believer to turn to the symbol of the "already here" and "not yet" of the kingdom of God.

Yet, Taylor is also sober about Christianity's ability to deliver. Despite this kingdom symbol, there are various "misprisions" that Christianity can inhabit: the misprision of Platonism, distorted notions of sacrifice, and the elimination rather than the transformation of desire.[74] Christianity, under the influence of Platonic philosophy, has despised the body, and exalted the renunciation of pleasurable desires through self-immolation, perpetuating a distorted notion of sacrificing that renounces ordinary pleasures.[75] Taylor lays some of the blame for these errors at the feet of a hyper-Augustinianism that celebrated self-mutilation.[76] He believes that such a legacy contributes to violence. Taylor further explores the relationship between suffering, sacrifice, and Christian salvation.[77] Part of the Christian legacy has been to

---

72. Ibid., 647, 653.

73. Ibid., 643, 647, 653.

74. Ibid., 643, 644, 646.

75. Ibid., 645.

76. Ibid., 652.

77. Ibid., 652–54.

understand sacrifice as a form of "punishment for the bad parts."[78] People
had always had a sense of falling short or "a sense of unworthiness" antecedent to physical suffering long before Christianity, and have asked how they
can make up for the unworthiness they feel.[79] Self-punishment has become
a response to suffering while believers engage in placating the gods for
purification. The numinous as terrifying motivates the believer to destroy
the impure.[80] According to Taylor, a simple and blunt Christian emphasis
on human evil can be ineffective and can strengthen "misanthropy."[81] This
leads back to the misprision that seeks to separate good and bad through
renunciation and purification. When people are asked to renounce more
and more for the sake of becoming pure, the most important insight of
Christianity is lost: God's initiative to create us and save us.

In contrast, the Christian experience is far from a warrior ethic or the
immanentism of secularity. God wills our good, including human flourishing, and wants to desacralize human violence.[82] The suffering of Christ
is about entering the forum of evil with an attitude of active resistance, to
transform evil from within through the power of love.[83] As such, the sufferings of Christ refuse to frame suffering in terms of antecedents but rather
in terms of a present response to a divine initiative and invitation, giving
meaning to God's resolve never to abandon humanity. For this ethic to be
fruitful in the lives of believers, the interpretation of the sufferings of Christ
needs to move beyond a juridical-penal understanding and a hermeneutic
of divine violence toward a valuing of complete human flourishing.

For Taylor, Christianity offers the possibility of affirming mutual benefit and responding to sensuality appropriately without the need for recourse
to violence or an authoritarian society. If Christianity is about overcoming
evil by turning evil to good, this cannot be done simply by imposing a code
or a rule of law and requiring obedience to that law, since discipleship means
going beyond a code or set of rules.[84] The path ahead is one of cooperat-
ing with the "pedagogy of God" in the form of a transformation that is not

78. Ibid., 647.

79. Ibid., 646. Taylor argues that suffering is often equated with personal
punishment.

80. Ibid., 647.

81. Ibid., 655.

82. Ibid., 649.

83. Ibid., 654.

84. Ibid., 701–3, 707.

simply engineering, or a reduction of our sensual self to some pathology, but a transformation of desire through a life lived through religious faith.[85]

Taylor offers a number of fruitful insights regarding the place of secularity in the Western tradition, especially in its ability to meet the problem of violence: secularity seeks equality before the rule of law, reaches for the goals of benevolence and justice, and aims to increase life by eliminating poverty, relieving suffering, and fostering prosperity. In the end, Taylor also acknowledges the unique religious insights that authentic Christianity can bring to the problem of violence.

## James W. Jones: A Psychological Perspective

Another perspective on the link between religion and violence comes through the lens of individual psychology: James W. Jones seeks to understand the link from the perspective of psychoanalytic theory. He asks: In practice, which factors of the developing self and the interaction of the self with the religious social and cultural milieu bring about a disposition for violence?

Jones acknowledges religion's capacity to both inspire and motivate people to great goodness. Yet, religious people also can cause great evil. He asserts that the propensity of ordinary people to commit extraordinary evil witnesses to the conjunction between religion and violence.[86] Jones follows the analysis of James Waller, who claims that we are able to work out what might shape the mind and heart of religious agents by examining the individual in his or her specific context.[87] Contextual elements include dispositional factors, such as xenophobia and ethnocentric factors; and pre-dispositional factors, which are shaped by cultural situations such as the cultural demonization of potential victims.

For Jones, one of the key factors in religiously motivated violence is the process of conversion that leads to a reorganization of the self, with a comprehensive change in worldview and identity.[88] The process of conversion is far from passive, but rather one that human beings willingly undergo, providing clear norms and prefabricated answers to the postmodern dilemma of personal identity.[89] The overall conviction is that the convert is a purposeful agent, who chooses a renewal in faith, in contrast to a pas-

85. Ibid., 673–74, 685.
86. Jones, *Blood that Cries Out*, 7.
87. Ibid., 7–29; Waller, *Becoming Evil.*
88. Jones, *Converting to Terrorism*, 5.
89. Ibid., 6.

sive person, who conforms to social pressures. Conversion experiences bring about a new sense of self especially amidst the anomie of postmodern societies.[90] The sense of being rootless is replaced by a sense of timeless tradition that feels more substantial to the shifting ideas of contemporary society. Whatever precipitates the process of conversion is multivalent, yet most people tell of a series of major stress factors leading up to conversion. While some merely drift into groups, many report high levels of emotional stress.[91] Studies find that converts report increased self-esteem, less depression and anxiety, and better interpersonal relationships after conversion and insertion into a new group.[92]

Jones outlines a number of themes that are common to religiously motivated violence. The first is the presence of humiliation and shame mediated through social circumstances. Jones gives a detailed study of Sayyed Qutb, a member of the Muslim Brotherhood, responsible, at least implicitly, for the promotion of an ideology of violence in Egypt and beyond. I will explore Qutb as an example of *ressentiment* in more detail in chapter 8. In studying Qutb, Jones asserts that humiliation was one of the greatest motivations for his ideas and actions.[93] The important issue is what religion does with shame and humiliation since "feelings of humiliation have been one of the most frequently cited 'root causes' of the turn to fundamentalism." [94]

Jones connects the idea of humiliation to Henri Kohut and the Object-Relations school of psychodynamics.[95] Jones, *pace* Kohut, underscores that:

> Humiliation is an injury to the person's sense of self and their self-esteem, a threat to the self. The psychologically threatened self responds with violence, just as the physically threatened self sometimes does especially if the self is inclined toward violence and lacks empathy for others. This parallels a finding from forensic psychology: men who batter or kill their wives or girlfriends often say openly that they felt they were losing control over their partners . . . This need for control often covers a psychological vulnerability that leads to violence when the self feels threatened . . . by the loss of control. Feelings of humiliation appear common in many of the oppressed groups that produce terrorists.[96]

90. Ibid., 7.
91. Ibid., 8.
92. Ibid., 10.
93. Jones, *Blood that Cries Out*, 36–40.
94. Jones, *Converting to Terrorism*, 13.
95. Jones, *Blood that Cries Out*, 132–35.
96. Ibid., 137.

Religious agents can take humiliating images such as those of Abu Ghraib and exacerbate the experience of being shamed through the lens of an idealized and punitive God before whom the shamed person feels even greater worthlessness. Idealization and an idealized figure are central to a humiliation-driven process. Jones, following Freud, connects patriarchal cultures, paternalistic images of deities, and guilt-laden religious expressions, where morality is worked out according to strict laws backed up by sacred power and dominance.[97] He asserts that the more "religion exalts its ideal or portrays the divine as an overpowering presence and emphasizes the gulf between the finite human beings and that ideal so that we must feel like worms not human, the more it contributes to and reinforces experiences of shame and humiliation."[98] These feelings increase the likelihood of violent outbursts. Distorted religion then becomes focused on submission to an overpowering presence, purification from one's sins, and a burning desire for divine favor.[99] The desire for divine acceptance can then be channeled by the religious community by "fomenting crusades, dehumanizing outsiders and encouraging prejudice" toward enemy targets.[100] The love for a demanding God replaces love for humans.[101] Alternatively, positive religion can also mute the violence of humiliation, encouraging compassion and empathy for the enemy, even one who may be the source of economic and social humiliation.[102]

The second theme that Jones describes as being common to religiously motivated violence is the rage for purification, again reacting to shame and humiliation. Jones states that "sacred values . . . are deeply held for non-instrumental reasons."[103] The actions of those who perpetrate religious violence are not usually founded in utilitarian aims alone but also in symbolic performances for the sake of purification, drawing on themes of birth and rebirth common in all religious cultures. Such a rebirth cycle must happen within history. Jones demonstrates the desire for rebirth from both Islamic and Christian martyrs' calendars, and from the image of the martyr borne up to paradise, purified and sinless. The idea that killing can be a means to redeem oneself or someone else is not unique and religious

---

97. Jones, "Why Does Religion Turn Violent?," 185.

98. Ibid., 169.

99. Jones, *Converting to Terrorism*, 15.

100. Jones, "Why Does Religion Turn Violent?," 170.

101. Jones, *Blood that Cries Out*, 123.

102. Ibid., 119.

103. Jones, *Converting to Terrorism*, 16.

terrorism provides the connection between martyrdom and the process of purification.[104] Death by martyrdom brings satisfaction to God. There is a link between purification, for the sake of holiness, and religious violence. The religious drive to sacrifice or to make one's life into one's cause wholly transcends all other meanings, and appears to go beyond any pragmatic or purely self-interested motivations.[105]

For Jones, the work of post-Freudian psychologists such as Ronald Fairburn alerts us to the enduring psychological mechanism of "splitting," first occasioned in early development, by which the ego is able to separate the all-good from the all-bad, sanitizing the internal image of the parent at the expense of its own self-worth.[106] Drawing on the work of Ruth Stein, who has analyzed the letter of Mohammad Atta,[107] Jones identifies a number of key psychological insights.[108] Stein traces the psychological process through a number of steps: an ambivalence toward the self, brought on by the oedipal stage, leads to an identificatory love by the son toward the father; the father rejects the son, causing self-contempt in the son; the son subsequently desires to eradicate what was rejected in a culture of censured maternal love (patriarchy); these rejected parts of the self become a source of humiliation, facilitated through religious rituals that emphasize self-deprecation and the eradication of impurity; the son's only recourse is to split off the bad parts of himself, aided by religion (image of the punitive God), and to project these bad parts onto others; they are externalized onto others violently, while increasingly submitting to the aggressor father. Jones concludes that some forms of fundamentalism are based on a violent, homoerotic, and self-abnegating father–son relationship that changes the exalted parental inner-object into a persecutory father-object to whom the son relates by means of both love and fear.[109]

Jones's third theme relating to religiously motivated violence is a desired union with God. Religious redemption is one of the primary motivators for violent action, sublating all other desires, resulting in a detachment from human empathetic connections and a reattachment to God alone.[110] This may be the beating heart of all religions, but, in this context, desire for

104. Jones, *Blood that Cries Out*, 47.

105. Ibid., 53–55.

106. Jones, "Why Does Religion Turn Violent?," 171, 186.

107. Atta was one of the people responsible for the bombing of the New York World Trade Center in 1993.

108. Stein, "Evil as Love," 393–420. Stein, "Fundamentalism," 201–29.

109. Jones, "Why Does Religion Turn Violent?," 188.

110. Ibid., 182.

union with God and the illusion of union attained through violent means are linked.[111] Jones asserts that this "process appears to be connected to the image of God that is at work here—the image of a vengeful and punitive and overpowering patriarchal being. The believer must find a way to relate to an omnipotent being who appears to will the world's destruction. The believer must humiliate himself before this demanding figure, feeling himself profoundly worthless and deeply guilty. And the punitive, omnipotent being must be appeased, placated. A blood sacrifice must be offered."[112] Jones links these themes of religious awareness to the development of the self. The social, cultural, and historical circumstances and the psychological processes evoked by these circumstances contribute toward the formation or deformation of the self,[113] distorting the ego's mature negotiation with others and giving rise to immature internal loci of control.[114]

Jones's fourth theme concerning religiously motivated violence is the possession of an apocalyptic vision. This vision is usually couched in the language of cosmic struggle between the forces of good and evil. Overall, Jones is concerned to present the psychological factors that may ground such visions and their narratives. He quotes from a number of authors, with whom he concurs, that an apocalyptic vision is usually inherently violent and religious at the same time. One of the most widespread beliefs held by such people who have such a vision is that they are at war with demonic and secular forces, whether they are attributed to a secular government or the wider public. Such a belief helps to form the mistaken assertion that no-one is an innocent victim.

The fifth of Jones's themes in religiously motivated violence is the demonization of others. Jones asserts that "the idea of sacred warfare makes possible the idea of a satanic opponent. Enemies who embody pure evil cannot be argued with or compromised with; they can only be destroyed. And as morally or spiritually subhuman, destroying them is not an immoral act but is rather, a moral duty."[115] Further, the overidealization of one's own tribe or gender in the name of religion provides a ready rationale for violence against the other, who is seen to be dehumanized and, having died a social death, can now be slaughtered with impunity.[116] Not content to

---

111. Jones, *Blood that Cries Out*, 61.

112. Ibid., 62–63.

113. Ibid., 118.

114. Jones, "Why Does Religion Turn Violent?," 179.

115. Jones, *Blood that Cries Out*, 44.

116. Ibid.

believe in waiting, people take an apocalyptic finality into their own hands and crusade against the evildoers and the unrighteous.[117]


## A Critique of James W. Jones

Jones provides a number of important insights from a psychoanalytic perspective regarding the relationship between religious development and deformation, the importance of significant others, and the intrapsychic development of the individual. Genuine psychological development influences genuine spiritual growth, while distorted psychological environments hamper mature spiritual formation. The psychoanalytical perspective helps us understand that if distorted aggression is to be avoided and growth is to be fostered, then we must address the psychological deficits in people from the early years of their lives, particularly in the relationship between parent and child. Yet psychological development occurs also within a community of faith with established beliefs and practices that may promote the deformation of the self through false symbols of God. When these symbols accentuate the image of God as remote, punitive, and angry, and are idealized to exert control and induce submission, then belief may well be a distorting influence.

The challenge is to articulate a larger developmental typology based on psychoanalytic parameters (especially at the oedipal stage of development) and its relationship to religious experience that would help identify phases of growth at key maturational moments and the particular barriers that stymie growth and leave unresolved elements. In the context of martyrdom and religion, while Jones is able to identify some of these psychological distortions, the challenge is to accurately evaluate the symbol of God in revealed religions and ask whether such symbols facilitate an authentic attachment to God and detachment from the world. I will argue in chapters 3, 7, and 9 especially that conversion, understood normatively, can better help us identify genuine psychological development within a community of faith.


## Mark Juergensmeyer: *Terror in the Mind of God*

My final author in this selective review of the literature concerning religiously motivated violence is the sociologist, Mark Juergensmeyer. From first-hand interviews, he postulates an empirical correlation between violence and religious expression, contending that religion seems to be

117. Ibid., 40–41.

connected with violence virtually everywhere.[118] His accounts give weight to the assertion that religion is, generally, part of the problem of violence, rather than part of the solution. So-called Christian bombers of abortion clinics, IRA and Ulster revolutionaries, religious Zionists, Muslim fundamentalists and Sikh militants demonstrate the link between religion and violence.[119] For Juergensmeyer, the critical question is whether their violent acts are primarily religious acts or political acts.[120] He notes the phenomenon of the "religionization of politics," that is, political policies are given greater legitimacy by religious symbol, imagery, and beliefs, as well as by the "politicization of religion," that is, religion intrudes into the public square for the sake of political change and protest.[121]

Juergensmeyer eclectically draws on the insights of many authors, including Sigmund Freud, René Girard, David C. Rapoport, Maurice Bloch, Ernest Becker, and Emile Durkheim, to assert the link between sacrificial violence and religion from psychological and psychosocial perspectives.[122] For Freud, violent religious symbols and rituals evoke and help vent violent impulses, performing a positive role in society.[123] For Girard, ritualized violence in archaic societies mediated through religious myths, rituals, and prohibitions have had a positive role in restoring social order.[124] Rapoport links religious messianic expectations and the radical transformation of history and society.[125]

Juergensmeyer is particularly drawn to the writings of Maurice Bloch, whose central insight is that sacrifice is an "empowering act" through which the victim can "surmount the fear of victimisation and become a conquering warrior and hunter."[126] Bloch offers a general theory of religion in which ritual takes the believer to a spiritual realm to encounter the transcendent so that the believer might return to the here and now and conquer it.[127] Groups that are disenfranchised personally and socially use violence as the means to

---

118. Juergensmeyer, *Terror*, xi; Juergensmeyer, "Religious Violence," 890.

119. Juergensmeyer, "Religious Violence," 891.

120. Ibid.

121. Ibid., 891.

122. Ibid., 892–93.

123. Juergensmeyer, *Terror*, 171; Freud, *Totem and Taboo*.

124. Juergensmeyer, *Terror*, 171; Girard, *Violence and the Sacred*.

125. Juergensmeyer, "Religious Violence," 897; Rapoport, "Messianic Sanctions for Terror."

126. Juergensmeyer, "Religious Violence," 893; Bloch, *Prey into Hunter*.

127. Bloch, *Prey into Hunter*, 4–5.

conquer other earthly powers on behalf of the deity.[128] Yet Juergensmeyer's assessment is that, while they may give the appearance of empowerment, such acts are in the end counterproductive. He turns to Ernest Becker, who postulates that many religiously motivated projects are simply attempts to avoid death and control chaos, and thus intrinsically they constitute a denial of death.[129] Lastly, Juergensmeyer draws on the social theories of Durkheim, who postulates a fundamental dichotomy between the sacred and the profane for religious believers, which in their minds gives rise to a conflict between the cosmic forces of good and evil.[130]

Juergensmeyer concludes that sacrifice is not the central context for viewing religious violence. Rather, "war is the context of sacrifice rather than the other way around."[131] Sacrifice and martyrdom are given their full significance within the symbolic context of cosmic war, which presupposes the dialectic of order versus chaos, good versus evil, truth versus falsehood.[132] Yet, in the end, Juergensmeyer admits that prominent thinkers who work in the field are "still groping towards a general theory of religion that will allow us to understand how the religious impulse of humanity is always a yearning for transcendence and tranquility, even when it fuels the most vicious aspects of human imagination. In the mind of God, if not in human reckoning, we are convinced that there is a link between violence and non-violence, between worldly order and transcendent order."[133]

Most importantly for my argument, Juergensmeyer presents four symbols as a set of interpretive lenses for understanding the link between violence and religion. I have chosen these symbols as the dominant framework for the following chapters and I will dialectically engage each of them in turn. The first symbol is cosmic war, which evokes an understanding within religious agents that the world is at war, a war that represents a struggle against "ideas, ideologies and political institutions."[134] Religious agents see themselves as soldiers engaged in a battle between good and evil. For example, Juergensmeyer relates how he met a group of young Sikh militants who were members of a martyr brigade in the Punjab, and when he asked why they become soldiers of God, they answered: "We're in a time of crisis . . . we're in a great moment of history and it's a time of conflict between good

---

128. Juergensmeyer, "Religious Violence," 893–94.

129. Juergensmeyer, Terror, 161; Becker, Denial of Death.

130. Juergensmeyer, Terror, 172; Durkheim, Forms of the Religious Life.

131. Juergensmeyer, Terror, 171.

132. Ibid., 171–72.

133. Juergensmeyer, "Religious Violence," 904.

134. Juergensmeyer, Terror, 151.

and evil, and truth and untruth, and religion and untruth. And we have a chance to make a difference."[135] When Juergensmeyer spoke to Mahmud Abouhalima, one of the bombers convicted of the 1993 World Trade Center bombings in New York, and asked him about the role of religion in public life, Mahmud answered, "You people are like sheep . . . You don't see what's going on. Your media just won't let you see it. There is a war going on, there's a war between truth and evil, and good and bad, of religion and unreligion, and your government is the enemy."[136] Both voices speak of the desire to destroy evil, restore good through violence, and change history.

According to Juergensmeyer, cosmic war imaginatively draws upon the great battles of the past and in the minds of believers relates such battles to a metaphysical conflict between good and evil. At the religious level, each person is either for God or against God, on the side of good or on the side of evil, participating in a culture of life or dealing in a culture of death, progressing either a national religious identity or a secularist agenda. There is a dualistic tendency characterized by a lack of a middle ground, establishing an all or nothing approach where usually the good of power is gained through violence.[137] It is characterized by an absolutist attitude where the end justifies the means.[138] The ideology of warfare sanctioned by God subsumes cultural understandings of cosmology, history, and eschatology, and constructs a religious justification for pursuing political power. The symbol of cosmic war postulates a victorious trial to be endured that rises up to a grand moment of social and personal transformation. For Juergensmeyer, religion provides a motivating influence for this change since one of the main purposes of religion is to create a vicarious experience of warfare, residing on a spiritual plane.[139]

Juergensmeyer's second symbol for understanding the link between violence and religion is martyrdom, by which a person makes a difference through a heroic and transforming death.[140] All acts of martyrdom function in such a way that they give religious and social recognition to the person and the group. Martyrdom requires sacrifice to be an act of destruction, going to one's death for what one believes.[141] Again, sacrifice has been a key feature of ancient and contemporary religions and Juergensmeyer, following

135. Juergensmeyer, "Bhindranwale to bin Laden," 22.

136. Ibid., 23.

137. Juergensmeyer, *Terror*, 152.

138. Ibid., 157.

139. Ibid., 160.

140. Ibid., 168.

141. Ibid., 170.

Girard, links religion to rites of destruction. However, the desire to conduct warfare comes first, followed by the organization of people according to a storyline of persecution, hope, and conquest that gives acts of self-sacrifice their meaning.

Juergensmeyer's third symbol is demonization, in which the enemy is identified as enemy, and their expulsion or annihilation is framed in the form of religious expulsions, usually by those who oppose them.[142] This involves a depersonalization of the enemy, rendering them complicit in evil, often using the language of Satan and satanic forces to describe them.[143] One of the main motivations for this characterization is to help stereotype whole groups of people and promote the idea of the "collective faceless enemy."[144] Some groups also make the link between the enemy and the realities of business, culture, and economic systems.[145] For example, the United States as a cultural, financial, and economic system of distorted power is a particular focus for Islamic terrorism.[146] Demonization also aids the process of empowerment. Power, marginalization, humiliation, and the regaining of power through violence are all interconnected.[147] This interconnection provides a context where religious language and political language become vehicles for increasing power, addressing simultaneously the humiliations and frustrations of people.[148]

Juergensmeyer's fourth and final symbol for understanding the link between violence and religion is warrior empowerment, by which the warrior or fighter is given religious, moral, and social justification for engaging in warfare. Juergensmeyer argues that people who engage in violence have been previously humiliated through lack of employment, economic deprivation, and political frustrations, but are now empowered by means of a reaction against humiliation.[149] This symbol is further solidified by an emasculating process within societies that produces a "hypermasculine response."[150] To die through an act of violence is better than dying from

---

142. Ibid., 174.
143. Ibid., 180.
144. Ibid., 178.
145. Ibid., 175.
146. Ibid., 181–85.
147. Ibid., 213.
148. Ibid., 198.
149. Ibid., 194.
150. Ibid., 208.

frustration and humiliation, thus putting "a daring claim of power on behalf of the powerless" into warriors' hands.[151]

Juergensmeyer further identifies two elements that establish the effectiveness of religious symbols.[152] First, the line between symbols and actual realities is often thin, pointing to the symbiosis between symbolic and real violence. Second, the symbolic story provides a structure whereby people can understand their life struggle in terms of hope and triumph. The symbol of cosmic war situates final victory in a future toward which the warrior struggles with hope.

Juergensmeyer describes terrorist acts as symbolic performances where the intention is to display "acts of deliberately exaggerated violence."[153] He contends that exaggerated religiously motivated violent acts are constructed events, often designed to numb the mind of the observer, and are more akin to mesmerizing theater.[154] At center stage are the acts themselves, stunningly abnormal and outrageously murderous, carried out in such a way that graphically displays the awesome power of violence, set within grand scenarios of conflict and proclamation. They are dramatic events or performative acts intended to impress their symbolic significance on others since power is more about perception than reality, more about symbol than rational strategy.[155] Juergensmeyer makes a broad connection between symbols and religion, asserting that public ritual has traditionally been the province of religion.[156] This is one of the reasons why performative violence comes so naturally to activists from a religious background. He cautions: when we take such religious acts seriously, the purpose of theater is achieved. Through these events perpetrators declare that their mission has its origins in God, and this mission intends to capture and reshape society to what it should be.[157]

Juergensmeyer seeks to evaluate the effectiveness of religion in influencing the perpetration of violent acts. On one side, religion is depicted as a problem when it encourages religious agents to be violent and militant.[158] He describes the way that religious agents take key notions from their traditions and interpret them to justify violence. Religious communities are

---

151. Ibid., 218.

152. Ibid., 168.

153. Ibid., 121–22.

154. Ibid., 124.

155. Ibid., 126.

156. Ibid., 126.

157. Ibid., 131.

158. Juergensmeyer, "Is Religion the Problem?," 1–2.

also problematic since they bring to a situation of conflict social validations that serve to prolong conflict: personal rewards, vehicles of social mobilization, organizational networks, and moral justifications for violence.[159] On the other side of the debate, Juergensmeyer acknowledges that religion addresses violence creatively. His position is expressed in a summary of various religious traditions—Christianity, Islam, Judaism, Hinduism, Sikhism, and Buddhism—and how each of these traditions generally advocates nonviolence, or violence only under certain conditions.[160] Religion stands with victims, and, where violence is perpetrated in the name of religion, it is a departure from true religion.[161] Juergensmeyer concludes with a moderate approach: "I do not think that religion is the problem. But I do think that the involvement of religion in public life is problematic."[162]

Juergensmeyer argues that religious agents will do virtually anything if they think violence has been sanctioned by divine mandate or conceived in the mind of God.[163] Religion has given power to terrorism and terrorism has given power to religion. At times, he admits a difficulty in distinguishing between terrorism that is religiously motivated and terrorism that is politically motivated and justified. At other times, Juergensmeyer finds it difficult to separate religious war and state-backed political wars, since they share common features to do with symbolism and affective intensity.[164] Yet he is struck with the intensity of the religious terrorist's quest for a deeper level of passionate spirituality than that offered by the superficial values of the modern world.[165] Juergensmeyer's conclusion is that it is not the spiritual intensity of religious terrorists that is unusual but their religious convictions, shaped by the sociopolitical forces of their time. Their movements are not simply aberrations but religious responses to social situations, and expressions of deeply held convictions.

Turning his mind to the global "rebellion" of religion, Juergensmeyer's assessment is that contemporary violence in the name of religion is a reaction to, or revenge for, the banishment of religion from the public space from the time of the European Enlightenment, currently fermenting in the context of a loss of faith in secular nationalism.[166] Religious leaders who

159. Ibid., 7.
160. Juergensmeyer, "Religious Violence," 899–903.
161. Juergensmeyer, "Is Religion the Problem?," 3.
162. Ibid., 4.
163. Juergensmeyer, *Terror*, 219.
164. Ibid., 148–49.
165. Ibid., 221.
166. Ibid., 229.

advocate violence are able to describe spiritual conflict in terms of good and evil, truth and falsehood, and salvation and damnation; and set these notions within existing social and political tensions. Religion becomes a vehicle for an ideology of social protest and resistance. For the religious agent, people and states are to be resisted especially when these assault the pride and identity of people, leading to alienation, marginalization, and social frustration.[167]

## A Critique of Mark Juergensmeyer

Juergensmeyer's symbols of cosmic war, martyrdom, demonization, and warrior power provide key categories by which academics understand the purposes and motivations of violent religious agents. However, the meanings given to these categories must be dialectically engaged. I will argue in chapter 4 that the symbol of cosmic war does not accurately describe the worldview of soldiers engaged in religiously motivated violence. In chapter 7, I will argue that martyrdom can be both authentic and inauthentic and I will identify norms for distinguishing false from true martyrdom. Further, when describing martyrdom, Juergensmeyer does not sufficiently engage his interlocutors on the subject of sacrifice as a subset of cosmic war. Is sacrifice simply a rite of destruction, and martyrdom simply equivalent to the destruction of the self, or can we understand self-sacrifice more authentically? I will argue that religious self-sacrifice need not necessarily be a distortion. In chapter 8, I will argue that it is important to distinguish the stereotypical process of demonization and the more difficult task of naming the demonic. Having named the demonic, religious symbols such as the Cross reveal to the Christian believer God's solution to the problem of evil. In chapter 9, I will argue that warrior/soldier empowerment can be both authentic and inauthentic.

Beyond qualifying the value of Juergensmeyer's symbols, a second criticism of his work relates to his accepting that people turn to religion to find order and meaning in their lives while yet he questions religion's role in the public space. He primarily understands religion in functionalist terms, asserting that part of the reason for global violence lies in the different ways religious communities understand the relationship between the sacred and the secular. Some believers are convinced that the political, economic, and technological considerations in a society should be directed by religious values. Other societies have reached a point of separation between the sacred and the secular, placing religious values in a private space and at the

---

167. Ibid., 171–74.

margins of the public square. Juergensmeyer asserts that one of the most important difficulties for societies today is the religionization of politics. As such he implicitly postulates that secular government should be primarily concerned with establishing the social order, while religious belief is best left to the private life of the individual. What he does not grasp is a role for religion in changing the social arrangements when these do not conform to the dignity of the person. These considerations suggest the questions: What is the proper relationship between the sacred and the secular? Which genuine sacralizations are to be promoted, and which distorted sacralizations dismantled? Are there forms of secularization to be encouraged and forms of secularization to be discouraged?[168] I will argue in chapter 3 that religion can be a cause of integral social transformation in society. Further, I will argue that social development cannot be found in the image of order alone but in a complex relationship between social order, cultural values, and the authenticity of those who inform religious communities.

A third criticism of Juergensmeyer's work is that he states that religion is both a pathway to peace and a means to increasing destructive violence. He adopts an empirical approach to religious expression and does not investigate a normative set of categories for appropriating religious faith. Can a normative understanding of religion be identified? I will argue that genuine religion as a response to the drive for self-transcendence cannot at the same time be a vehicle for fueling violence. Further, I will argue that a normative understanding of religion can be identified, for without such normativity the empirical approach alone will end up mixing both the intelligible and the unintelligible data of experience and attempt to rationalize what does not make sense.[169]

Finally, implicit in the symbol of cosmic war is the desire to change history by establishing a new order through violent means. I will argue for an alternative, nonviolent heuristic for understanding human history and informing historical change that requires an interrelationship between religious, personal, cultural, and social integrity.

---

168. Lonergan, *Papers, 1965–1980*, 259–81.

169. See MacIntyre, *After Virtue*, 209. He states that "(un)intelligible actions are failed candidates for the status of intelligible action; and to lump unintelligible actions and intelligible actions together in a single class of actions and then characterise actions in terms of what items of both sets have in common is to make the mistake of ignoring this."

# Conclusion

In this chapter's selective literature review on the conjunction between religion and violence, we have noted four particular perspectives. Given the trajectory of Girard's thought (the first perspective), we may ask: Is all desire doomed to be rivalistic? Can Girard's insights regarding the scapegoat mechanism give us some understanding of escalating violence? In an era where people have moved beyond religion and the sacrificial system that once maintained order in religious societies, what could take its place? Or what does the dimension of transcendent Christian revelation bring to rivalistic mimetic theory? In response to these questions, I will argue for an explanatory account of desire that includes both the importance of desire formed intersubjectively as well as the desire of the human spirit to know and value, a realist position toward evil, and an understanding as to how the grace of God can liberate desire from mimetic rivalry.

Taylor creates a dialogue between secular humanism, immanent counter-Enlightenment humanism, and Christianity, in order to address violence in the world. He argues that Christianity has important insights into how we might address human suffering and the problem of evil through an appeal to faith in the gift of God's love as the means and the end of transcendence. I, in turn, will argue that Christianity does speak to the concerns of modernity: the importance of reason, affectivity, and empowerment. And I will argue that the romantic set and the tragic set possess a combination of insights and oversights when it comes to addressing the problem of violence.

Jones's psychological perspective affirms that we are better able to understand religious violence from the perspective of psychoanalytical psychology and the important process of conversion. His insights suggest a number of questions, including: How does psychological knowledge help us practically to deal with the situations of humiliation, shame, and guilt that are often present in people's lives? I will argue that the process of conversion can be understood not only empirically but also normatively.

Finally, Juergensmeyer's sociological perspective is the most crucial for naming the four symbols of religiously motivated violence that I will examine throughout the major part of this book. His insights suggest a number of questions: How legitimate is it to talk about religion in empirical terms alone? Does a space open up for talking about authentic and inauthentic religion? If there are such things as authentic self-transcendence and authentic religion, how do we recognize inauthenticity? If religious violence is characterized by themes of cosmic war, martyrdom, demonization, and warrior empowerment, do these themes help us to address violence? I will argue that it is possible to give an explanatory account of the distinction between authentic and inauthentic religion, and that we can then give a heuristic explanatory account of meaning-making in history so that we may identify when there is social and cultural breakdown, and how to bring about authentic progress.

# 3

## Lonergan, Religion, and Violence

THE INSIGHTS PRESENTED BY Girard, Taylor, Jones, and Juergensmeyer have provided us with enough evidence to support the proposition that some forms of religious expression both motivate and justify the violent actions of religious agents. However, the survey of these authors' works also leads me to assert that it is not enough simply to demonstrate empirically that people are motivated to commit violent acts by religious images, symbols, and doctrines. It is also important to dialectically engage religious images, symbols, and doctrines so as to judge whether they are conducive to authentic living, whether they are authentic understandings of a particular religious tradition, and whether, as categories chosen by academics, they accurately reflect the imagination, understanding, and historical life of religious agents. If these categories are not conducive to authentic living, then it is also important to identify those categories that are.

Therefore, my argument here must address three interrelated aspects. First, it must address the dimension of religious agents as dramatic subjects, their use of violence to change their historical circumstances, and their employment of religious tradition to motivate and justify violence. Second, it must address the work of scholars, especially their evaluation of religious agents, and offer an assessment as to whether scholars' narratives accurately interpret the mind of religious agents. I argue that unless authors understand their own understanding by attending to their own performative praxis, then categories such as cosmic war, martyrdom, demonization, and warrior empowerment will prove to be inadequate for diagnosing the causes of, and hence overcoming, violence. Third, I must address how genuine religion may heal violence and help people transform history.

As a first observation, we can say that violent religious agents engage in shaping human history through becoming martyrs and warriors. We may ask: What principles exist to direct our making of human history? How are we to understand the interrelationship of these principles within persons, communities, and cultures? If people are committed to changing the shape of history, then they are working out of some understanding, however implicit, of human history. Their view of human history is shaped by the religious tradition that they have inherited. A person's implicit view of history may flow out of the distorted ontological assertion that violence will not only change the course of history but that violence is intrinsic to social reality.[1] On this worldview, violent conflict is understood to be central to the dynamics of change.[2] For example, Juergensmeyer and Jones employ the symbol of cosmic war to describe the phenomenon in which religious agents seek to change social and political institutions through religiously justified violence. In chapter 4, I will argue that when religious agents understand human processes solely in terms of the grace–sin dialectic, they will be unable or unwilling to see a large number of variables and the relations among them needed to cultivate order. I will argue that this viewpoint will not be conducive to human well-being and derives from an ethic of control, ultimately destroying people, their cultural products, and social institutions.

This first observation invites some understanding of the interrelationship between human well-being, cultural integrity, social institutions, progress, and decline. In the present chapter, I will argue that Lonergan's insights provide a heuristic account of human history that is normative and dialectical. It is normative inasmuch as such as Lonergan's account provides a framework for explaining the relationship between persons, the development of cultural integrity, and social institutions. It is dialectical inasmuch as this account helps us identify personal, cultural, and social breakdowns and ways they might be addressed to reestablish flourishing. This heuristic account hence provides a set of conceptual tools to assess how religion can be a means to a genuine making of history.

By way of a second observation, we may understand the role of authentic religious agents only by providing a heuristic account of genuine religion. Such an account would enable us to distinguish a distorted religious heritage from an authentic religious heritage. While Juergensmeyer and Jones do not discount completely the healing power of religious communities, they focus on the breakdowns brought about by adherence to distorted religion. Generally, they are not concerned to develop a heuristic account of authentic religion even though they accept the need to develop a coherent

---

1. Melchin and Picard, *Transforming Conflict*, 28.

2. Ibid., 29.

theory of religion. Again, Lonergan provides a heuristic account of genuine religion as a framework for diagnosing authenticity and inauthenticity. In chapter 8, I will give an account of how to pastorally engage one's enemies and I will demonstrate that the Christian symbol of the Cross can be a source of human healing when retrieved through the lens of religious love.

As a third observation, we may ask: Can a religious tradition that promotes conflict and violence concretely create a good or better human reality? What would be an alternative tradition that might bring about a better human reality? We may say that concrete historical religious traditions with their own approaches to hermeneutics, narratives, principles, inspirations, and leadership models are always a mixture of authenticity and inauthenticity. Therefore, we need to ask whether concrete religious traditions that are inherited by religious agents help to evoke actions that are truly conducive to human flourishing. Since the symbol of warfare is central to conflict, I will provide a constructive Christian understanding of warfare in chapter 6, an authentic understanding of Christian martyrdom and its relationship to sacrifice in chapter 7, and a Christian understanding of soldiering in chapter 9. Lonergan highlights the importance of a dialectical engagement with traditions, whether they are purposely distorted by religious agents to serve their own ends, or have been handed down in a distorted manner through religious communities over many centuries.

To explore the issues raised by these observations, let us turn now to the philosophical and theological writings of Bernard Lonergan and of those influenced by his writings, especially Robert M. Doran. As we saw briefly in chapter 1, Lonergan's major works, *Insight* and *Method in Theology*, address the problem of making the world a better place by understanding insight, the differentiations of consciousness, normative meaning, biases, conversion, the importance of feelings and values, historical consciousness, the scale of values, and the role of religion.[3]

## The Process of Self-Appropriation

We have seen that one important consideration is whether the assessments by academics concerning religiously motivated violence accurately interpret the mind of religious agents. Researching data around religiously motivated violence is only one aspect in coming to an explanation and evaluation of what is going on and what can be done to bring progress. Making sense of such descriptions through social, cultural, and psychological theories presumes that we have accepted the underlying presuppositions

3. Lonergan, *Method*, 27–52.

and assumptions of such theories. Lonergan suggests that scholars must be attentive to themselves as researchers.

Accordingly, Lonergan's notion of self-appropriation invites the researcher to self-knowledge. Lonergan states that self-appropriation is the effort to discover the kind of person that one is and involves the cultivation of a self-presence, that is, "a person present to [oneself] for others to be present to [self]."[4] He employs an ocular metaphor, asserting that "what is important, in other words, is the looker, not the looked at, even when the self is what is looked at."[5] By self-appropriation, one is able to deal with an ultimate point of reference from which one can deal with many other questions.[6] Self-appropriation concerns the subject as subject and the awareness that, when the subject intends an object, the subject can concomitantly be present to or attend to oneself as a subject.[7] Therefore, the metaphor of "looker" should not be taken to mean that self-appropriation is accomplished through a form of introspection, as if one could take a long and hard look at oneself.

This shift of focus is possible since consciousness is a quality distinct from, yet immanent in, intentional acts, nonintentional states and trends, and preintentional, affective, and volitional phenomena.[8] Self-appropriation means that we are engaged in a reflective practice by which we can analyze what we are experiencing when we are feeling, symbolizing, learning, choosing, and loving. This reflective practice reveals a presence to self as empirical when simply experiencing, a presence to self as intelligent when understanding, a presence to self as rational when making judgments, and a presence to self as existential when deliberating, making decisions, and choosing a loving course of action.

Intellectual self-appropriation is grasping what really is going on when we know, and involves a sustained self-awareness or heightened self-awareness of our concrete performance.[9] This process makes demands and begins in a "sufficiently cultural consciousness," one that is aware of the complexity and range of human knowing.[10] Within all our efforts to learn

4. Lonergan, *Lonergan Reader*, 352.

5. Ibid., 353.

6. Ibid., 359.

7. Lonergan, *Collection*, 209–10.

8. Lonergan, *Insight*, 344; McCarthy, *Crisis of Philosophy*, 234. Such an understanding of consciousness suggests a distinction be made between a prereflexive experiential consciousness and a reflexive intentional analysis.

9. Lonergan, *Method*, 11–14. Lonergan's approach is more an analysis of the performing subject than a conceptual analysis.

10. Ibid., 22.

and to know about the world, there lies an ideal about knowing and knowledge. Since the seeking of any knowledge is the seeking of an unknown through questioning, Lonergan states that the implicit ideal of knowledge is the ideal of each person as asking questions, being intelligent, having insights, formulating hypotheses and concepts, weighing evidence, making judgments, and deliberating about choices.[11]

Moral self-appropriation involves attending to self as one is deliberating on values, choosing what is better and more loving, and making the self more aware of one's possible growth in freedom in such a way that "to be aware of possibility is to be anxious."[12] This intending is noticed when we are oriented toward values by way of feelings, through such questions as: Is this worthwhile to pursue or not? Can I do better? Existentially, we are also present to ourselves as experiencing biases within consciousness that prevent insights from emerging.

Religious or spiritual self-appropriation helps us articulate the importance of God's solution for the problem of evil, a problem that brings about personal and cultural breakdown and solidifies the social problems of violence and alienation.[13] Religious development brings us into the awareness that there is a divinely originated solution to evil offered to our freedom as a gift, whose acceptance makes possible a new direction for growth, a capacity for discerning the will of God, and transformation.[14] In religious self-appropriation, presence to self is a matter of articulating what is going on when we are in love with God and how this love has an effect on the whole of human consciousness.[15] It is our self-understanding grasped by the love of God and oriented toward what is ultimately valuable.

Through the self-appropriation of one's intellectual, moral, and religious consciousness, scholars would be able to assemble, review, evaluate, compare, and identify the underlying roots of diverse accounts and reach foundational categories for understanding the link between religion and violence. Intellectual self-appropriation, moral self-appropriation, and religious self-appropriation have the potential to form a community in dialogue that would seek to shape an authentic critique of culture.[16]

---

11. Lonergan, *Lonergan Reader*, 351–52.

12. Morelli, "Appropriation of Moral Consciousness," 186.

13. Doran, *Intentionality and Psyche*, 396–97.

14. Ibid., 398–401.

15. Ibid., 407.

16. Lonergan, *Insight*, 663–67. Lonergan names such cultural acts of critique as "cosmopolis."

To deal with questions as profound as the link between violence and religion in our concrete performance, not only the scholar but also the religious agent needs a commitment to self-reflection and self-knowledge. Over the course of this book we will see that an unrestricted state of being in love with God sustains moral commitment and intellectual self-appropriation, while engagement in violence derails our orientation to God, moral authenticity, and critical thinking. Though a lack of self-appropriation does not prevent people living good lives, nevertheless its presence enables persons to express more accurately what they are thinking and doing when they are being religious. Without such a commitment, religious agents are vulnerable to accepting destructive feelings uncritically, to being deluded by blindspots, and to being entrapped by an unwillingness to seek the truly good; and they are prey to appealing ideologies and distorted inherited traditions. Admittedly, it is very difficult for religious agents to be engaged with themselves as knowers and valuers when they are being buffeted affectively by violence. The feelings and thoughts that occur in times of conflict and violence arise quickly and carry us forward with emotion into a practical drama, often shaping and reshaping us into greater violence. It is especially difficult to negotiate an open inquiry into what is better when distorted feelings, such as terror in the face of death, or desires for revenge, motivate our practical actions. Beyond this, there is the difficulty of appropriating what is happening in human consciousness given a set of cultural and social conditions that promote a bias toward a practical and commonsense approach to human knowing and doing.

Lonergan is well aware of these challenges and understands the problem of appropriation as concerning the tasks of learning, identification, and orientation.[17] The task of learning is about the slow acquiring of habitual insights or sufficient understanding so that a person can move from one viewpoint to another—a process of education facilitated by committed mentors in contexts of social stability and development. The danger in religious communities where education is minimal is that religious authorities might use words as weapons of power. There may be an implicit attitude that believers must not think for themselves but simply receive religious beliefs as imparted to them. The task of identification is the process of locating in oneself the data that confirm the account of what one is doing when one is feeling, knowing, and choosing, through a heightening of consciousness, and involves a shift in focus from the object being intended to the subject intending. The task of orientation highlights that though we may be capable of intelligent inquiry and critical reflection, we may still "fail to orient our-

17. Ibid., 582.

selves towards truth, [so that] we both distort what we know and restrict what we might know," pointing to the dialectic between a biased desire to know and a disinterested desire to know.[18]

## The Structure of Intentional Human Consciousness

In both *Insight* and *Method in Theology*, Lonergan provides an explanation for the structure and operations of intentional consciousness that become foundational to appropriating the intrinsic norms for uncovering the intelligible, the real, the genuinely worthwhile, and the path toward self-transcendence.[19] Human experiencing, knowing, valuing, and deciding are all parts of a dynamic structure, a self-constituting whole made up of several parts.[20] Each part is related to the other parts of the structure such that if one part breaks down the other parts are affected. Much violence is perpetrated on the basis of flawed perception, incorrect understanding, and false judgments mistaken for reality, such that the false is held to be true and other relevant questions are ruled out. This leads to delusional attitudes that keep inaccuracies in place, potentially worsening a situation. On the other hand, by attuning ourselves to the operations of human consciousness, we may achieve self-transcendence, moving beyond illusions and half-truths about reality, toward what is truly good and worth doing.

Human knowing and acting is a compound of four distinct yet inter-related levels within consciousness: the levels of experience, understanding, judgment, and deliberation.[21] Empirical consciousness, or the level of experience, technically understood, has conscious experience presented as data, the data of sense and the data of consciousness.[22] To the extent that one is guided by wonder and is attentive to the relevant data of a given inquiry, one is better able to understand. Conversely, the failure to attend to the relevant data leads to a lack of understanding. The precept for this level is: be attentive.

The questions that arise from empirical consciousness (What is it? How is it so? Why is it the case?) lead to the second level of intellectual consciousness (concerned with acts of understanding, direct insights, and inverse insights), which gives rise to hypotheses, formulations, and concepts. Understanding requires that we experience a field of data, wondering,

18. Ibid., 582–83.
19. Lonergan, *Method*, 11.
20. Ibid., 14.
21. Ibid., 9–10.
22. Ibid., 9.

inquiring, being curious about the data, ruminating over the data, waiting for insight, and conceiving. This level attempts to get to the nature of things and the intelligible content of a specific set of data. The precept for this level is: be intelligent.

These insights and formulations give rise to questions for reflection or verification (asking: Is it so?) that are concerned with existence or reality, constituting the level of rational consciousness or judgment. We return to our original insight anticipating that if our insight is correct, we will find sufficient evidence to verify it. A correct judgment following the posing of questions for reflection and the weighing up of evidence culminates in a reflective insight in which all conditions have been fulfilled to render a judgment. For Lonergan, a grasp of the objective veracity of judgment rests upon a grasp of the virtually unconditioned, namely, that all conditions needed for that judgment have been fulfilled. The precept for this level is: be reasonable.

Further questions arise beyond a judgment of truth concerning deliberating, valuing, and choosing (Is it worthwhile or valuable? What am I going to do?), which constitutes the fourth level, of rational self-consciousness or moral consciousness.[23] At the level of moral consciousness one is concerned with intending the truly good and truly valuable so that knowing leads to doing and the subject moves away from satisfaction as the criterion for what is good and toward what is genuinely valuable. Accordingly, the precept for the fourth level is: be responsible.

## The Patterns of Experience and the Differentiation of Consciousness

From this account of the operations within consciousness, Lonergan focuses on appropriating the polymorphic nature of our consciousness.[24] Polymorphism is constituted by a number of patterns of experience that orient our understanding, judging, and deliberating in various directions: biological, esthetic, artistic, intellectual, practical, dramatic, mystical, and religious.[25] Empirical consciousness is prepatterned by our interests and concerns toward a specific orientation. While in a particular pattern(s), under the influence of its dominant concerns, our presence to self is affected. According to our habits of openness to broader patterns of experience, our grasp of truth and value will either advance or recede in any context. For

23. Ibid., 34–36.
24. Lonergan, *Insight*, 410.
25. Ibid., 202–12.

example, a person constituted predominantly by the biological pattern has as his or her main concern biological survival so that faced with threat or fear, he or she is concerned simply to protect his or her life. It is possible also for patterns to coexist, for example, when the dramatic as well as the religious patterns dominate the experiential flow, a person can think and act both religiously and practically. One implication is clear: cultural meanings and values influence the concerns of the subject, and the different combinations of patterns within the subject shape the differing personal horizons, and these, in turn, shape cultures. The exclusion of certain patterns through less developed or even distorted cultures may result in the lack of needed insights in the realm of fact and moral values.

It is also possible to recognize within consciousness various realms of meaning. These differentiations account for our control over the products of meaning that constitute our identity and mediate the difference between reality and illusion, value and disvalue. These realms are called: common sense, theoretic, interiority, and transcendent.[26] Doran states that conflict within cultures "is partly a matter of clashes of persons of variously differentiated consciousness . . . Conflicts between cultures are often a function of differing combinations of conscious differentiations [for these] exercise a prevalent influence in establishing operative sets of meanings and value to guide different ways of life."[27]

The realm of common sense is concerned with our day to day practical lives.[28] Commonsense knowing and valuing are practically oriented through descriptive thinking, expressed in ordinary everyday language, and are concerned with the way an issue affects us now. In the ordinary and good sense of the word, commonsense thinking is egocentric, intellectual, widespread, practical, and intersubjective. The person of common sense asks: How do I do this in the most practical way to address this issue for us here and now? Religious expression in commonsense thinking is the identification of religious experience with its outward manifestations: the external (this text), the spatial (this land), the specific (this way of life), and the human (this community).[29] In terms of spiritual transformation, there may have been a time when being practical was enough to sustain people; however, there are indications today that such an approach is not enough to overcome the distortions in community and culture perpetrated by violence.

---

26. Lonergan, *Method*, 81–85. Lonergan also proposes another differentiation, the realm of art. See Lonergan, *Insight*, 187; *Method*, 303–4.

27. Doran, *Dialectics of History*, 537.

28. Lonergan, *Method*, 81.

29. Doran, *Intentionality and Psyche*, 52.

Yet, our understanding of and solutions for religiously motivated violence require "fully differentiated consciousness," which Lonergan was convinced "is the fruit of an extremely prolonged development."[30] Common sense is not concerned with complexity, long-term solutions to problems, an ultimate resolution of issues, or the optimum way of thinking, evaluating, and acting. Indeed, people may even resentfully brush aside or ignore any attempts to raise questions that are concerned with long-term solutions. Lonergan puts the matter urgently: "If man's practical bent is to be liberated and turned toward the development of science, if his critical bent is to be liberated from myth and turned towards the development of philosophy, if his religious concern is to renounce aberrations and accept purification, then, all three will be served by a differentiation of consciousness, a recognition of the world of theory."[31]

The realm of theory gives rise to more explanatory ways of thinking, knowing, and valuing in all fields of study and is illustrated in religious traditions by the introduction of dogmas, theology, and juridical terms.[32] Rather than understanding how this issue relates to oneself or this group practically, theory is concerned to reach a systematic exigency by introducing terms and the relations between the terms so as to expand one's understanding of issues. The explanations reached are meant to deliver objective knowledge and morality that go beyond the immediate practical interest of this subject or community. Theory and common sense are often mistakenly pitted against one another rather than seen as complementary ways of knowing.

The realm of interiority makes it possible for us to distinguish between common sense and theory.[33] Interiority moves from consciousness of self and of objects of the world to self-knowledge such that one grasps the structure and operations of knowing and valuing, and the relationship between psyche and spirit. The move to human interiority means that through our faithfulness and attunement to intrinsic norms, knowledge of truth and values is attained. Interiority helps us identify and value which operations within consciousness are active in any given moment, especially as we move from the realm of practical common sense to the realm of theory, with its technical and precise knowledge. An interiorly differentiated consciousness allows us to develop the categories of all our knowledge, whether for philosophic or religious knowledge.

---

30. Ibid., 257.

31. Lonergan, *Method*, 258.

32. Ibid., 82–83.

33. Ibid., 83.

Finally, Lonergan identifies the realm of transcendence as our experience of surrendering to the Divine with devotion, prayer, and acts of love.[34] The gift of God's love is therefore itself a realm of meaning, transforming us through the experience of the forgiveness of sin, cultivated by a life of prayer and self-sacrifice and then "intensifying, purifying, clarifying, the objectifications referring to the transcendent whether in the realm of common sense, or of theory, or of other interiority."[35] As consciousness differentiates, theoretical questions about the transcendent will emerge. With the differentiation of the person into common sense, theory, and interiority, self-appropriation leads not only to operations of experiencing, understanding, judging, and deciding but to religious experience.

The realms of meaning help us appreciate the insufficiency of practical commonsense knowing (whose focus is getting a job done) alone, as well as the insufficiency of theory alone, with its technical precision and specializations. The realms also highlight the importance of not only being religiously and morally upright but also of being able to articulate intelligently and with precise self-knowledge what is going on in human consciousness. Yet the realms of meaning articulate a ground beyond both theory and common sense that would help us avoid relativism. The realms also reveal that the process of human development is not only about human creativity and self-transcendence but the power of God acting in our lives. The power of God becomes the ground for doing what God wants, choosing responsibly, and gaining an accurate knowledge of God.

## Values, Feelings, and Traditions

In *Method in Theology*, Lonergan explores more fully the notion of value, the concrete good, and its relationship to feelings.[36] Value is what is intended in questions that arise for deliberation, promoting the subject to full consciousness and a happy conscience until one reaches the sustained self-transcendence of the virtuous person.[37] Lonergan acknowledges the link between feelings and judgments of value such that feelings are an apprehension of value.[38] He distinguishes intentional and unintentional feelings. Intentional

---

34. Ibid., 83–84.

35. Ibid., 266.

36. Lonergan, *Method*, 34–37.

37. The key question is the question that intends the good: Is it worthwhile? Is it truly or only apparently good?

38. Lonergan, *Method*, 30.

feelings intend or apprehend an object.[39] Feelings as an apprehension of values have two main objects. Intentional feelings may simply reveal an object to be agreeable or disagreeable, satisfying or dissatisfying. Alternatively, intentional feelings may reveal an object to be both valuable and satisfying. Finally, intentional feelings may reveal values to be worthwhile but dissatisfying.[40] Questions for deliberation follow our preapprehension of value and these questions are prompted not only by what may be agreeable to us but what is truly good, "principles of benevolence and beneficence, capable of genuine collaboration and of true love" that match the full reach of the transcendental notion of value.[41] Feelings of love and mutual generosity through deliberation carry us toward moral self-transcendence.

Lonergan is also aware of the danger in not attending to feelings: the pulls and counterpulls,[42] the distorting mechanism of suppressing feelings, the repressive mechanism of *ressentiment*,[43] and the distorting influences within community that discourage us from feeling empathetically toward others. Unless we question our feelings, there exists the possibility of hating the truly good and loving what is truly evil.[44] Feelings of revenge arising from reactive anger and hatred may feel satisfying or agreeable but through deliberation will be judged not to be truly good for self or communities as a whole.

Lonergan also recognizes the importance of symbol, stating that a symbol is an image of a real or imaginary object that evokes a feeling or is evoked by a feeling.[45] Affectivity is carried by images or evokes images, and images give rise to insight. Symbols reflect a person's connection to a culture, to family, and to God and these connections affectively promote either authenticity or inauthenticity. Symbols such as cosmic war, martyrdom, warriorhood, God, or Satan are often inherited through a tradition before they are critically engaged, eliciting many different kinds of affective responses, including love or hate, joy or sorrow, patience or anger, sweetness or bitterness.[46] As I mentioned earlier, I intend to dialectically engage four key symbols from Juergensmeyer to evaluate whether such symbols have been authentically appropriated and whether the practical insights that follow from their appropriation truly promote human living.

39. Ibid., 30–31. Here, Lonergan includes a list of intentional feelings.

40. Ibid., 31.

41. Ibid., 35.

42. Lonergan, *Third Collection*, 190, 192.

43. Lonergan, *Method*, 33.

44. Ibid., 38, 40.

45. Ibid., 64.

46. Dunne, *Lonergan and Spirituality*, 64–65.

In Lonergan's article, "Creating and Healing in History," moreover, Lonergan frames the task of achieving what is valuable in terms of two movements within consciousness: the vector of creativity, a movement from below upward, and the vector of healing, a movement from above downward.[47] In *Insight* and *Method* he invites the reader to appropriate his or her own creativity from experience, to form questions, formulate understanding, and judge truth and value. However, there is a movement from above downward, of affectivity from love to responsibility, and from reason to understanding and experience. Later, I will argue that when we are grasped by God's love, decisions, values, and thinking take us in a particular direction. Dunne states that this "affective movement tells us what is worth investigating. It tells us who is worthy of our trust."[48] This movement expands our moral horizon to include the hopes and fears of others.[49] It expands our intellectual horizon through our sharing questions with others and our sharing of common knowledge.

## Horizons, Orientations, Freedom, and Relations

Lonergan presents four other realities that condition the formation of one's values, namely, one's horizon, orientation, freedom, and personal relations. One's horizon is the sum of one's beliefs, concerns, attitudes, and commitments and is structured by the interplay of two interrelated poles: one's acts of consciousness with their orientation, and the objects intended by these acts of consciousness. Orientation or concern refers to the manner by which feelings and patterned experiences have a significant influence on the way human consciousness is oriented experientially in a certain direction. The concerns of one's life are the felt orientations that dominate the direction of one's knowing and doing.[50]

Lonergan distinguishes between essential freedom and effective freedom.[51] Essential freedom makes us human and is a deeper resource within us, marking us as being made in the image and likeness of God. Effective freedom means that the operative range of our essential freedom is restricted by our horizon.[52] Authentic freedom is our orientation to the truly good and an important category in any discussion about religiously motivated

47. Lonergan, *Third Collection*, 100–9.

48. Dunne, *Doing Better*, 59.

49. Ibid., 133.

50. Lonergan, *Method*, 51–52.

51. Lonergan, *Insight*, 643–45.

52. Shute and Zanardi, *Moral Decision Making*, 111–16.

violence since the exercise of freedom involves a choice to constitute oneself in a particular direction.

Lonergan also notes the importance of personal relations, including those with leaders and role models, and interpersonal formative influences.[53] He states that "personal relations vary from intimacy to ignorance, from love to exploitation, from respect to contempt, from friendliness to enmity. They bind a community together, or divide it into factions or tear it apart."[54] The personal relations that make up the fabric of our lives will influence our orientations, possible conversions, and breakdowns. Equally, orientations and possible conversions and breakdowns will influence the personal relations that we seek to make a part of our lives. While the orientations of our lives sum up the concerns that we feel, commonly we pick up these concerns according to the way that we respond to people.

## The Presence of Bias

If our horizons, orientations, and effective freedom set a framework for the range of questions that can be asked so as to arrive at judgments of value, bias names the process of derailment that blocks relevant questions for human well-being. Within the individual and community, a number of biases can emerge that escalate violence and hamper practical solutions to meet needs, blocking our ability to learn. Biases result in the possibility that people can lack the willingness to learn to the point that they lack the knowledge and skill to ask important and relevant questions so that they may practically address escalating violence. Lonergan names four biases: dramatic, individual, social (or group), and general bias.

### Dramatic Bias

When repression does not allow all memories, feelings, and images to emerge from our psyche, we are subject to dramatic bias.[55] We block questions from emerging without noticing that we do so. Dramatic bias is played out in our psychic lives. When we speak of such bias we acknowledge the power of fear and anxiety to dominate our practical search for solutions to problems. Our ability to ask questions is dependent on images associated with feelings. Dramatic bias blocks relevant images from coming into con-

53. Lonergan, *Method*, 50.
54. Ibid., 50.
55. Lonergan, *Insight*, 214.

scious experience. A lack of relevant images means a lack of insights, which can condition negatively the possibility of changing violent behavior.

## Individual Bias

When we are more attentive to what will benefit our own desires and needs over those of other people, we are subject to individual bias. We intentionally avoid correct understanding through an act of suppression.[56] Individual bias or egoism occurs when an individual, overcome by his or her own ego-centered desires, puts aside a full use of intelligence for cooperative living to look after his or her own interest. Such a person is smart enough to design and implement courses of action that will enable him or her to outsmart others through exploitative behavior. He or she must also engage in enough suppression so as not to allow relevant questions to emerge that might steer him or her toward a better course of action.

## Social Bias

Social or group bias operates when we are more protective of the interests of a particular group (one's nation, class, race, or gender) and focus on attaining stronger social and cultural ties.[57] Social bias is constituted by a group's increasing desire for self-preservation and power over other groups or individuals (tribalism). Such groups can point to the precarious position they find themselves in and argue that they have no other choice but to act by the rules and objectives formulated to perpetuate their group. Depending on the character of the group, actions taken can either be reforming or revolutionary. In the latter, social conditions break down to such a point that one group overpowers another group, and, in the case of escalating violence, the oppressed often become the oppressors. Thus, social bias solidifies in a society whose social conditions may be oppressive toward particular groups, inviting its own reversal but without the guarantees that the new arrangement will be free of violence.

## General Bias

A lack of willingness to seek long-term solutions to problems, or to conduct an in-depth investigation of problems that would require a movement out of

56. Ibid., 244–47.
57. Ibid., 247–50.

commonsense thinking to more theoretical thinking, constitutes general bias.[58] Long-term solutions often require giving full reign to intelligent thinking. Without fully intelligent thinking, fear, manipulation, and violence become the distorted pathways for keeping people subdued or for keeping them from bringing about change. The solution is for intelligence to be liberated in its commonsense and theoretical dimensions and for wonder to become the dominant concern in consciousness so that intellectual detachment and impartiality become central.[59] The ramifications of general bias are massive. We end up not being able to distinguish what makes sense for living from what does not make sense. There is no criterion or authority for discerning the truth. What people judge to be progress is seen by people one generation later not to be progressive at all. The result is the brushing aside of relevant and ultimate but difficult questions. The disinterested desire for truth and value is abandoned and in its place a hard pragmatism dominates.

## Conversion

Conversion is a radical change in the orientation and concern of one's life from distorted meanings and values that arise from bias to authentic meanings and values, and is experienced as either a dramatic event or an ongoing process.[60] Lonergan distinguishes three kinds of conversion: religious, moral, and intellectual. Robert Doran adds a fourth: psychic conversion.[61] Lonergan's intellectual enterprise was punctuated by the awareness that there was a rising tide of cruelty and violence in the world that needed to be addressed and he was convinced that religious, moral, and intellectual conversion were pivotal. In the previous chapter, I noted that James W. Jones described the process of conversion and its centrality in the life of the person. I argued that Jones's account of conversion was empirical and descriptive, therefore unable to approximate Lonergan's normative dimensions of conversion. Without a normative understanding of conversion, we are unable to distinguish conversion from breakdown.

58. Ibid., 250–51.
59. Lonergan, *Topics in Education*, 86–88.
60. Lonergan, *Method*, 52.
61. Doran, *Intentionality and Psyche*, 25–70.

## Religious Conversion

Lonergan defines religious conversion as the experience of falling in love with God, a self-surrender to God without the loss of self, a transformation of our horizon through the power of unconditional love, a basic fulfillment of our conscious intentionality.[62] The fulfillment of intentionality brings peace and joy, and love of neighbor and self, while a lack of fulfillment can result in cynicism, the urge to dominate, and despair and violence. Religious conversion is the core of religion, healing people so that their moral and intellectual creativity might be released. Such an event is gift, not achievement. One may be able to sense the goodness in oneself as made good and valued by God.

Religious conversion leads to a sense of the "we" between God and us, a genuine friendship. It may lead to a courageous stance, taking a different path, and to engaging in the task of working through complex problems. This experience brings a certain completion into our lives and becomes a powerful undertow to our deciding, valuing, understanding, and living, conditioning cultural values, which in turn condition social values. It facilitates the emergence of new insights and a new willingness to put them into practice.


## Moral Conversion

Lonergan defines moral conversion as the change in the criterion by which one makes commitments and choices in one's life. He states that "moral conversion changes the criterion of one's decisions and choices from satisfactions to values."[63] When we were children, we made choices according to the criterion of reward and punishment, associating good choices with pleasure and bad choices with pain. Moral conversion moves us beyond this sort of measure to assert that authentic choices are based on objective values. Basing our lives on these values may mean that we will suffer as a consequence of the stance we take, and, conversely, simply following the way of satisfying choices may not always be the right direction to take.[64] The opposite of moral self-transcendence is sin, resulting in moral impotence.

62. Lonergan, *Method*, 105, 240.

63. Ibid., 240.

64. Ibid., 104.

## Intellectual Conversion

This mode of conversion is "a radical clarification and consequently, the elimination of an exceedingly stubborn myth concerning reality, objectivity and human knowledge. The myth is that knowing is like looking, that objectivity is seeing what is there to be seen and not seeing is what is not there and that the reality is what is out there now to be looked at."[65] This myth overlooks the distinction between the "world mediated by meaning" and "the world of immediacy."[66] Through intellectual conversion we can recognize three very distinct philosophical positions on human knowing: naïve realism, idealism, and critical realism.[67] The naïve realist mistakenly attributes the objectivity of knowing to one aspect of knowing, namely, the experiential. This gives rise to the mistaken idea that what is given in immediate experience is real. The idealist includes understanding as well as sense data but retains the notion that the world mediated by meaning is not real but ideal. The critical realist "can acknowledge the facts of human knowing and pronounce the world mediated by meaning to be the real world; he can do so only in so much as he shows that the process of experiencing, understanding, and judging is a process of self-transcendence."[68] The criterion of intellectual objectivity is not looking at images but bringing questions to what one is experiencing, achieving acts of understanding or insights, and judging insights based on the fulfillment of the pre and post conditions for that insight to be verified with some degree of possibility, probability, or certainty.

## Psychic Conversion

Doran took Lonergan's cognitional theory, his three conversions, and his discussion on differentiations of consciousness, as well as his remarks on symbols, dreams, and censorship, to develop an understanding of psychic conversion. Consciousness is the entire arena of internal experience, encompassing sensations, emotions, images, spontaneous responses to others, understanding, insights, judgments of truth, values, and decisions. The unconscious is the complex array of neural pathways in the body, with its physical, chemical, and biological substratum. The human psyche cannot ignore organic demands.[69] The latter serves to pattern the energy of the

---

65. Ibid., 238.
66. Ibid.
67. Ibid., 239.
68. Ibid.
69. Doran, *Dialectics of History*, 183.

unconscious into symbols, feelings, and images.[70] Freud asserts that the psyche, existing between the neural pathways and conscious thinking, exercises a censorship function. He postulated that this "psychic censor" had a predominantly repressive gatekeeper function, while Lonergan asserts that the psychic censor is constructive unless distorted through bias.[71] Girard's mimetic account highlights the intersubjective formation of the sensitive psyche. For Doran, psychic conversion is the movement away from the repression of feelings and images within the psyche, and a movement toward the constructive and smooth flow of images and feelings needed for understanding, judgment, and decision.[72] Psychic conversion facilitates one's ability to know what one is feeling, and how feelings are related to particular symbols, questions, insights, and ideas. This conversion has to do with the boundary between what is conscious (and not yet known) and what is unconscious. The censorship between the unconscious and the conscious operates to open and shut the door when new insights are required and new values need to be affirmed, especially when symbols have mutilated or degraded reality.

## The Existential Subject and Historical Existence

So far, this account of Lonergan's and Doran's analyses has focused primarily on an understanding of the subject as subject through his or her religious, moral, intellectual, and psychic consciousness as a source of human authenticity and as the starting point for reversing the cycles of decline in society.[73] From here to the end of the next section, which deals with Lonergan's scale of values, we will consider the subject in history.

Living history is the interplay and choices of actual people.[74] Thomas McPartland notes that questions to do with personal and communal moral identity raise the issue of human historicity and therefore of the subject in history: the set of meanings, values, and choices from the past that inform one's perspective in the present to shape the meanings and values of the future.[75] Yet each individual remains in a dialectical relationship with an inherited knowledge, a set of values, and a way of life. Each community

70. Ibid.

71. Lonergan, *Insight*, 216.

72. Doran, *Dialectics of History*, 85–86.

73. Lonergan, *Insight*, 251–67.

74. Dunne, *Doing Better*, 178. Dunne distinguishes living history from written history.

75. McPartland, *Philosophy of Historical Existence*, 43.

presents a set of functioning priorities that are a mixture of authentic and inauthentic tasks. By means of such priorities, a community mediates meanings and values through acculturation, socialization, and education. Further, the individual is conditioned by the community just as the historical development of communities is conditioned by individual development.

If we want progress in human development, we ought to assess not only the political, economic, technological, and cultural context of a society but also these structures as they facilitate the emergence of shared experiences, understandings, judgments, and decisions constitutive of community.[76] The goal of historical development is fidelity to the norms of inquiry under the concrete and unique circumstances that people find themselves a part of. When higher integrations of community can be achieved, these become the points of identity from which new questions for inquiry might emerge. Within a religious perspective, history is also at the crossroads between time and eternity, and the finite and the infinite, which means that higher integrations of communities are grounded in a sustained self-transcendence made possible by the participation of the human spirit in transcendent mystery.[77]

## Progress, Decline, and Redemption

Progress is embodied in effective social structures, cultures of integrity, and authentic personal formation. These elements, working together, help us to arrive at intelligent insights and responsible action. Decline is the process of breakdown, a flight from understanding and irresponsibility. Moral impotence and an intellectual flight from understanding persist, and people are unable to change them by their own power. If progress and decline were the only factors in the human story, there would be no way to achieve sustained development so as to overcome violence within communities and individuals.

Only God's redemptive grace can curtail the inroads of sin and bias. By means of the love of God poured into our hearts, God provides a solution to the problem of evil through a new good of willing called "charity."[78] We share, through analogy, in God's own knowledge of God, the world, human destiny, and our part in creation through a new good of knowing called "faith."[79] We share in God's vision for a new social order despite frustrations, setbacks, and the inroads of bias through a new good of

---

76. Ibid., 47.
77. Ibid., 50.
78. Lonergan, *Method*, 107, 115.
79. Dunne, "Faith, Hope and Charity," 59.

striving called "hope" and so we possess the courage to keep on persevering despite setbacks.[80]

## The Scale of Values

Lonergan's notion of integrity in human living concerns human feelings that respond to values on the basis of an ascending scale or hierarchy or preference of values. Such a scale of values will be an important set of categories for developing a "pure" pathway of progress "from a moral horizon based on spontaneous preferences through to a hierarchical series of ever more self-transcending preferences."[81] The scale of values is one element in providing a heuristic structure for the relationship between persons, cultures, and communities.[82] A grasp of the scale of values is based on moral conversion. Lonergan sets out the various levels of value, and their precise relationship to one another, achieved only through self-appropriation distinguishing vital, social, cultural, personal, and religious values. Lonergan states:

> Not only do feelings respond to values. They do so in accord with some scale of preference. So we may distinguish vital, social, cultural, personal and religious values in an ascending order. Vital values such as health and strength, grace and vigor, normally are preferred to avoiding the work, privations, pains involved in acquiring, maintaining, restoring them. Social values such as the good of order, which conditions the vital values of the whole community, have to be preferred to the vital values of individual members of the community. Cultural values do not exist without the underpinning of vital and social values but nonetheless they rank higher. Not on bread alone doth man live. Over and above mere living and operating, men have to find a meaning and value in their operating. It is the function of culture to discover, express, validate, criticize, correct, develop, and improve such meaning and value. Personal value is the person in his self-transcendence as loving and being loved as originator of values in himself and in his milieu, as an inspiration and invitation to others to do likewise. Religious values finally are at the heart of the meaning and value of man's living and man's world.[83]

---

80. Lonergan, *Method*, 117.

81. Ibid., 162.

82. The knowledge of the "skeleton" of what is yet to be discovered is called the "heuristic" structure. See Flanagan, *Quest for Self-Knowledge*, 14.

83. Lonergan, *Method*, 32.

Doran takes Lonergan's scale and makes intelligible the relationship between the levels of the values in terms of movements up and down the scale.[84] Doran argues for a heuristic account of human development in terms of a complex interrelationship between person, culture, community, and the action of God. Such an account can help us to identify a normative process of development within any social matrix, and to recognize breakdown and what may need to be done to restore creativity.

## Lonergan's Notion of Dialectic

Shifting our focus slightly from Lonergan's scale of values, it is useful briefly to examine his understanding of dialectic, which helps us to understand opposed principles, or drivers, of change and development. Lonergan states that "dialectic is a pure form with general applications; it is applicable to any concrete unfolding of linked but opposed principles that are modified cumulatively by the unfolding; it envisages at once the conscious and unconscious either in a single subject or in an aggregate and succession of subjects; it is adjustable to any course of events, from an ideal line of pure progress resulting from the harmonious working of the opposed principles, to any degree of conflict, aberration, breakdown and disintegration."[85]

In light of Lonergan's characterization of dialectic, we may note several points. First, as a pure form, dialectic does not give concrete answers to tensions within human living.[86] Dialectic helps provide an *a priori* heuristic structure in processes that are characterized by opposing principles of change where the principles are modified cumulatively by the unfolding.[87] Persons, cultures, and communities progress over time by grasping that development comes about by opposed but linked principles of change. There are at least two principles at work modifying each other while at the same time modifying the developing reality. Therefore, there is both a tension between the principles and an actual change in the constitutive nature of the principles.

Second, Lonergan asserts that at the heart of human development stands the law of limitation and transcendence. As the principles of limitation and transcendence are held in creative tension, influencing one another cumulatively, there exists movement and rest, the operation and integration of development. The pole of transcendence is the operator and the pole of

84. Doran, *Dialectics of History*, 97–106.

85. Lonergan, *Insight*, 269.

86. Ibid., 268–69.

87. Ibid., 217.

limitation is the integrator.[88] This creative tension highlights an important difference between change and development. Change without normative development can be blind. In the natural world such change happens often, but in the human world change brings about development only when guided by intelligence and responsibility. Genuineness involves allowing the creative tension between limitation and transcendence to be brought into human affairs and into consciousness.[89]

Third, the breakdown of the tension can be toward either pole of the dialectic, constituting a failure in genuineness.[90] Neither pole must be dominant. Doran develops Lonergan's notion of dialectic. When the principles are held in a creative tension, there occurs what Doran calls the dialectic of *contraries*, where progress and growth result. When the principles are not held in tension and one opts for one side of the tension over the other, there occurs what he calls the dialectic of *contradictories*, and each of the poles is distorted.[91] In the case of contradictories, the only authentic choice is the choice for the good and a restoration of the creative tension.

A fourth point in light of Lonergan's—and Doran's—thought is that the integrity of dialectic is a function, not of one or the other of the constitutive poles of the dialectic but of some third principle or higher synthesis.[92] In the scale of values, the integrity of social values is a function of the integrity of culture. The integrity of cultural values is a function of the saving meaning of the Gospel and personal value. The authenticity of the person is a function of God's gift of grace.

Our challenge is to understand the normative direction of development in the relationship between persons, cultures, and community. If change is not simply going to increase decline in society and if people are going to develop authentically, then there must be a way to evaluate change according to some intrinsic norm. If we understand historical development in terms of the way persons constitute themselves through their growth in truth and value, then the notion of dialectic will help identify the manner in which normative change might occur between persons, culture, and community.

A fifth point follows up Doran's account: it brings both human historical consciousness and the grace of God together as two aspects or dimensions of the one real world. He calls this account "a theological theory of

88. Ibid., 476.
89. Ibid., 477–78.
90. Ibid., 478.
91. Doran, *Dialectics of History*, 80–82.
92. Ibid., 88–89.

history."[93] This theoretic structure gives greater explanatory power to Lonergan's scale of values and the relationship between progress, decline, and
redemption. For our purposes, since we are dealing with the link between
violence and religion, the question becomes: In what way can such an account help us understand authentic human development and an authentic
making of human history so as to overcome violence? In what way does
such an account help us understand breakdown in human development and
human histories, and what may be needed to restore progress?

## Vital Values

To return our focus more exclusively to Lonergan's scale of values, we note
that he regards vital values as concerning those things that we desire for
human existence, including health, housing, food, clothing, learning new
skills, and work. These vital values ensure self-preservation, propagation,
security, and comfort.[94]

## Social Values

These values are the means by which we deliver our vital values in a recurrent
manner. Social values are made authentic through the integral dialectic of
community. The primordial basis of community is our spontaneous bonds
of affection. The natural sympathy between people who make up a nation,
tribe, and state, as well as parents toward their children, is paramount. This
spontaneous sense of belonging, which is the basis of community, becomes
even richer through common experiences, understandings, judgments of
truth and value, and commitments.[95] Society is also a necessary element
of community growth and development and is constituted by the elements
of politics, economics, and technology.[96] Society also is made intelligible
through everyday culture.

    Therefore, the dialectic of community brings into tension two prin-
ciples: the spontaneous bonds of connection and belonging that we feel,
understand, and value (the pole of limitation) and that ground all community life; and the political, economic, and technological systems of practical

---

93. Doran, "System and History," 652.`
94. Doran, *Dialectics of History*, 94.
95. Lonergan, *Insight*, 237–38.
96. Doran, *Dialectics of History*, 359.

intelligence (the pole of transcendence).[97] Such an explanation of social values avoids a number of errors. It avoids the error which assumes that community is about togetherness and belonging without the practical commonsense intelligence that generates social systems. It also avoids the error which prioritizes practical skills and devalues a sense of belonging, as in social contract theories.

Within a distorted dialectic of community, there is an interrelationship between violence and social conditions. Violent and oppressive structures deprive people of vital values: food, clothing, and health. When people are deprived of vital values the conditions for the possibility of discovering and finding direction in life are thwarted. Such oppressive and unjust structures pattern the experiences of people. Lack of food, shelter, and clothing means that people cannot think properly, and growth in authenticity is hampered. Anxieties and fears mount up in the face of an uncertain future. A lack of education means that people feel unprepared for living with others, eventually depriving them of work and a means to living, especially in a competitive environment. If community provides a context for living, then the breakdown of social values may provoke people to commit acts of rage and revenge to redress the escalating sense of powerlessness. These dynamic and interrelated principles are true at the macro level of nations as well as at the micro levels of groups. Integrity in such a community consists in the creative tension between the principles within the dialectic of community. A dominance of practical intelligence signals an undermining of social cohesion. A dominance of connectedness and belonging creates economic, technological, and political stagnation.

## Cultural Values

The integrity of the dialectic of community is maintained by cultural values. Such values inform the direction we take in our lives. Culture appeals to our understanding of what we have judged truthful and worthwhile. The level of culture is a higher viewpoint than the social level. It exercises a measure of discovery, expression, validation, criticism, correction, and development.[98]

Doran, following the scholarship of Eric Voegelin, puts forward three available patterns of cultural meanings and values as ideal types: cosmological, anthropological, and soteriological. [99] As ideal types, these cultural patterns are never fully present in any one historical culture but these types are

97. Ibid., 361.
98. Ibid., 506–7.
99. Ibid., 507–13.

able to help us identify tendencies within cultures. For Doran, an integral dialectic of culture is constituted by the linked but opposed principles of cosmological (the pole of limitation) and anthropological (the pole of transcendence) meanings and values.

The cosmologically oriented cultural type finds the paradigm of order in cosmic rhythms. The individual gains integrity by imitating the group and the group imitates the cosmos.[100] The cosmos designates the undifferentiated completeness of reality, such that immanence (the finite world) and transcendence, the earthly and the divine world of gods and goddesses, are acknowledged not distinguished. The divine and the natural worlds are experienced and understood as one interpenetrated order. Glenn Hughes states that "the 'primary experience of the cosmos', then, is an experience of all of reality as an interpenetrating oneness. And 'cosmological' cultures, which include all early human cultures, are those in which the apprehension of the natural world is still dominated by a sense of its oneness with ultimate meaning. In these cultures, therefore, divine reality is symbolized, without any sense of impropriety as a multiplicity of cosmic forces and things, including divine personages manifesting themselves as earth, sky, celestial objects, winds, waters, animals, plants, humans."[101] Cultures expressing this typology symbolize their meanings and values in nuanced oral traditions and rituals whose artistry often escapes commonsense Western thinkers of today.

The cultures of ancient Israel, ancient Greece, China, and India reached a point of breakthrough beyond the cosmological type toward an anthropological type in which the ground of human existence was transcendent, beyond the world of things. The new standards sought by philosophers were a set of values to guide and judge personal, social, and cultural order (and disorder) in society, where the paradigm of order was reason or a transcendent God. Here, the group gained integrity from the individual and the individual attuned his or her understandings and values to rational discourse and/or God, who was discovered within.[102] As the transcendent became differentiated from worldly reality, however, so a greater speculation on and specification of the natural and human world developed. The categories of the natural and supernatural, the sacred and secular, symbolize this differentiation in which the natural is given its own proper autonomy.

With the anthropological breakthrough, there is a differentiation between immanence and transcendence. We recognize ourselves as raised to participation in a radically transcendent mystery of absolute truth,

100. Ibid., 510.

101. Hughes, *Transcendence and History*, 155.

102. Ibid., 187.

goodness, and holiness.[103] This partnership is experienced as a single movement within consciousness but within this one movement we may distinguish two poles. The first pole is the divine partner, who initiates the search and serves as the ultimate goal. The second pole is the human partner, who questions, understands, fears, hopes, and cooperates or resists cooperation with the divine partner.[104] When it comes to shaping community to meet the needs of people, the power engine of this cultural type is the human ability to reflect, gain insight, acquire theoretical reasoning (as distinct from commonsense practical reasoning), and exercise human freedom. This type has a tendency to hold up the importance of the individual, as it has a greater confidence in the power of the individual to change the course of history. Through practical and theoretical insights into the issues of food, clothing, health, shelter, education, and personal relationship systems, social groupings are able to provide and deliver the conditions for authentic human living.[105] The result is a greater mastery of fate and the environment.

Due to the persistent problem of evil, the integrity of cultural values is made possible only by soteriologically oriented meanings and values. For Christians, such a saving influence is captured through the Hebrew and Christian Scriptures that reveal the mysterious law of the Cross.[106] The soteriological influence is made possible because grace elevates and heals nature.[107] Grace helps us to appreciate and achieve moral integrity, to reason so that we may be authentically reasonable, and to be sensitive to the biological rhythms of the body and the life of feelings. Cultural integrity is possible when there is authentic personal value—when people are converted religiously, morally, intellectually, and psychically.

## Personal Value

The fourth level of Lonergan's scale of values is the level of personal value.[108] Following Lonergan, Doran affirms that personal integrity is achieved through maintaining the creative tension between body/psyche and intentionality.[109] This integrity is the normative source of meaning in human history. The integral dialectic between psyche and intentionality leads a person

103. Ibid., 184.

104. Ibid., 188.

105. Doran, *Dialectics of History*, 512.

106. Lonergan, *Papers, 1958–1964*, 24–28.

107. Doran, *Dialectics of History*, 518.

108. Ibid., 179–85.

109. Ibid., 211–26.

to growth and development in feeling, understanding, judgments, and commitments. When the creative tension between these two principles is broken and either principle dominates, then the person slides into inauthenticity.

Through Lonergan's account, I have presented an explanatory set of categories by which to understand the development of the subject, and the subject's emergence as either a failed or an authentic person within the dialectic of community. Community sets a number of conditions that stimulate vital human spontaneities and orient the person's imagination and intelligence. Whether these spontaneities rise up to create a dignified life or whether they evoke destruction in violence depends on, among other things, the kind of influences coming from community. Their failure to find solutions to vital and social needs contributes to an atmosphere of fear and rivalry, and overflows into further acts of violence. This culminates in demonically destructive illusions that postulate creating a new order by simply destroying what was there before, a postulate that simply increases social and psychic disorder. This approach to change participates in the illusion of integrating good and evil, amounting to a psychic capitulation to disorder. By contrast, the way to recovery requires that we acknowledge the negative energies that remain in the psyche. Their healing requires we own the truth of our destructive behaviors, guilt, and shame, and cease to hate and vent our spontaneous affective disorders, yet cooperate with the healing vector of grace toward responsible and intelligent living.

Further, in the process of making moral decisions, the *ethic of control* is a very unhelpful framework out of which to operate. According to Crysdale, the ethic of control assumes that moral actions produce clear and definite results as opposed to the more humble goal of creating the conditions that would make it possible for transformation to take place in both the short and the long term.[110] The moral agent mistakenly assumes that decisive action against evil renders the agent invulnerable to further threats, delivering the satisfaction of immediate victory and success and the ability to generate results through imposing its will on others. The ethic of control relies on a clear and certain plan to rid the world of a current problem so as to protect one from further threats, while presuming a monopoly of power that defines action as the ability to obtain desired quantifiable results.[111] The utopian goal sought appears to offer immediate results and guarantees of effectiveness despite the dangers that may accompany such action. Mistakenly, the ethic of control assumes that we are autonomous agents in direct control of the outcomes of our actions, creating values at will rather than

110. Crysdale, *Embracing Travail*, 42.
111. Crysdale, "Risk, Gratitude, and Love," 152.

discovering values that have already been discerned as valuable from our tradition, and believing that the end of our deliberation is merely the good, blind to any value that may exceed human well-being.

In this way, the ethic of control is a manifestation of a distorted sense of personal value. The ethic of control can capitulate to violence.[112] In the face of this capitulation, it can be difficult for moral agents to face the possibility that they are acting as perpetrators, violently scapegoating others for their own desired ends. Those who proceed by an ethic of control understand hurtful consequences as mere "collateral damage" to be "managed" while they achieve "controlling outcomes."[113] The difficulty in this position is that we can neither coerce others into having insights and taking responsibility nor can we manipulate a religious change of heart in others. The dynamic unfolding of the human world and history cannot simply be subject to a "mechanical determinism in which justice operates as a mathematical equation."[114] Such a mechanism is reflected in situations where the unrighteous are punished by God's agent, influencing the emergence of even more harmful consequences by simply shifting the conditions of power.

Lonergan is aware of the difficulty in unraveling "at a stroke the tangled skein of intelligibility and absurdity in concrete situations," and how little is gained by seeking to respond to the perpetrator of violence with more violence.[115] In this way, Lonergan can understand the shortcomings in an ethic of control. When the response to violence is simply more violence, the dialectic of winners and losers emerges and losers do not want to remain losers. To replace one set of violent conditions by another is most likely to replace the old with a new and unstable scheme.

What happens, however, if there is a breakdown in the virtuous habits of people? What happens when we are paralyzed in moral impotence and lack the willingness to develop authentically? The integrity of personal values is made possible by love and grace, hence the dimension of religious value.

## Religious Value

This fifth level in the scale of values corresponds with much of what was said earlier in the section on religious conversion.[116] Religious value is not about

112. Crysdale, *Embracing Travail*, 45–46.

113. Crysdale, "Playing God?," 256.

114. Crysdale, "Law of the Cross," 213.

115. Lonergan, *Insight*, 712.

116. Doran, *Dialectics of History*, 177–79.

reflecting a commitment to any one church, doctrine, or way of life; rather, religious value is that dimension of human experience, understanding, and valuing that relates us dynamically to the ultimate source of love, goodness, and truth. We experience this love in the gifts of forgiveness, peace, joy, and justice. Religious value generates groups that establish processes that facilitate a connection with the sacred. Prayer, times of retreat, personal spiritual formation, and pastoral spiritual care are just some of the ways that persons can grow in virtue and character with regard to the ultimate end of human life in God. We will explore religious value more extensively later in this chapter.

## The Scale of Values, Creativity, Breakdown, and Restoration

Doran comes to a number of conclusions about this heuristic account of the relationship between persons, culture, and community. First, in a healthy society, practical intelligence exists in dialectical interaction with the sense of belonging to constitute an integral dialectic of community. Second, Doran states that "the dialectical integration of the social order is a function proximately, of the everyday level of culture," but apart from everyday culture, there is the superstructure of society, which lies in the "distinct dimension of culture, the reflexive, objectifying component."[117] Third, the vector of creativity can be derailed because of the inroads of sin. Personal sin and bias are exposed through the self-interest and injustice they generate. Social sin can take hold. We may become efficient but lose the ability to be effective or, alternatively, we may cling to a social identity to the exclusion of a practical intelligence that will meet the vital needs of people. Cultural sin and bias are exposed in the short-term expediency that influences our thinking, judging, and commitments. Societies become dominated by the values of self-preservation, comfort, and security, and exist with a greater sense of fear.

Fourth, Doran affirms the relations of mutual conditioning between the values. New social institutions are imperative for overcoming social disorders yet this may require a shift toward new cultural values since the integrity of social institutions is a function of the meanings and values that inform them. Since authentic culture gives direction to the social processes that are put into place, "personal integrity emerges in the context of cultural traditions, but cultural integrity is impossible without persons of integrity to promote them."[118] Integrity of culture is impossible without persons standing back, asking questions, coming to understanding, and making judgments of truth, judgments of value, and decisions, often at a personal cost.

117. Ibid., 95.
118. Ibid., 95–96.

Grace perfects the natural endowment we possess in reason and human freedom. But that natural endowment cannot be sustained along a path of authentic development without grace.

Fifth, because of personal, cultural, and social breakdown, the vector of healing and restoration is needed. God's grace, or religious value in all its many manifestations, reaches into human history. Immediately grace heals human hearts and minds. More remotely, grace frees our reason to seek the truth. Our seeking of the truth must not be regarded as merely a "private realm of existence without relevance" to restoration at the cultural and social levels of history.[119]

Lastly, in Christian terms, this account of human flourishing gives greater explanatory power to the symbol of the reign of God: the divinely originated solution to evil in the world. Christ's mission is to advance the reign of God. The practical solution to the problem of evil must be commensurate to the extent of breakdown. In the symbol of the reign of God and in the life, death, and resurrection of Christ, God gives us the solution. Unless a graced humanity is healed morally, intellectually, affectively, and psychically, a more valuable, reasonable, and intelligent social project cannot be carried out.

## Religion and Religious Experience

While in *Insight* Lonergan develops philosophical arguments for the existence of God, in *Method*, he shifts his focus toward a philosophy of religious experience that would complement his philosophy of God and thus provide a more rounded philosophy of religion. Lonergan links the search for the Divine and our knowledge of the Divine to self-transcendence, authenticity, being in love, and participation in divine life.[120] While the levels of consciousness are empirical, intellectual, rational, and existential, religious experience is existential and deals directly with the drama of our lives and the changing of human history through our being in a dynamic state of love. Religious consciousness sublates moral and intellectual consciousness so that what is captured at the lower level is not lost but integrated into a new, enriching synthesis at a higher level.[121] At the level of unmediated experience, the experience of the transcendent is an experienced awareness prior to any expression of it. At the level of understanding, the person begins to move into a world mediated by meaning through expression in the form of

119. Ibid., 99.
120. Lonergan, *Method*, 105.
121. Ibid., 241.

image, symbol, art, or language. At the level of judgment, each formulation is tested and verified by means of critical thought, heading toward objects of knowledge. However, the declarative meaning of religious myths and the imperative meaning of religious magic may go astray so that the cult of the sacred seeks "reinforcement in the erotic, the sexual, [and] the orgiastic," separating itself from the pursuit of self-transcendence.[122]

Lonergan's analysis of genuine religion focuses on the gift of love as centrally important to an explanatory account of religious experience. The potential for self-transcendence reaches its highest expression in the act of being and falling in love. Lonergan refers often to Romans 5:5, about the love of God being poured into our hearts by the Holy Spirit. Through this gift of love, we enter into a subject to subject relationship with God. This love grounds prayer, theological reflection, and religious expression. Lonergan understands love as one person's response to the value of another. Love takes us out of ourselves to seek the good of the other. While an orientation toward God may be implicitly present in every question, correct understanding, and judgment of value, the act of being in love with God is the fulfillment of our questing and as such is a very different reality from anything else in life.

From within the Catholic Christian tradition, Lonergan understands the experience of being in love with God as being without reservation and restriction. This sort of love is not a product of our own making but the work of God and a participation in the divine life, having the power to re-shape our horizon of beliefs, values, feelings, concerns, and strivings.[123] This explanation is a normative approach to conversion that stands in contrast to the approach adopted by James Jones, as outlined in chapter 2, which characterizes conversion simply as a transformation or change of the self. Further, according to Lonergan's approach, this act of being in love might be consciously experienced but not necessarily objectified. Since this gift is not the product of our knowledge and choice, this love has the power to undo our previous relative horizon of knowing, and to draw us into an unknowing, transforming what we consider to be worthwhile. It is an experience of mystery, at times overwhelming, like a room filled with music of "notable intensity."[124]

For Lonergan, in terms of intentional process, the experience of being in love with God is not equivalent to the data of experience at the level of

122. Lonergan, *Papers, 1965–1980*, 45.

123. Lonergan, *Method*, 106.

124. Lonergan, *Third Collection*, 125.

empirical consciousness.[125] Rather, it is experience that is identical to consciousness itself, with the subject present to him- or herself in each of his or her own operations.[126] It is the experience of personal consciousness being drawn to God at the level of existential consciousness and, as such, it leads us to take responsibility for our lives and our world, affirming what is truly worthwhile and spurring us on to do good in the world. Further, religious experience as gift differs from the knowledge of faith or beliefs, which is a more explicit recognition and cognition. While adverting to religious experience as a transcultural core that grounds all true holiness and that is universal to all religions, Lonergan does not neglect specific religious expression or superstructure.[127] As Gregson notes, it is transcultural in accord with the reality to which the formulation refers, yet formulations may vary from one cultural setting to another.[128]

## Faith, Hope, and Charity

The experience of being in love in an unrestricted manner allows the full flourishing of the gifts of faith, hope, and charity. Lonergan names these gifts or virtues as needed elements in healing the distortions within community.[129] Faith is the judgment of value born of religious love. Faith is not simply trust in God, or the specific assertion of doctrine. As Dunne argues, faith is the prior act of appreciation that discerns and welcomes God, allowing us to gaze in wonder, welcome stories about God, and discern concrete proposals as worth doing in the light of God.[130]

Hope is a confident desire born of religious love.[131] Hope longs for the full good and all truth. It longs for a glorious outcome to human history despite the frustrations, setbacks, and limitations of human being and doing. Hope's desire is confident because of faith. Faith gives a judgment of value and truth concerning God, enabling us to commit to a way out of our difficulties and setbacks. Hope renders desire confident in the face of this truth.[132] Hope supports faith by giving an affective movement toward value judgments and consolidates faith by a confidence embodied through

125. Lonergan, *Method*, 106–7.

126. Gregson, *Meeting of Religions*, 60.

127. Lonergan, *Method*, 283.

128. Gregson, *Meeting of Religions*, 62.

129. Lonergan, *Insight*, 740–50.

130. Dunne, "Faith, Hope and Charity," 57.

131. Ibid., 60

132. Ibid., 61.

anagogic symbols, enabling us to carry on through the uncertainty of the present.[133]

Finally, charity is an active love for a person or community through which the subject impelled by the gift of God's love becomes affectively self-transcendent through falling in love and becomes morally self-transcendent through acts of benevolence and beneficence.[134] Ultimately, we come to understand and value such acts of love as an overflowing of God's love for us, impelling us to act.[135] Charity becomes the decision to act on judgments of value made in faith and to act on confident desires made in hope. Further, the active love that flows from charity reaches down to transform the whole of one's subjectivity so that a person is engaged in loving not only while attending to the beloved but at all times.[136] For this reason, being in love with God and others is a "state"[137] that is understood not in any individual event of any kind but by observing regular acts of love over time. For this reason, the data of love includes both the data of consciousness, such as feelings of joy and peace, and the data of external performance, such as acts of kindness, self-control, and turning the other cheek.[138] The touchstone of authentic loving is the ongoing movement of the self toward the other, while the touchstone of religious love is the ongoing movement of self toward God and toward others for the sake of God. Finally, being in love is a dynamic state.[139] Love knits together operations and feelings within consciousness into a functional whole yet moves the person from the consolidation of the present toward growth and a more coherent self-transcendence.[140]

Insofar as we practice the virtues of faith, hope, and charity, we are drawn to the Divine Mystery in different ways. While each virtue has an impact on the way we are toward people, events, and human existence, these virtues also shape the way we are toward transcendent mystery. Faith values the terminus of our judgments of value and truth. Hope is the confident expectation of arriving at this terminus in a way that will satisfy our heart's longing. Charity makes a decision to move toward this terminus with thanksgiving, praise, and appreciation through a personal encounter with God, who draws us into a partnership.

133. Dunne, *Lonergan and Spirituality*, 125.

134. Lonergan, *Method*, 289.

135. Dunne, "Faith, Hope and Charity," 51.

136. Lonergan, *Method*, 32.

137. Ibid., 33.

138. Ibid., 289.

139. Ibid., 106–7, 119.

140. Ibid., 289; Wilkins, "Grace and Growth," 733–34.

## The Incomprehensibility of God and the Problem of Evil

Despite the gifts of faith, hope, and charity, religious consciousness sustains the tension between the finite and the infinite with difficulty. In our encounter with the Divine, however, there are two matters that have the potential to overwhelm us and derail our growth. First, there is the incomprehensibility of God emphasized more in the *via negativa* of religious traditions. We can know much more about what the Divine is not than about what the Divine is and so we experience a felt absence of God. The Creator is so radically different from the creation that knowing the Divine is characterized by elimination, forgetting, unknowing, without images and symbols, in darkness. Yet even as the apophatic way speaks in negative terms of our knowing God fully, Christian tradition notes that such experiences receive their nourishment from the gift of divine love. We reach a chasm between ourselves as finite and God, who is infinite. Lonergan implies that dread accompanying this experience of chasm is often associated with a punishing and wrathful deity in cultures that operate out of earlier stages of meaning. In later stages of meaning, cultures understand the experience of dread as related to the call to holiness.[141]

The second matter that may overwhelm us is the problem of evil. The chasm between ourselves and God becomes existentially powerful when we are confronted with the problem of violence and evil. We fail to comprehend evil because it lacks meaning altogether.[142] I will explore the unintelligibility of evil more thoroughly in chapter 8, on demonization. To some it might seem that the Divine allows us to get away with unspeakable violence, prompting us to mistakenly think that the Divine Mystery is a power beyond history with a totally unknowable will. From here it is a small step to asserting that God is the source of evil. Dunne states that we can easily fall into the confusion of not knowing whether "our terror [at the unknowingness of God and the triumph of sin] is an ordered response of a creature to its creator" or of allowing the terror to shape a disordered response of bias grounded in illusions.[143] This latter option denies that God is all good. Doran notes that this option is found in the writings of Carl Jung, who asserted that God is both good and evil.[144] One response to this assertion is to say that, since God is both good and evil, and we are in the image of God,

141. Lonergan, *Method*, 113.

142. Crysdale, *Embracing Travail*, 147–48.

143. Dunne, *Lonergan and Spirituality*, 125.

144. Doran, *Intentionality and Psyche*, 433.

then, evil and good can be reconciled in our lives, thus adopting a mistaken assertion that evil is given a necessary place in our hearts.[145]

The blending of evil with a benevolent God is problematic for Christianity, Judaism, and Islam. Good and evil are not contraries or opposites held in tension but contradictories needing a rejection of evil and a holding to goodness. Further, the mystery of evil is rooted not in God, but in the failure of human agency. Doran asserts that the "age of the martyrs is anything but over. The overcoming of evil, then, is not a matter only of coming to greater consciousness, even if self-appropriation is a moral demand of our time. And achieving greater consciousness will not relativize good and evil, but rather will sharpen our ability to differentiate what is worthwhile from what is worthless, seductive, [and] malicious. The process of coming to greater consciousness is a process of conversion. It involves a more discerning rejection of what is evil, not to compromise with evil in our lives. Good and evil remain contradictories."[146]

The gift of grace grounds the solution to the problem of evil. Charity acknowledges a relationship between creature and Creator characterized as being in love. Faith provides some assurance to the truth of things despite the incursions of evil. Hope gives us a confidence to carry on despite a lack of certainty. Hope may not eliminate fear but it does help us to distinguish the fearful darkness of sin and the incomprehensibility of Divine Mystery. So, while temptation may be a counterpull leading us to despair, hope is another pull resisting temptation by envisioning a divine victory over sin and a divine presence that is immanent yet transcendent. Our symbols of hope, thus, become important and effective helps so that we might desire with confidence the reign of Divine Mystery.

## Faith and Religious Belief

Lonergan makes a distinction between religious faith and religious belief: religious faith is the knowing that proceeds from being in love with God, and religious belief emerges when the illuminated believer chooses to speak or write about these religious experiences mediated through some mode or manner of expression (art, language, and symbol).[147] The religious believer may share his or her commitment to the revealed word, which is also the gift of God, with others, never going against one's natural reason yet perfecting natural reason and drawing others to desire, understand, and judge who

145. Ibid., 442.
146. Ibid., 444.
147. Ibid., 118.

God is.[148] In the end, "the judgements of value relevant for religious belief come from faith, the eye of religious love, an eye that can discern God's self-disclosures."[149] Inasmuch as an older wisdom exists, often equating faith with religious belief, Lonergan distinguishes them so as to interconnect the two.

## The Dialectical Nature of Religious Development

For his understanding of religion, Lonergan appeals to an analysis by Friedrich Heiler concerning seven aspects common to religions generally: the transcendent reality; the transcendent reality immanent in human hearts; the transcendent reality as supreme beauty, truth, and goodness; the transcendent reality as characterized by love and compassion; the path to union with this transcendent mystery through self-denial and prayer; the demand of this transcendent mystery that we love our neighbors and even our enemies; and lastly, the ultimate fulfillment of the believer in the knowledge of God and union with God.[150] All these common features are "implicit in the experience of being in love in an unrestricted manner."[151]

For Lonergan, the dialectical character of religious development implies that Heiler's analysis of religion "will be matched in the history of religions by their opposite."[152] Following each of these features of religion with the goal of highlighting possible aberrations, Lonergan recognizes that there are schools of prayer and asceticism that overemphasize the transcendence of God or even name this reality as nothing, in this way devaluing the personal dimension of love. The lack of a personal dimension between God and us promotes remoteness and incomprehension and fails to create trustfulness toward God. This may give rise to excessive fear, psychological anxiety, insecurity, and uncertainty. This insight was alluded to by James W. Jones in chapter 2. Further, while acknowledging an ontological divide between this world and divine perfection, an overemphasis on divine transcendence can also feed into the conviction that history is beyond repair and can be corrected only through an apocalyptic and violent event. When the personal love of God is not fully acknowledged, the terror induced by an overemphasis on the transcendence of God can provoke a demonic turn to acts against those we consider to be less righteous. I will examine this more closely in chapter 5, on the warfare aspect of cosmic war.

148. Ibid., 85–99.
149. Ibid., 119.
150. Ibid., 109.
151. Ibid.
152. Ibid.

Conversely, an overemphasis on the immanence of God can rob ritual and symbol of their proper function, privileging what is done to the subject over what is given freely through grace by God. It can portray the idea of a divine impotence in relation to the practical problem of evil through identifying God with nature and natural disasters with God's divine punishment. Further, when the love of God is disconnected from moral, intellectual, and psychic self-transcendence, we can easily be lost in an experience of love as erotic and orgiastic, rendering our criteria for choosing rooted in what are merely agreeable and satisfying feelings.[153] When love is not directed to the good, it can easily disregard the neighbor and do what is best for itself.

Religious development is therefore dialectical. It is ever a journey from inauthenticity to authenticity through intellectual, rational, and existential self-transcendence. Yet Lonergan's account of religious love also states a very sober warning about religious aberration:

> Religious development is not simply the unfolding in all its consequences of a dynamic state of being in love in an unrestricted manner. For that love is the utmost in self-transcendence and man's transcendence is very precarious. Of itself, self-transcendence involves tension between the self as transcending and the self as transcended. So, human authenticity is never some pure and serene and secure possession. It is ever a withdrawal from inauthenticity, and every successful withdrawal only brings to light the need for further withdrawals. Our advance in understanding is also the elimination of oversights and misunderstandings. Our advance in truth is also the correction of mistakes and errors. Our moral development is through repentance from our sins. Genuine religion is discovered and realised by redemption from the many traps of religious aberration.[154]

While we may correctly evaluate a religious experience, we may still refuse to respond. People can go through the motions of rituals and worship but their actions may be empty or, worse still, a device for one group to exploit another. Religious knowers and choosers are also open to the four biases leading to inauthenticity. Religious schemes of worship and faith formation need the growth of moral and cognitive development to underpin them.[155] Lonergan signals that religious development requires vigilance to overcome incorrect understanding, to move beyond error to judgments of

153. Ibid., 111.

154. Ibid., 110.

155. Flanagan, *Quest for Self-Knowledge*, 251.

truth, to progress in moral excellence, and to acknowledge the gift of divine grace that enables a universal willingness for the good.

## Horizons and Difference

Lonergan asserts that there are three kinds of differences within the relative horizons of human consciousness either within the same religious tradition or across different traditions: complementary, genetic, and dialectical.[156] When we speak about complementary differences, we are asserting diversity since such differences add to existing insights that make for better living. A person brings differing perspectives and sets of questions to concrete problems. The more diverse the set of questions the more likely it is that insights will emerge to meet the challenge in the problem. Genetic or developmental differences are successive stages in some process of development. Each successive stage presupposes the previous stage while being a development of it, acknowledging that people can be at various stages of physiological, psychic, intellectual, moral, and religious maturity. These differences account for growth in personal maturity and developments in cultures. Let us now focus more on genetic differences and then also on dialectical differences.

## Genetic Differences and Cultural Shifts

In focusing further on genetic differences, I want to highlight in particular the cultural shift from classicism to historical consciousness.[157] Earlier I noted that Lonergan distinguishes the everyday precritical culture from the emergence of critical culture. "Classicism" is the term Lonergan gives to certain cultural orders and products that had been held up as universal; normative; and a permanent achievement in philosophy, art, and ethics; and that had emphasized unchanging essences.[158] In classicism there is a tendency to dogmatism over an acceptance of genuine pluralism and, ultimately, a "built-in incapacity to grasp the need for change and to effect the necessary adaptations."[159] In this way, classicism privileges a cultural product over the dynamic human spirit behind the product, and a way of knowing that relies on deductive logic from first principles over the context of a situation that gives rise to new questions, new theories, and new concepts. As Olkovich

156. Ibid., 236.
157. Lonergan, *Third Collection*, 179.
158. Olkovich, "Conceptualism," 38–40.
159. Lonergan, *Second Collection*, 182.

notes, this deductive reasoning within a conceptual system cannot account for the evolution of new ideas; it is the result of a conceptualist cognitional theory.[160] The level of abstraction is such that the conceptualist overlooks the importance of the immediacy of the data and the concrete mode of understanding, that is, from data to understanding and judgment.

In contrast to classicism, Lonergan states that historicity is "what man makes of man" in his concrete self-realization.[161] Cultural achievements and social institutions are not fixed but change according to circumstances. Each change is a change of idea, judgment, and evaluation that may lead to progress or decline. Historically minded culture replaces the idea of a permanent cultural product with a program of change. It begins from an empirical notion of culture, humanly constructed, ongoing, and diverse. The empirical notion itself begins with the particular human contexts, with their diverse concerns and questions, moving in different directions. Lonergan takes his stand on the invariant and normative structure of human intending that leads to genuine human performance. Yet this normative source is not the only source of meaning since norms can be violated. The subject can be inattentive, unintelligent, unreasonable, or irresponsible.[162]

The shift from classicism to historical mindedness represents a massive cultural change that presents a significant challenge to religious communities. The antipathies between various groups within societies and across societies are a result of the radically different approaches to cultural meanings, particularly religious meaning, across the various religious traditions.[163] The decisions of religious agents as to whether to engage in violence will be partly influenced by where the community to which they belong finds itself along this cultural shift.

## Radical Differences

Within religious cultures, radical differences result when people treat the same issue but come up with contradictory positions or values.[164] They are usually the result of the dialectic of contradictories arising from the breakdown in the dialectics of persons, culture, and community. Bias and willfulness suppress questions that could give rise to intelligent thinking. The more that bias suppresses questions, the more likely it is that insights

160. Olkovich, "Conceptualism," 46–47.

161. Lonergan, *Third Collection*, 170.

162. Ibid., 176.

163. McInerney, "Religion and Violence," 14.

164. Lonergan, *Method*, 236.

will not emerge. Conversion is tantamount to the transformation of values. Radical differences come about because people are at different points of conversion.[165] For example, lacking religious conversion, some people respond to questions about God with atheism or agnosticism. Life is, then, not experienced so much as gift but as an empirical fact and is lived with no ultimate meaning. Freedom may simply mean the liberty to do what one pleases within the confines of distorted religious and secular laws. Alternatively, people may join a religious community on the basis of being attracted to the social and cultural practices of the community, without experiencing any religious conversion.

Lonergan does not underestimate the importance of religion to reverse the effects of decline and bias. Yet, he also has a healthy realism about the destructive power of distorted religion. Even as falseness or lack of genuineness in religion comes about due to a distorted religious expression, the consequences can still be fatal for a whole society.[166] While distorted religion adds to the problem of evil, Lonergan is also well aware that the active elimination of religion, by whatever political/social ideology or self-alienation, represents the tragic mutilation of a reality that potentially could reverse decline. Lonergan notes:

> Moreover, this elimination of a genuine part of the culture means that a previous whole has been mutilated, that some balance has been upset, that the remainder will become distorted in an effort to compensate. Further, such elimination, mutilation, distortion will of course be admired as the forward march of progress, while the evident ills they bring forth are to be remedied not by a return to a misguided past, but by more elimination, mutilation, distortion. Once a process of dissolution has begun it is screened by self-deception and it is perpetuated by inconsistency . . . Different nations, different classes of society, different age groups can select different parts of past achievement for elimination, different mutilations to be effected (and) different distortions to be provoked. Increasing dissolution will then be matched by increasing division, incomprehension, suspicions, distrust, hostility, hatred and violence.[167]

165. Ibid., 237–42.

166. German Bishops Conference, "Statement," 1–2. For example, it has been argued that the Catholic Church's failure to purify itself of its anti-Semitic biases prior to World War II contributed to the evil of the Holocaust.

167. Lonergan, *Method*, 244.

## A Dialogical Engagement between Religious Traditions

Despite the occurrence of human biases and the conflict such radical differences may incite, religious traditions founded on self-sacrificing love have the power to undo violence and decline. Lonergan states that "it is not propaganda and it is not argument but religious faith that will liberate human reasonableness from its ideological prisons. It is not the promises of men but religious hope that can enable men to resist the vast pressures of social decay. If passions are to quieten down and if wrongs are to be not exacerbated, not ignored, not merely palliated, but acknowledged and removed, then human possessiveness and human pride have to be replaced by religious charity, by the charity of the suffering servant, by self-sacrificing love."[168]

Yet the problem of violence is not the responsibility of any one tradition. The solution to the problem invites the combined energies of all major religions working together. Lonergan asserts that the religious experience of the Christian as the objective manifestation of God's love in Christ is specifically different from religious experience generally.[169] Yet religious conversion grounded in God's love becomes the foundational experience behind all religious traditions and creates a platform for interreligious dialogue. Self-transcendence is achieved in a distinctive manner relative to one's own religious faith and can be understood fully only within that interpretive context.

## Conclusion

Drawing on the work of Lonergan and the scholars influenced by his thought, we have worked through an understanding of religious human formation and deformation in this chapter by means of a number of positions about the human person, culture, community, and religion. These will help explicate the link between religion and violence.

In the interim, we may conclude, first, that the processes of self-appropriation and self-transcendence are equally important to people in our current societies. These societies are marked by violence, yet they are also marked by people who want to choose responsibly, judge wisely, and work out what God wants and does not want. Self-appropriation helps us discover a great deal about the dynamics of human consciousness: the patterns of experience, the differentiations within consciousness, the transcendental method, and the intellectual and psychic operators within human

168. Ibid., 117.
169. Lonergan, *Philosophy of God and Theology*, 67.

consciousness. Second, while there is a normative source of meaning in human history as the creative tension between psychic and intentional consciousness, an account of the total source of meaning in human history must identify the many ways that norms are violated by individuals, societies, and groups.

Third, historical mindedness is the awareness that people have a collective responsibility for the creation of the human world. Historicity of subjects is founded on the insight that the good is concrete and is realized in responsible decisions. Lonergan presents a comprehensive model of foundational elements that might give rise to a set of issues in any moral situation, including: feelings and values; freedom; horizon; concern and orientation; and religious, moral, intellectual, and psychic conversion. Fourth, Lonergan gives an explanatory framework for a normative understanding of history through an objective hierarchy or scale of values—vital, social, cultural, personal, and religious—that helps us to realize what is better in itself from what is merely preferable. The notion of dialectics provides the insight that there are two principles at work at the level of personal, cultural, and social values, while the creative and healing vectors give us a model for identifying progress, breakdown, and restoration in human history.

Fifth, Lonergan asserts that religion has a very important part to play in shaping human history, such that, theologically, the divine dimension of human life does not erase the human but helps persons fulfill their transcendental intending toward the true and the good. To arrive at an understanding of religion, we start by understanding the nature of religious experience in its relationship to human consciousness; the gifts of faith, hope and love; the unknowingness of God; and the problem of evil. Sixth, Lonergan asserts the dialectical nature of religious development, thus providing a sober account of the problem of religious aberration in which the will of God can be distorted and misunderstood. Seventh, all claims made by various religious communities among themselves individually are in need of careful scrutiny, particularly when they are used to justify violence. The link between religion and violence provides a challenge to any dialogue between believers of various traditions, as they try to get to the root of their divisions and conflicts, toward religious meanings and values that are held in common so that the problem of violence can be addressed.

In the next chapter, we will explore the first of four symbols that are used by authors to describe the religious horizon of subjects who engage in violence, namely, cosmic war.

# 4

# A Dialectical Engagement with
# Cosmic War: Cosmos

IN THE PREVIOUS CHAPTER, I outlined a theoretical framework for authentic and historical meaning-making based on Lonergan's creative and healing vectors within the scale of values. The creative vector constitutes the movement from below upward, from vital, to social, cultural, and personal values. The need to realize vital values on a recurrent basis gives rise to questions at the social level to address the needs of sustainable living. Sustainable living invites questions at the cultural level so that a direction conducive to human living might be found. Questions at the cultural level draw forth our capacity for personal self-transcendence.

This creative vector is, however, subject to the inroads of sin and bias in such a way that questions at lower levels reaching up into higher levels render diminishing returns. In the face of breakdown, healing and restoration are needed. In the Christian perspective, God's grace enters human history through authentic religious communities and their symbols, sacred texts, art, way of life, and narratives. Grace heals the human heart through restoring the creative tension between body, psyche, and spirit. This creative tension enables a fuller cultural flourishing so that new cultural meanings and values emerge. New cultural values heal institutions and give rise to new social institutions that seek to realize on a recurrent basis the vital values that enable sustainable living.

The role of religious values is most significant in this healing and restoring process. Lonergan argues that the grace of God has the power to reshape attitudes, beliefs, values, and feelings through a being in love that transforms all our values: proximately, at the personal and cultural levels, and, remotely, at the social level of human communities. The experience of being in love with God permeates the whole of consciousness and invites us to take responsibility for the transformation of the world. However, religious aberration is the sober warning that authenticity cannot be taken for granted. The process of self-transcendence is always found in the tension between the self as transcending and the self as transcended. As I noted in the previous chapter, human authenticity is ever a withdrawal from inauthenticity, toward greater authenticity. It is my contention in this chapter that religiously motivated violence is one form of religious aberration. Religious development is, as I have noted, dialectical. For religious development to occur, we must recognize bias and overcome the effects of sin.

In the literature review in chapter 2, we saw that several authors— Juergensmeyer, Jones, and others—present a set of symbols to help understand religiously motivated violence, namely, cosmic war, martyrdom, demonization, and warrior empowerment. By engaging these symbols dialectically, I will test whether they are simply aberrant, or in what manner, if any, they may become symbols of transformation toward intelligent and responsible living.

In this chapter, I will begin to engage dialectically the symbol of cosmic war. This symbol potentially shapes the religious, personal, and cultural horizons of religious agents involved in violent means to bring about historical change. My goal is to identify the insights and oversights of these religious agents, distinguishing authentic from inauthentic engagement, and to dialectically engage the symbol so that we may better understand the data of religiously motivated violence. I hope to demonstrate that the symbol of cosmic war as described by Juergensmeyer and supported by Jones and others encapsulates some insights into the performance of religious agents motivated by violence but also contains a number of oversights.[1]

The symbol of cosmic war also has the potential to produce a distorted understanding of the cosmos and of the relationship between the cosmos and God. Hence in this chapter I will examine the meaning of cosmos as understood by religious agents motivated to violence. I will begin by examining the shift in the meaning of cosmos between cultures that are cosmologically oriented and those that are anthropologically oriented. Each of these two cultural types captures a set of insights about the cosmos. A creative tension between these two cultural types can be achieved only through a soteriological influence that gives rise to an understanding of cosmos that does not have to be understood simply from the perspective of the struggle between good and evil but can be understood from the perceptive of human

---

1. Kimball, *Religion Becomes Evil*; Aslan, *Win a Cosmic War*. Both Kimball and Aslan use the symbol of cosmic war in the same way as Juergensmeyer and Jones use it.

self-transcendence, open to the possibility of grasping truth through acts of meaning, willing, and acting for justice, grounded in self-sacrificing love. I will also examine how our cultural and social contexts informed by soterio-logical meanings and values can help us navigate the relationship between the secular and the sacred.

## Juergensmeyer's Symbol of "Cosmos"

Cosmic war is a symbol used by scholars to describe religious people who are convinced that they are engaged in a metaphysical conflict between good and evil. It represents a central metaphor for Juergensmeyer and others.[2] In a religious context, this symbol involves the conviction that a mighty spiritual power, God, who wills order in the world, is locked in spiritual struggle with a power, Satan, who wills chaos.[3] The earthly battle then represents a participation in a divine struggle. God informs the side of good against the side of evil, and the God-fearing believer is drawn into this battle, siding with the forces of good. Juergensmeyer identifies cosmic war as a theopolitical theme influencing the worldview of those engaged in religiously motivated violence. He chooses the image "cosmic" because the battles engaged by believers are "larger than life."[4] What makes this earthly struggle particularly savage is their connection to a divine struggle that fills them with enthusiasm for the spiritual confrontation of evil on earth.[5] Juergensmeyer bases his assessment on studies of religious agents such as Reverend Michael Bray, of the Army of God; Master Asahara, of the Aum Shinrikyo; and Rabbi Kahane, founder of the Kach Party in Israel. Each of these people communicates an inner conviction that the world has gone awry, and calls for acts of desperation to reverse the situation of evil.[6] I will explore the idea of *warfare* in the next chapter.

2. Treverton et al., "Exploring Religious Conflict." The RAND Corporation is a nonprofit research organization providing objective analysis and effective solutions that address the challenges facing the public and private sectors around the world. In this document the authors explore terrorism through the central symbol of cosmic war.

3. Cohn, *Cosmos, Chaos*, 105, 114.

4. Ibid., 149.

5. Ibid., 150.

6. Ibid., 152–54.

## Key Questions

The term *cosmos* suggests a number of questions: What does the term mean? How do we make sense of this idea within cosmological and anthropological cultural types? Does the religious agent's understanding of cosmos locked into a struggle of good against evil help him or her to create a better world? What enrichment could a distinction between the natural and supernatural add to our understanding of cosmos and to the practical actions of religious agents? How does Lonergan's account of natural and human processes in the world differ from the account of religious agents motivated to violence, as understood by Juergensmeyer? How does Lonergan's understanding of world processes influence our understanding of the relationship between the sacred and the secular?

## The Meaning of "Cosmos"

At the outset, I argue that the term "cosmos" is analogous and not univocal. Hughes asserts that cosmos is the primary constant, the whole of reality in which consciousness participates, the context from which all meaning flows.[7] Drawing on Doran's refinement of the cultural dialectic in chapter 3, I argue that cosmos holds a different understanding within cosmologically and anthropologically oriented cultures.

## The Cosmological Cultural Type and Cosmos

Within cosmologically oriented cultures, the ground of all meaning, the creator and sustainer of life, is not clearly distinguished from nature. The world encountered is a world through which an epiphany of the Divine is realized, and every part of it has a completeness of meaning that serves to remind us of the whole so that the "primary experience of the cosmos" is the "interpenetrating oneness of all things."[8] In the drama of living, everything pales in comparison to the Divine, symbolized as the mysterious power of the gods or of the highest or "hidden" god, while every place and event potentially becomes an epiphany of the Divine.

In cosmologically oriented religions, gods are understood to be useful and practical to humans. The gods are either benign or malignant based on their desire to provide the tribe with the means for human flourishing:

---

7. Hughes, *Transcendence and History*, 183–85.

8. Ibid., 155.

safety, life, health, prosperity, and descendants.[9] Social order is the product of an organic unity between human flourishing and ritual worship such that when this oneness is broken, chaos is felt by the tribe as a separation from the gods.

The compactness of this undifferentiated consciousness gives rise to a symbolic commonsense understanding of order and chaos, recorded in religious narratives and enacted in mythic rituals, the latter mediating a passage from one way of being to a new and better way of being. Commenting on the work of Mircea Eliade, Joseph Flanagan states that each person becomes complete in a second birth through the performance of rituals that have a superhuman origin, reformed in accordance with the ideal image revealed in myth.[10] In chapter 2, I noted that both Girard and Taylor draw attention to the ritual nature of war, which has the effect of concentrating violence, relating it to the sacred and giving the act of killing a numinous depth, while, at the same time, heightening the excitement and inebriation resulting from killing.[11] This is also Juergensmeyer's position: religious activism and divine warfare are linked.[12]

In contrast, I noted from my account of Lonergan in chapter 3 that the heart of genuine religious performance is love of God and others. The contrast between a religious activism motivated by love and a religious activism oriented to warfare can be clearly grasped only through religious and moral conversion. This contrast is further grasped through intellectual conversion, by which the subject moves beyond the elemental meaning of religious experience toward a critical reflection and evaluative control of meaning as a means to distinguish knowledge of God from the religious experience of God. Mythopoetic narratives are elemental in meaning, describing the ultimate beginnings of the present social order, and often depicting a golden age of harmony between humans and the gods.[13] These commonsense narratives reveal how society came into existence in some ultimate sense. Such narratives start at a point of divine-cosmic origins, proceed to legendary events that merge with recent history, and conclude with the establishing of the society as it is known at the time of the author's writing. If the founding religious narratives of social order were couched in the form of redemptive violence, then the imitation of the gods and their fierce battles informed and

---

9. Taylor, *Secular Age*, 689.

10. Flanagan, *Quest for Self-Knowledge*, 244–45. See Eliade, *Cosmos and History*.

11. Taylor, *Secular Age*, 688.

12. Juergensmeyer, *Terror*, 149.

13. Hughes, *Transcendence and History*, 46.

underpinned the formation of warrior cultures.[14] Disorder could be overcome by imitating the battles of gods, as portrayed in mythic narratives, through combining creation myths with combat warfare myths.[15]

Walter Wink notes that warfare as distinct from random and small-scale violence became common between approximately 4000 BCE and 3000 BCE.[16] An example of a creation myth that emphasized violence and conflict has been dated in Babylonian culture to around 1250 BCE; it is known as the *Enuma Elish* myth. Though based on older traditions, this myth depicts the birth of the cosmos from a battle to the death between Marduk and Tiamut, with creation emerging from the carcass of the slain Tiamut. According to Wink, the lesson from this myth is clear: the creation of the world and violence are interconnected, humans came on the earth as part of a world organized by violence, and humans consequently perpetuate violence in their deeds to establish order.[17] Indeed, the creation of the world is an act of violence, in which chaos precedes order, evil precedes goodness, and humans are created from the blood of an assassinated god.

Commenting on Paul Ricoeur's reading of this myth, Wink proposes that the ultimate outcome of it is the identification of the enemy with those whom the gods opposed and vanquished.[18] Wink further assesses this creation myth as highly militaristic, since Marduk's purpose as king was to bring order and to subdue nations through war. This myth enshrines a primitive theology that identifies the enemy with the powers of chaos, and may be the first articulation of the doctrine that might makes right.[19] Politics derives from the Divine, and salvation is a political identification with, and imitation of, the god of order against the god of chaos through violence. The enemy, who is evil, does not subscribe to our god and war becomes the means to punish evil. As I noted in chapter 2, Girard argues that there is a relationship between sacrifice, religion, and social order in pre-Axial religious societies through the killing of a sacrificial victim, usually an outsider, considered guilty for the disorder, and through whose killing order is restored once again.[20] While such worldviews might be religious, sacred, and symbolically ordered, they may not lead to full human living.

---

14. Wink, *Engaging the Powers*, 13–17.

15. Cohn, *Cosmos, Chaos*, 42–45.

16. Wink, "Myth of Redemptive Violence," 266–67.

17. Ibid., 268.

18. Wink, *Engaging the Powers*, 16; Ricoeur, *Symbolism of Evil*, 193–98.

19. Wink, "Myth of Redemptive Violence," 269.

20. Girard, "On War and Apocalypse," 1–12.

I argue that Juergensmeyer's use of "cosmic" to characterize the horizon of violent religious agents reveals a central misunderstanding about contemporary religiously motivated violence, namely, that religious agents motivated by violence operate primarily out of a cosmologically oriented framework, one that perpetuates an archaic form of religion in which warfare, violence, and the divine will are intimately linked. Juergensmeyer draws significantly from scholars who have studied the religious practice of substantially cosmologically oriented cultures. René Girard, James G. Fraser, E. B. Tylor, and Maurice Bloch describe these religious cultures from diverse perspectives: the centrality of ritual sacrifice in religion as a means to establishing order through a scapegoat (Girard); religion as a means of bribing the gods (Tylor); religion as a means of rejuvenating the gods (Fraser); and religion as a means to empower believers (Bloch).[21] Juergensmeyer's primary focus is the religious agent who achieves order primarily through violence. However, Juergensmeyer does not recognize the possibility of an anthropologically oriented framework for religion that would provide the conceptual tools to understand differently the horizon of religious agents. The compactness of the cosmological mindset does not allow for a large enough set of possibilities and conceptual tools to accurately understand world processes, the problem of evil, and one's relationship to God. Juergensmeyer does not grasp that cosmologically oriented religions alone, cut off from the influence of an anthropological orientation, cannot provide commentators or believers with sufficient conceptual tools to move beyond commonsense correlations between religious adherence and violence.

I would suggest an alternative hypothesis. The violent religious agents of today are not operating from a pre-Axial religious mythology; rather they have made a moral judgment about good and evil done to them. They have decided that God is against evil done to them and against the perpetrators of that evil, and thus they are justified in using violence to overcome them. In this case, religious agents see themselves as simply imitating God's hatred of evil, but with a set of actions that do not open them to a new future. They misunderstand God's purpose as one that destroys evil, and, in the process, they diminish God by portraying mere power and not goodness as the proper means to overcome evil.[22]

Whether the assessment of good and evil is accurate and whether the use of violence to counter violence will bring social transformation comes from an understanding not fully available within a cosmological framework. Under the impact of anthropological meanings and values, an

21. Juergensmeyer, "Religious Violence," 891–92.
22. Gregson, "Faces of Evil," 128.

understanding of both cosmos and religion is transformed. Without a clear understanding of the importance of soteriological meaning to address the problem of evil through the power of transforming love, cultural integrity will be difficult to sustain. When the creative tension between the cosmological pole and the anthropological pole collapses, the collapse toward the cosmological pole tends to correlate religious belief with social living, or, alternatively, the collapse toward the anthropological pole tends toward a wall of separation between religion and social transformation, and/or reduction of religion to morality.

## The Anthropological Cultural Type and Cosmos

In anthropologically constituted cultures, there emerges a different understanding of cosmos, one that is shaped by a view of reality that distinguishes the body from the soul, the finite from the infinite, immanence from transcendence, and good from evil.[23] When anthropological cultural elements began to emerge during the Axial period (800 to 200 BCE), religious traditions moved beyond a simple correspondence between the need to worship the deity and the need to be sustained.[24] The cosmos became the world, the universe, creation, and the theater of history, differentiated from the divine.[25] Hughes notes that with this shift there is still a need to account for the presence of divine reality within finite reality and that "nothing in this discovery negated the human experience of *the oneness of reality.*"[26] What emerges is a conceptual autonomy of the finite and the infinite without a complete separation, since the finite participates in the life of the infinite.[27]

It follows that some sort of symbolic evocation of the divine presence within created reality continues to be healthy for human living, attested to in the sacramental character of certain places, things, and persons.[28] Through analogical thinking, reality becomes a sacramental sign of the infinite God and it is only in and through the things of the world that we are able to approach the Divine Reality.[29] Without these symbolic evocations, we run the

23. Hughes, *Transcendence and History*, 157.

24. Pre-Axial and Axial ages of history are terms originally used by Karl Jaspers, whereby "axial" represents a deep cut or dividing line in history dated at about 500 BCE. Jaspers, *Origin and Goal of History*, 1–2.

25. Wink, *Engaging the Powers*, 51.

26. Hughes, *Transcendence and History*, 157.

27. Ibid., 160.

28. Ibid., 161.

29. Ibid., 162.

risk of draining the world of divine significance and negating the relationship between God and humans that has been there from the beginning. Myths still have their place as an elemental language of felt images that evoke the search for truth, values, and God. However, mythic symbols are no longer a direct means for knowing the will of God or understanding the divine purpose without subjecting them to reasonable and responsible reflection.

Alternatively, our ability to establish the good is diminished when we reject the transcendent dimension, resulting in a one-dimensional physical universe, a situation reflected in immanentist and materialist worldviews. As I outlined in chapter 2, Taylor gives a philosophical and social analysis of such worldviews within the West. These worldviews represent a distortion toward the anthropological pole within the cultural dialectic. This reality is captured by the symbol of idolatry, and is demonstrated in aberrant and degrading myths that postulate a universe without God (atheism) or a universe in which God is irrelevant (deism).[30] Our adherence to such aberrant myths could lead to a loss of critical meaning and a failure in critical assessment when it comes to understanding the final purpose and goal of human living. As these interpretative tools fall into disuse, a growing incapacity to distinguish between true and false inspiration, the profoundly spiritual from demonic intoxications, may also occur.[31]

One example of this aberrant thinking is found in the West following the Enlightenment. Science has been able to discover the natural world desacralized from any religious meaning. However, the old order of hierarchical sacralism gave way to bureaucratic secularism, capitalist industrialization, and an empirical reason identified solely with measurement and technical manipulation. Within this context, an aberrant myth about the cosmos emerged following the Industrial Revolution: the symbol of cosmos as machine. McPartland notes that "when the cosmos is a machine of matter in motion, operating according to mathematically determined mechanical laws, then the polis is, as Descartes perhaps ironically imagined in his *Discourse on Method in Theology*, a machine to be constructed, refined and reformed by Enlightenment social engineering."[32] By means of such a myth, "scientific progress would propel moral progress" and a virtuous society would be created spontaneously, modeled on "geometric precision," resulting in a culture that does "not seem to do justice to the evil propensities of unredeemed humanity," and often leading to a "totalitarian practicality."[33]

---

30. Ibid., 163–64.

31. Ibid., 165.

32. McPartland, *Philosophy of Historical Existence*, 128.

33. Ibid., 129.

This mechanistic symbol of the cosmos reflects an understanding of the created order, both natural and human, as determined solely by laws systematically worked out, substituting a dialectical practical reason with scientism, technocracy, and instrumental rationality standing in stark contrast to the idea of a cosmos that reflects the goodness of God.

## The Soteriological Dimension and Cosmos

As I noted in relation to Lonergan's scale of values and Doran's refinement of it, the cosmological and anthropological poles of the cultural dialectic are held in creative tension through soteriological meanings and values. In cultures influenced by a soteriological component, the meaning of the cosmos opens up the possibility of acknowledging the action of the transcendent order within worldly existence. These two orders interpenetrate in such a way that God enters human history in grace through human interiority. In the Christian biblical tradition, the word "cosmos," or world, has an analogous meaning and its commonsense symbolic meaning is found in the biblical text. Hence, first, the world is simply God's creation and as such manifests the saving wisdom of the Creator. Belief in the wisdom of the Creator opens the way for appreciating a poetic beauty in the nature of creation as we move from below upward: the physical and chemical to the complex biological; from the neural manifolds in the human body to the emotional and symbolic; from our ability to ask questions to our capacity to be intelligent, reasonable, responsible, and in love. Such wisdom has a higher probability of being discovered under the influence of grace and through the theological virtues of faith, hope, and love. In chapter 3, I noted that Lonergan argues for the intrinsic intelligibility of reality: we ask questions for understanding, judgment, and responsible living, and this questioning implicitly signals that not only is there an intelligent order to be found but there is a human order to be achieved that reflects the mind of God.

Second, there is a religious understanding of the world as darkened by sin due to self-assertion over against God, a world of greed, despair, frustration, and hatred—a world without love. This is not meant to signal an evil creation, since matter by its nature does not resist God, nor should it promote a renunciation of material reality in favor of the spiritual. However, the universal extent of evil makes clear that the power of evil has the capacity to infect all manner of relationships extending to the whole universe, distorting social, cultural, personal, and religious realities. In chapter 3, I stated that Lonergan asserts the reality of evil to be a radical unintelligibility in the world leaving us ultimately unable to understand why a person commits an evil act.[34] I will expand on this understanding in chapter 8.

Third, there is an understanding of cosmos, captured in the Gospel of John, where we are told that "God so loved the world that he gave his only Son that all who believe in him may have eternal life" (John 3:16, NRSV). Christians are exhorted not to be *of the world* but *in the world* (John 15:18–19). This graced revelation by God effects the transformation of a situation characterized by evil through the power of self-sacrificing love. Through religious, moral, and intellectual conversion, as explained in chapter 2, God graces humankind to build cultures and communities of integrity. The victory of these insights is never a foregone conclusion or the product of coercion, but a process of reasoned persuasion, loving encounter, and self-appropriation through the various conversions. The grace of God helps us remain in the creative tension between infinite and finite—between transcendent divine reality and the world as the place of sacramental encounter.

In this way, theologically, the cosmos is understood and accepted as the world created by God, made sinful and fallen by humankind, and redeemed by the glory of God so that it may be conformed to its intrinsic goodness. The Christian understanding of cosmos acknowledges the reality of matter and spirit as created by God and for communion with God. This Christian belief means that all people share coexistence "not only in the wonder of the physical cosmos but in the transcendent reality of the divine creation."[35] The experience of the cosmos as oneness remains a constant even with the distinction between the Creator God and the creation, while "this distinction *always presupposes the fact and truth* of the prior apprehension of a comprehending whole within which these distinctions are made."[36] Violence fractures the mutual coexistence and cooperation intended by God in the creation.

## The Grace–Sin Dialectic

Juergensmeyer and others explicitly assert that those who engage in religiously motivated violence simply privilege an interrelationship between warfare, religion, and social order. If this were the case, then religious agents would primarily understand violence as a central tool of religion, which is clearly not the case, a judgment attested to by the richness of human living created through religious communities.

34. Lonergan, *Insight*, 716.
35. Hughes, *Transcendence and History*, 46.
36. Ibid., 158.

How then can we best understand the horizon of religious agents motivated by violence in our present context? I argue that their horizon emerges out of an understanding of cosmos predominantly shaped existentially by the grace–sin dialectic, which, in the case of such agents, has the effect of distorting their understanding of the world. This dialectic establishes a constitutive meaning in the lives of religious agents who view the world as a battleground between their identity and the identity of others whom they consider to be evil. The danger with this dialectic is that if one is not part of the realm of the religious, then one is in the realm of sin, leaving God-fearing humanity with one choice, that is, to battle against evil and to establish religious alternatives to social order. Believers motivated in such a way may even establish alternative institutions, roles, and ways of life, not only asserting them to be better and more aligned to God's will but often seeking to implement such forms through a religious totalitarianism, thereby restricting the effective freedom of persons. Implicitly, the opposition between grace and sin combines a felt existential conflict with an imperative to save the world from a threat perceived as able to cause the destruction of humanity and the world.

In the Christian tradition, as Ormerod states, the grace–sin dialectic is found within the writings of St. Augustine, who describes our existential situation as either under the authority and law of God or under the authority of sin.[37] However, this dialectical distinction presents too easily a "black and white account of the human condition" in which one is "all sin" or "all grace." The danger with such a commonsense descriptive account of the human condition is that it can easily lead to a form of dualism whereby the finitude of our human state becomes identified with sin itself. If one's horizon is limited by a commonsense understanding of the dialectic, shaping descriptive theology, then there is a tendency to be suspicious of any human motivation, reason, and valuing that does not have a religious origin or intent. The consequence is a distorted understanding of the cosmos, emphasizing an essentially corrupted human nature having nothing to contribute to social and cultural progress in its own right.

If the person's orientation is shaped by the grace–sin dialectic then, believers operating out of a dramatic and practical pattern of experience predominantly pay attention to particular sins and practical ways of overcoming them through an act of trust in their received religious traditions. This narrow horizon within the believer, usually shaped by social and cultural biases, is indirectly related to a lack of orientation, learning, and development. By widening one's patterns of experience into the mystical, esthetic,

37. Ormerod, *Creation, Grace and Redemption*, 112.

and intellectual patterns of experience, complementing the dramatic and practical patterns, the possibility for other insights to emerge increases. Without access to the full range of patterned experience, the conditions are created for a possible distortion of the dramatic pattern through occluding the possibility of other insights from other experiences.

Lonergan talks about differences in knowledge that come about through the differentiations of consciousness and the realms of meaning. He postulates that a fully differentiated consciousness is able to move between the realms of meaning with ease, even if a person with such consciousness is very rare. Hughes argues that when commonsense claims omnicompetence within the realm of transcendence as a way of coming to knowledge about God, then all other realms of meaning including the realm of transcendence are reduced to external social occasions, with their ritual conformities.[38] Similarly, when the realm of transcendence becomes omnicompetent in human consciousness, then the other realms of meaning can easily become irrelevant, illusory, or evil.[39]

This lack of differentiation in consciousness further confuses one's knowledge of God since the procedures and specialized language of one realm of meaning become the criteria for navigating one's way through other realms of meaning, leading to an uncritical blending of various languages concerning the knowledge of the transcendent across realms. This problem has direct bearing on the manner by which religious agents symbolize God and on whether that symbolization corresponds to the truth about God and what God asks of believers. The sensory, affective, or pragmatic criteria that form the basis of commonsense judgments can be coopted as the sole criteria for truth claims and for what is real.[40] When the realm of common sense becomes omnicompetent, images of God that are very practical and affective, such as might be found in stories and mythic tales, can be misconstrued. A set of guiding clues for practically and immediately guiding one's concrete relationship to God cannot adequately answer questions about God that require a more theoretic differentiation.

For example, R. Scott Appleby postulates a link between knowledge of God and violence. Commenting on Rudolph Otto's phrase *mysterium tremendum et fascinans*, Appleby states that the numinous can evoke a myriad of felt responses: demonic forms, thrilling and vibrant affects, strange excitement, ecstatic feeling, and beauty, glory, and the barbaric.[41]

---

38. Hughes, *Transcendence and History*, 200.

39. Ibid., 201.

40. Ibid., 202.

41. Appleby, *Ambivalence of the Sacred*, 28–29.

His conclusion is that, due to the nature of religious experience, we are to abandon the expectation that such a numinous power will bring only a force for peace. Since the experience of God is felt as both attractive and overpowering fear, it is easier to justify violence for fear of being punished by God.

Appleby has a valid insight; however, it is best understood within Lonergan's insights into religious knowledge and realms of meaning. The possibility of coming to a knowledge that misunderstands our experience of God is more probable when religious agents remain in the realm of common sense alone and at the level of elemental symbolization. A fuller knowledge of God and of the purposes of God requires believers to move freely between all realms of meaning according to the methods and objects peculiar to each realm, integrating the realms of common sense, theory, and interiority with the realm of transcendence. If the other realms were to be explored, then in the realm of transcendence we would sense ourselves first being grasped by unconditional and unrestricted love, with the call to dreaded holiness.[42] The call to dreaded holiness is the heart of our fear and awe of God. In the realm of interiority, we would sense ourselves reaching up toward the mystery of God as the ultimate to be known and to be loved, beginning at the level of experience with its qualities of attraction and awe, through the unrestricted scope of questioning, to the level of understanding, and verified at the level of judging through critical thought. At the level of evaluating, deciding, and acting, we would take control of our lives, seeking authenticity through being in love with God and others and would come to evaluate the experience of awe as the relationship that changes the way we live.[43] The unrestricted desire to know and to value that moves the subject from wonder to order in the universe is "also the root of hope that there *is* an order to the universe."[44] In the realm of theory, we would grasp intelligently the mystery of God's relationship to the world and the properties and the regularities governing their interaction through a systematic explanation and technical language differing from, yet complementing commonsense images, symbols, and myths.

## The Natural and Supernatural

I have argued that the grace–sin dialectic can too easily lead to a negative view of the world through a black and white account of the human condition, potentially leading the believer into espousing a dualist position.

42. Lonergan, *Method*, 115, 209.
43. Ibid., 109.
44. Doorley, "Nonviolence, Creation and Healing," 102.

Lonergan presents a number of insights that lead to a richer understanding of the cosmos. In chapter 20 of *Insight*, he explores the possibility of a different solution to the problem of evil through a supernatural and divine revelation. Yet especially in his earlier work, *Grace and Freedom*, and throughout the whole of *Insight*, Lonergan accepts the distinction between the natural and supernatural within the universe of being, a theoretical distinction that was largely the discovery of Philip the Chancellor of Paris in the early thirteenth century and that was subsequently elucidated theologically by Thomas Aquinas.[45]

The theorem of the supernatural helped theologians discover what they precisely meant by grace and sin in a systematic manner. The theorem also implied the validity of the term "nature," and as Frederick Crowe asserts, with the recognition of the natural order, there followed an understanding of a rightful and relative autonomy for the social and cultural levels from religion. According to Crowe, we realize that "the human race was created human with a need for hunting, fishing, for song and dance, for mathematics, science, philosophy, [and with] whatever lies within its potency for development."[46] We are able to cultivate our fields and build our houses, marry, create communities, function as nations and explore the boundaries of space, all by means of God's providence, proportional to our human nature, but without necessarily needing divine grace. The human processes of the cosmos are good in their own right, with the potency in human nature to create techniques to grow food, to govern ourselves, to gain wisdom, and to educate the next generation.[47] If we can say "yes" to the intelligibility and goodness of the universe, then we can place our hope in the ultimate goodness of the universe, accepting suffering as a part of the human condition and not despairing in the face of sinful desires that obfuscate our pure desire to know and value. Hope rests on the unrestricted character of our desire, even as we are mindful of our human limitations and all attempts to undermine the good that occur through sin.[48]

## Lonergan and World Processes

Drawing on Lonergan's understanding of the scale of values and the mutual conditioning between the social and the cultural dialectic, I would like to suggest an alternative understanding of world processes that would also

45. Lonergan, *Grace and Freedom*, 17, 20, 158, 165.
46. Crowe, *Level of Our Time*, 420.
47. Ibid., 421.
48. Doorley, "Nonviolence, Creation and Healing," 103.

enrich our understanding of the cosmos, and that would counter the hypothesis that integral social and cultural change can be brought about by destroying evil through violence.

Lonergan presents an understanding of the natural and human world in terms of processes that avoid any reduction to physical, chemical, and biological processes alone, as well as any determinism by fixed laws.[49] In terms of understanding natural processes in the world, scientists seek to have knowledge of the world in two complementary ways: classical and statistical methods.[50] Through classical intelligibility, scientists observe a long series of events or clusters of events and seek direct insights into the functional correlation among the data, anticipating an intelligible universe according to systematic processes. In this way a pattern or regularity in the data provides a unified explanation, as for example in the case of the law of gravity. However, the metaphor of law can lead to what Lonergan calls "oversight into insight."[51] The oversight is that one could easily overlook an important feature of equations and other correlations, namely, that these correlations are highly conditioned. Depending on the environmental conditions, classical correlations can manifest themselves quite differently. "Law" does not mean an unconditional imperative, whether we are speaking about laws of physics or chemistry. These laws do not control events; rather, their "role in determining events is conditioned by conditions that are outside their control."[52] The stability of regularities depends on the fulfilling conditions.

Apart from regular patterns occurring in large, complex, and conditioned cycles, there are nonsystematic and random events. While cycles of complexity occur, the conditions for their fulfillment arise and fall away in random fashion. Statistical intelligibility focuses on how often these regularities occur and under what conditions. The statistical scientist focuses on attaining insight into concrete data and nonsystematic processes and so is concerned to work out the frequency of events in a place and time. Statistical method also goes beyond determining actual frequencies to discovering ideal relative frequencies, which are called probabilities.[53] By calculating the probabilities of events happening, we understand the world as governed not only by systematic processes but also by underlying concrete conditions, novelty in situations, and unsystematic processes. The nonsystematic

49. This insight is shared by Charles Taylor, summarized in my exposition in chapter 2.

50. Lonergan, *Insight*, 60–88.

51. Ibid., 70.

52. Byrne, "Evolutionary Science," 904.

53. Ibid., 907.

or random nature of these events is defined not absolutely but in relation to some pattern of events. Randomness is relative to a pattern, whether a systematic correlation or an ideal frequency. Byrne explains that if, for example, a relatively random series of mutations coincidentally happens to have adaptive advantage in the environment, then it will shift the probabilities of survival and propagation of its processes.[54] Therefore, we make sense of the world by means of classical and statistical intelligibility. Some events occur according to an order or regularity while their underlying conditions occur according to some probability.

Lonergan's notion of schemes of recurrence helps us to grasp the interaction between regularity and conditions. A scheme of recurrence is a series of events that are linked cyclically through a series of conditionals that are no longer coincidental: if A occurs, then B occurs; if B occurs then C occurs; and if C occurs . . . then A will recur.[55] Each reaction in the cycle constitutes one of the key conditions for the occurrence of the next reaction in the cycle. In this case, A is not the only condition for the occurrence of B; rather, it is the last condition required for B. Lonergan also notes that even longer and more complex series of conditioned schemes of recurrence can occur and these can involve sub-loops and alternative pathways. For example, the complex scheme that makes up the circulation of water on earth conditions the possibility of the nitrogen cycle of plants, which, in turn, conditions the possibility for the digestive systems of animal life to arise. These schemes are at once more than the sum of their physical, chemical, and biological processes, yet they depend on these processes for their existence.[56]

Lonergan calls this evolving process "emergent probability."[57] It is emergent since cycles emerge, function, and survive as long as the conditions are there for their continuation. Emergence is dependent on the continuing functioning of schemes that are prior recurrent schemes. At the same time, development cannot move forward without the prior schemes being transformed by the later schemes. Therefore, there is a delicate interrelationship between prior conditions and even while prior schemes are being transformed. Emergence is probable since the random assembly of conditions occurs according to ideal frequencies. And it is an emergent probability since, once cycles begin to be set in place at one level into

54. Ibid., 908–10. All interrelated cycles of the universe are some combination of the laws of psychics, chemistry, and biology, and are explainable "in terms of the prior conditions randomly brought together at particular places and time" (910).

55. Lonergan, *Insight*, 141.

56. Crysdale and Ormerod, *Creator God*, 33.

57. Ibid., 144–62.

recurrent schemes, there is an increased probability for the emergence of the next level and more complex cycles.

## Lonergan and Human World Processes

Lonergan goes on to show the relevance of emergent probability to human living and decision making. Human affairs are also shaped by emergent probability, which postulates particular desires realized recurrently through an invariant structure made up of two elements: a good of order, and values.[58] In other words, persons are not simply conditioned by their environment but are also the conditioners of their environment and themselves.[59] More importantly for our exploration of the link between religion and violence, at the level of social values, the good of order consisting of technology, economy, and polity is the process that will deliver particular goods on a recurrent basis.

The good of order is made up of two factors: a general structure and an intrinsic principle of change guided by insights and communal decisions. The general structure is characterized by three elements: a regular recurrence of particular goods, coordinated cooperation and operation due to a set of conditions, and authority.[60] First, schemes of recurrence permeate the human world, where regularities are crucial and where humans do not have to wait for conditions to be right to bring about change. Through reflective and dialectical insights persons can affect the emergence of practical insights. For example, there are schemes of recurrence that are constitutive of a functioning family system or for the delivery of recurrent goods within a complex society, such as the good of education and health.

Second, regular recurrence systems need the coordination and operation of many people working together. Coordination and operations happen because certain conditions are fulfilled: people possess the required skills, affective habits (feelings), cognitional habits (acts of meaning), and volitional habits (choices). Schemes happen because institutions and the material means of facilitating operations have realized them. Such coordination often relies on interpersonal relations of status and leadership emerging within the group so that some authority and leadership directs the operations. While there are orderly patterns of human meaning that perpetuate themselves, there are other patterns that rely on the persistence of underlying conditions. Last, what is determined to be the good of order concretely

58. Lonergan, *Topics in Education*, 32.

59. Crysdale, "Law of the Cross," 207.

60. Lonergan, *Topics in Education*, 34–36.

functioning raises the question of value: esthetic, moral, and religious.[61]
The invariant structure of the human good requires values to sustain it, to
provide people with direction for the processes, and to constitute authentic
human living.

Lonergan's insight into schemes of recurrence and the emergence and
survival of new integrations highlights that emergent probability is not the
same as automatic progress.[62] I argue that changing conditions of society
through violence is inherently unstable. Lower manifolds can remain coincidental while higher integrations can become unstable and break up into
various parts; or they can become rigid, thus not allowing new integrations
for new situations. For new ethical integrations to emerge within a community, new insights and a new willingness to act for justice are needed.
For this to occur, the moral evils, irrationality, and distorted values of the
recurring schemes that perpetuate bias need to be faced head on and to be
dissolved, together with the distorted human aspirations that justified them.
The lower manifolds of images and feelings within consciousness needed
for insight can be blocked by dramatic bias, while the higher integration
of insights may not find the social structures of cooperation and leadership to support their survival. Similarly, a society cannot move forward
if it is under the influence of general bias that precludes the full development of intelligence. According to Lonergan, our "incapacity for sustained
development"[63] makes us mindful that evil is never fully eliminated and
that what is needed for progress is "a higher integration of human living."[64]

Since the human world is subject to the distortion of bias, the emergence of a higher integration is more likely when people are open to religious conversion, to the grace of God that enables a being in love with God
and others. This religious conversion potentially provides the conditions
for greater religious, moral, and intellectual self-transcendence addressing
the biases in each of us, especially group bias, which hampers cooperation.
At the cultural level, we question, evaluate, and criticize whether the social process is truly good, and focus on the meanings and values that give
people and their institutions direction. The importance of reflective judgment and human solidarity sustaining intellectual and moral development
are paramount. The good of order must be responsible, free, and attentive
to esthetic value such that its value shines through the products and the
institutions that make them. The good of order is more likely to emerge

61. Ibid., 36–38.

62. Lonergan, *Insight*, 653–56.

63. Ibid., 653.

64. Ibid., 655.

when underpinned by religious values so that the demands of conscience before God are met.

If emergent schemes are to promote human development, we must be open to redemptive love, faithful to the transcendental precepts, intelligent with regard to the interrelationship between social institutions and cultures of integrity, and attentive to the fragile and tentative nature of human processes. If this were to happen, there would be a greater likelihood that a shift would occur toward authentic human living, that is, toward a community that respects difference and promotes inclusiveness. To bring about inclusive communities, people need to set up the right conditions conducive to the occurrence of insight, communication, persuasion, consensus, and action so that the possibility for conversion can arise, mindful that we are also embedded in the systems we seek to change.[65] To do otherwise is simply to act through a will to power, focused on pragmatism and the shifting of power relations, often by means of violence.

We can therefore understand the dynamism of world processes according to an explanatory framework that Lonergan calls "finality."[66] Finality is "the upwardly but indeterminately directed dynamism" of world processes, both natural and human.[67] I will focus on the human world symbolized in its social institutions and cultural values. First, as a notion denoting how human development unfolds, finality is a heuristic notion. It does not answer all our questions but tells us the elements likely to be involved so that we might seek out answers to our questions.[68]

Second, the human world's unfolding is dynamic.[69] The human social and cultural world is subject to interactive change and development. There are stable patterns within institutions and cultures but these are altered as conditions change. Third, finality asserts that dynamism is directed to higher integrations. The levels of the human good begin in lower levels and head toward higher integration from the physical, to the chemical, to the botanical, to the zoological, to the vital, to the social level, and finally to cultural values. What exactly emerges is not predetermined but dependent on the contingent conditions in the situation. Fourth, the dynamism is indeterminately directed. Though systems join together into more complex arrangements, what will emerge next is not determined beforehand. We can

---

65. Crysdale, "Law of the Cross," 207.

66. Lonergan, *Insight*, 470–76.

67. Ibid., 497.

68. Crysdale and Ormerod, *Creator God*, 69–70.

69. Ibid.

measure the probability or ideal frequency of something emerging but what actually occurs is known only when it comes.

Fifth, the drive toward a good of order that will deliver recurrent goods requires a number of elements working together effectively. A recurrent pattern of integrity in people willing to act intelligently and responsibly is essential for directing institutions toward the common good and away from mere power and violence. However, it can also be the case that recurrent patterns of destructiveness can result in the breakdown of systems and decline. Yet what emerges and survives does so according to schedules of probability. The dialectic of grace and sin may provide a set of categories for articulating an existential response to decline; however, the decision to eliminate sin by destroying it will not be adequate to the task of developing people of integrity needed to rebuild institutions and cultures.

One example of a scheme of recurrence that sought to undo the destructiveness of the cycle of violence can be found in the Truth Commissions established in post-apartheid South Africa. In the wake of massive injustice during apartheid South Africa and at a time when people needed to work together toward a new unity under the flag of a new and emerging South Africa, the Truth and Reconciliation Commission was established as a possible way to bring together people into a united community. In the apartheid years, Black South Africans had been victimized, resulting in a community divided by group biases. As a scheme of recurrence, the commission sessions shifted the probabilities toward people hearing the truth, letting go of their anger and violence, and ultimately mourning for themselves and those who had been killed at the hands of the apartheid regime. The establishing of this political process through the work of the commission institutionally made possible the conditions for: a process of truth-telling; an arena for the voiceless, traumatized victims to have their voice; the shaming of perpetrators for past wrongs; and the possibility of breaking the cycle of violence.[70]

## The Sacred and the Secular

Just as the natural/supernatural distinction opens the possibility of a legitimate exploration of the natural, so the secular/sacred distinction further enables us to explore the natural order with particular reference to the possibility of legitimate secular social and cultural orders. These distinctions help illuminate the dangers that militant or extreme religious fundamentalists have highlighted through social critique, but have often overreacted to, challenging us to identify the legitimate insights fundamentalists present.

70. Ormerod, *Creation, Grace and Redemption*, 158–61.

Distinguishing the secular social and cultural orders from the sacred order so as to better understand the relationship between these various orders helps us find a more authentic understanding of the cosmos.

It must be said that the terms "secular" and "sacred" often used by Western democracies to secure a wall of separation between religion and the state do not help. Alternatively, the strong adherence by militant fundamentalists to their religious identity has been partly a reaction against the kind of Western secular cultural values outlined by Taylor, and partly a reaction against the technological, political, and economic inequalities. Such groups have spoken loudly and acted publicly when their self-identity as a minority group has been under threat by a more dominant cultural group seeking to eliminate or absorb them, thus negating the minority group's distinctiveness. John Dadosky states that, while Lonergan did not speak much about fundamentalism, he did speak about the importance of authenticity in human living; and the danger both of obscurantism, which blocks the asking of all relevant questions, and of adherence to religious identities that reflect partial truth.[71]

Lonergan frames the possible tensions between the secular and the sacred in terms of four provocative distinctions: a sacralization to be dropped, a secularization to be welcomed, a secularization to be resisted, and a sacralization to be fostered.[72] Drawing on insights from Girard, Doran notes four theological and moral standards by which we can measure this fourfold distinction presented by Lonergan.[73]

The standard for sacralization to be dropped in human affairs is any attempt to use the name of God, or the word of God, or any sacral object to justify persecution, exclusion, and scapegoating.[74] Examples of the negative face of this distinction are religious fundamentalist groups who sacralize the political dimension so that the ideal society becomes one in which the political and religious realms are oriented to the same proximate goals and are, thus, not sufficiently differentiated. In such an arrangement, conversion can be subtly forced on unbelievers, watering down religious conversion to simply entry into a faith tradition, leading to violence committed in God's name and justified on the basis of establishing order. Following Lonergan's account in chapter 3, an exclusive reliance on a soteriological self-understanding (grace) too easily repudiates the validity of anthropological truth. The social and cultural orders contain both anthropological and cosmological truths.

---

71. Dadosky, "Sacralization."

72. Lonergan, *Papers, 1965–1980*, 264.

73. Doran, "Essays in Systematic Theology 24," 1–42.

74. Ibid., 2.

When a community of faith engages in an overreliance on soteriological self-understanding, there is a danger that the orientation to meaning, truth, and goodness, which is a key to the anthropological breakthrough, will be easily repudiated. For example, the problems associated with a traditionalist leadership within militant fundamentalism privileges a form of tradition promising a return to a golden age. Shaped by a classicist mentality and a literalist approach to the interpretation of a text, this stance does not allow new questions that contradict the prevailing militant orthodoxy.

Doran asserts that the standard for a sacralization to be fostered in human affairs is the adherence to Lonergan's account of the mysterious law of the Cross.[75] I will expound this mysterious law more fully in chapter 6, on the suffering servant, and in chapter 8, on demonization and the symbol of the Cross. This approach would lead believers of all persuasions not to despise human values but to lift them up, to be *in the world* yet not *of the world,* to accept that God favors all victims of history, calling them to be God's servants. To be of service is to accept a legitimate pluralism and to respect genuine values without wanting to sacralize them according to a particular religious tradition.[76]

Doran draws attention to another form of humanity, one grounded in a self-understanding of human subjects that can mediate the differentiations of consciousness explored in chapter 3, promoting an "intercultural dialogue," "mutual enrichment," the acceptance of a plurality of values toward responsibility and freedom "returning to our own difference enriched by what we have learned in the process."[77] Lonergan gives this the name "cosmopolis."[78] Cosmopolis is not any specific institution or group but a new and dynamic integration of the subject whereby acts of intellect and willingness move a person forward to new questions, yielding new situations committed to reason, for the sake of implementing the dialectic of community. By contrast, according to Doran, post-historic humanity is characterized as "the expansion of the imperialistic realities of our time into totalitarian exploits that would lock our psyches and imaginations and questioning spirit into ever more rigid straitjackets, so that 'one-world' would be realised by the power of force and violence."[79]

75. Ibid., 2–3.

76. Lonergan, *Papers, 1965–1980,* 265.

77. Doran, *Dialectics of History,* 37–38.

78. Lonergan, *Insight,* 263–67.

79. Doran, *Dialectics of History,* 37. The notions of world-cultural humanity and post-historic humanity are ideal types. Doran, "Theological Grounds," 105–22.

For Doran, the standards for a secularization to be welcomed are the transcendental precepts, the affectivity of wonder, doubt, and anxiety accompanying intentional consciousness, reaching up toward the love of God and neighbor.[80] For example, some religious fundamentalists, on the one hand, appreciate and make use of the products of new technologies to communicate their message, sometimes to accentuate the negative aspects of particular cultures and, at other times, to communicate their cultural outlook by contrast. On the other hand, such groups often feel confronted by new insights in the field of hermeneutics that challenge them beyond a naïve realist and literalist interpretation of their sacred texts.[81]

For Doran, the standard of secularization to be resisted is any attempt to condemn carriers of the genuine religious word, in whatever tradition, by efforts to locate human living and perfectibility solely on the basis of human resources, as had been the case in totalitarian regimes of the twentieth century.[82] An authentic understanding of the cosmos cannot simply be reduced to the idea of the machine, changed and manipulated according to a will to power. Such an account would simply perpetuate violence, seeking to put down violent reactions to disempowerment by more force. From Taylor's account of secularization in the West, we can identify the limitations of both secular and counter-immanent Enlightenment humanism as a comprehensive answer to human living, to violence and as a limitation to the challenge of transcendence. According to Dadosky, the kind of secularization to be especially resisted in Western countries is the phenomenon of hyperculture carried by mass commercial interest, a primary vehicle of homogenization, where, through the amplification and control of media, the envy for consumption and consumerism is accentuated while the particular human values of minor cultures are diminished.[83]

## Conclusion

To summarize this first chapter on the understanding of cosmos, we may recall, first, that the understanding of cosmos as part of the symbol of cosmic war has a different meaning in cosmologically oriented and anthropologically oriented societies. In largely cosmological cultures, there

---

80. Doran, "Essays in Systematic Theology 24," 3.

81. Dadosky, "Sacralization," 520. As an example, the Wahhabi branch of Islam admits little need for a developing understanding of texts beyond the static interpretation of the Koran and Sunnah.

82. Doran, "Essays in Systematic Theology 24," 4.

83. Dadosky, "Sacralization," 521–22.

is an interpenetration of material, human, and divine realities. In largely anthropological societies, there is a distinction between finite and infinite, immanent and transcendent. Through the soteriological turn, the cosmos becomes that reality created by God for our salvation, with its own poten-tiality and intrinsic goodness, and for our communion with God, in which all that is created shares coexistence in the creation brought into existence and sustained by God. Inasmuch as Juergensmeyer asserts that religious agents motivated by violence mirror on earth some struggle by God against evil in heaven, then he is asserting their self-understanding to be mythic. Juergensmeyer bases his conclusions on a cosmological understanding of religion and cosmos, thus not attending to the realm of possibilities within soteriological and anthropological meanings and values. To this extent, his account of religion and violence is truncated and inadequate.

Second, I have argued, however, that such agents operate out of a con-ceptual understanding of grace and sin that goes beyond mythic knowing. Such an understanding presents a grave danger: the misunderstanding of cosmic dualism and consequently a lack of an appreciation of cosmos in all its richness as a potentially emerging set of processes. At the level of cultural values, there is a long and slow process before new institutions of learning and authentic persons emerge. People whose religious horizon is shaped by the grace–sin dialectic are often reacting against a mechanistic imagina-tion that postulates a social and cultural milieu that can be controlled by power, thus setting the stage for a retaliatory, religiously motivated violence. However, these milieus produce a distorted religious tradition that experi-ences God as punitive, angry, and violent. In contrast, an experience of God founded on an unrestricted and dynamic being in love with God, ground-ing all religious expression and sublating moral and intellectual conversion, opens the believer to different virtues and different understandings of what constitutes reality. The important distinction between the natural and su-pernatural helps us to grasp an understanding of world processes grounded in recurrent schemes, highlighting that human development does not hap-pen by forceful control but rather by creating the conditions that would make possible free and authentic transformation.

Third, through Lonergan's insights on sacralization and secularization, we are able to construct a heuristic for the kind of cultural and social world against which religious fundamentalist groups rightfully and legitimately react, and the kind of cultural world that legitimately should be fostered both in religious communities and wider society. Lonergan implies that rad-ical problems require commensurate solutions and since religious violence is a problem in the "very dynamic structure of cognitional, volitional and social activity," then it too will require a radical solution.[84] The problem is not primarily social but gives rise to the social surd, and from the social surd it receives "its continuity, its aggravation, [and] its cumulative character."[85] Therefore, the problem cannot be solved simply by presenting a correct philosophy, theology, or ethics since "precisely because they are correct, they will not appear correct to minds disoriented . . . they will not appear workable to wills with restricted ranges of effective freedom . . . they will be weak competitors for serious attention in the realm of practical affairs."[86] Nor is the problem solved through establishing a benevolent despotism to enforce a correct philosophy, theology, and ethics. Even if force can be used to correct the immoral individual or group, it does not follow that it can correct the general bias of common sense.

In the next chapter, I will examine the horizons of religious agents who postulate warfare as a solution to the problem of overcoming evil.

84. Lonergan, *Insight*, 653.
85. Ibid., 654.
86. Ibid., 654.

# 5

# A Dialectical Engagement with Cosmic War: Warfare

IN THE PREVIOUS CHAPTER, I argued the importance of a dialectical engagement with the idea of *cosmos* within the symbol of cosmic war. We saw that the designation of *cosmic* war that linked violence, divine will, and warfare within a cosmologically oriented mindset was imprecise, especially when dealing with religious groups who demonstrate that their cultures have achieved, if only partially, an anthropological breakthrough. A better, more nuanced understanding of the religious agent's horizon would be to categorize it in terms of a grace–sin dialectic but that carries the danger of cosmic dualism, and consequently a lack of appreciation for the complexity and dynamism of the cosmos as a potentially emerging set of processes. Further, the experience of God founded in an unrestricted and dynamic state of being in love grounds all religious expression sublating moral and intellectual conversion, opening the probability that believers might develop different virtues and cultural meanings of how reality is constituted.

In this chapter I will critique the symbol of "warfare," often justified through appeals to religious traditions, and argue that examining the moral horizons of religious believers gives us a more comprehensive understanding of their actions in relation to warfare. These horizons are pragmatism,[1] militarism, pacifism, and just war, with the potential for each of these to merge with religious apocalyptic consciousness. I will examine the way in which state and nonstate agents use religious imagination to justify war-

---

1. The literature considered refers to images of war. One image is called realism and equates to a political realist or pragmatist approach to policy. Because of the technical meaning of realism within Lonergan's thought, I shall consistently refer to this position as pragmatism, noting where the terminology of particular authors may differ.

fare for the purposes of retaliation, empire building, and reclaiming lost territory, exploring both Western and Islamic perspectives. But I will leave it to the next chapter to examine a Christian understanding of religious apocalyptic consciousness that helps shape an intelligently and responsibly religious imagination concerning warfare.

As we saw in chapter 2, Girard's concept of sacred violence leads to the belief that through the destructive power of violent acts by religious communities, order and peace can become a reality. Warfare is therefore justified as a means for establishing order, while religion is complicit in validating warfare. I argued that Lonergan's account leads to the conclusion that the problem is, in part, inauthentic religion. This leads commentators who do not distinguish between genuine and false religion to misidentify the cause in "religion." The argument that religion is the problem is further weakened by the way religion and politics are poorly differentiated and are interrelated. Where religion and politics are completely separated, the danger is that the problem of evil within society is not sufficiently addressed. Where religion subsumes politics and does not allow politics its own proper relative autonomy, the danger is that acts of war are related to images of the violent will of God. Where the political realm subsumes religion, the danger is that distorted political actions manipulate the social dynamics of religion so as to justify war and religious identity corresponding to political identity.

Juergensmeyer asserts that the central metaphor for viewing religiously motivated violence is warfare since "war is the context of sacrifice rather than the other way around."[2] The world is brought to order through warfare mediated by religious agents who often correlate actual warfare with the sanctioned will of God so that the enemy of God, perceived as destroying a cultural heritage, way of life, and communal identity, is brought to subjugation.[3]

According to Juergensmeyer, the idea of "warfare" for the religious agent evokes the image of a great enemy and a participation in an all-consuming battle where no compromise is possible, the stakes are high, and an all or nothing response is required.[4] He argues that the texts of religious traditions often use the imagery of warfare since "the task of creating a vicarious experience of warfare—albeit, one usually imagined as residing on a spiritual plane—is one of the main businesses of religion."[5] For

---

2. Juergensmeyer, *Terror*, 171.

3. Ibid., 149–63. Juergensmeyer draws examples from Hinduism, Islam, Judaism, and Christianity to highlight the ways in which believers correlate warfare with belief in their sacred texts.

4. Ibid., 152.

5. Ibid., 160.

Juergensmeyer, therefore, those engaged in religious violence envision the struggle of war as primarily religious rather than political and economic: a battle between transcendent beliefs and worldly goals, between religion and antireligion. At the same time, only war holds out the hope of victory over antireligion and the means to achieve victory historically.[6] Disorder is only ultimately corrected by God, who is beyond killing and being killed.[7] As a post-Enlightenment thinker, Juergensmeyer is committed to the separation of religion and politics and, therefore, engages in his own form of dualistic thinking rather than exploring what might be an authentic relationship between religion and politics. Whilst agreeing with Juergensmeyer's assessment that certain groups might use religious meanings and values to justify warfare in certain historical circumstances, I argue that using warfare to establish social order and political power is based upon a very complex and diverging set of unhelpful positions.

With Juergensmeyer, I argue that political cultures justified by religious traditions that promote actual warfare as a means to establish order will not be able to provide new cultural meanings and new social institutions to meet the needs of a community on a recurrent basis. Rather than make a simple correlation between religion and warfare to explain the data, against Juergensmeyer I propose that an examination of the moral horizon of subjects and the place of religious and moral conversion helps us to better understand decisions for or against warfare.

To that end, I will examine five moral horizons: pragmatism, militarism, pacifism, just war, and apocalyptic consciousness. Though Juergensmeyer and others rightly put forward examples of believers who advocate warfare to advance theocratic societies, he omits to mention that secular states who advocate a separation of church and state are also capable of using implicit religious rhetoric to justify and motivate their claims for war. I will demonstrate how distorted religious meanings can underpin the justification for warfare by church and state, with particular reference to the United States of America and its decision to invade Iraq in 2003. I will especially argue that the justification for war by militant Islamic groups is founded on a narrow interpretation of jihad, which, in the long run, distorts the religious tradition of Islam, founded on love of God and neighbor. I will dialectically engage the notion of jihad, arguing for an alternative understanding to that held by radical groups.

6. Ibid., 158.
7. Ibid., 161.

## Warfare and the Moral Horizon of the Subject

The phenomenon of warfare can be approached from psychophysical,[8] economic, technological, sociopolitical,[9] cultural, and religious perspectives. In Lonergan's account of the concrete subject, the relative horizon of the subject marks the effective limits of the subject's feelings, understanding, and values through a prepatterned set of experiences that shape the questioner's insights and decisions. Anthony Coates presents four "images of war" that describe both the horizon of subjects contemplating warfare and the intended object: realism, militarism, pacifism, and just war.[10] These are not so much images as they are a set of expectations, judgments of fact and of value that structure the subject's horizon and shape responses to war. I will explore Coates's images, dealing with the first three in this section and just war in the next chapter. Finally, I will include in my analysis another horizon of meaning that often uses battle imagery to structure the moral response of religious agents, namely, religious apocalyptic consciousness, and examine how it can distort decisions and actions and, in the next chapter, how it can be authentically appropriated.

## Realism/Pragmatism

The relative horizon of pragmatism is influenced by an attitude of skepticism toward moral norms or prescriptions around warfare, especially when those norms are applied to the actual circumstances of conflict.[11] On Coates's view, the pragmatist claims that the moralist view ends up creating longer periods of conflict, fueled by moral puritanism and dangerous utopianism,[12] whereas the pragmatist prefers to work within the constraints and possibilities of power, and strives toward the balancing of power between states, where security and self-preservation are the key values to advance the national interest of one's country. This leads Coates to describe pragmatism as the "prevention of domination and the fostering of equilibrium."[13] While the pragmatist may not be keen to begin a war

---

8. Scarry, *Body in Pain*, 90, 128.

9. Kleiderer et al., *Just War*, 6. These authors put the emphasis on the relationship between warfare and politics.

10. Coates, *Ethics of War*.

11. Ibid., 18. Coates uses the term "realism" here but, as previously mentioned, I shall refer to this position as pragmatism.

12. Coates, *Ethics of War*, 18–19.

13. Ibid., 20.

for moral reasons, before knowing clearly the outcome in terms of power relations, once engaged, the moral limitations of ordinary human living do not apply and the pragmatist is dominated by the pragmatic considerations of power and interest.[14] This leads Coates to say that "war is hell and moral theorists delude themselves if they imagine it can be other than it is."[15] The conduct of war becomes an instrumental means for pursuing the national interest of the state and maximizing political gain, where national interest is the default position of leaders.

Steven Lee grounds the political justification of the realist in Hobbesian political theory.[16] Hobbes argued that in the state of nature, people without government are brutish and at war with each other. The solution to this chaos is a social contract among members, creating a central coercive government to maintain the rule of law. Since, however, there is no world government, nations constantly feel threatened by other nations, who act out of the desire for competitive advantage, who engage in provocative actions against one another, and who mistrust one another. The basis of morality for political decisions is physical security, comfort, and self-preservation, and other moral consideration cannot have priority if the long-term security and self-interest of the people is not first upheld.

I argue that the pragmatist position contains a number of weaknesses. First, the realist or pragmatist mindset, which is grounded in power relations, can easily lead to incalculable destruction precisely because it fails to attend to moral imperatives in the conduct of war. This mindset can too easily put aside the distinction between combatants and noncombatants, arguing erroneously that noncombatant deaths are simply collateral damage. While there may be a number of noncombatants killed indirectly in war, there should be no intentional targeting of civilians, even if such actions would lead to a quicker end to conflict. Similarly, the pragmatist position seems to disregard proportionality, that is, the principle that militaries must use only that amount of force necessary to overcome the enemy in proportion to their level of resistance and compliance, and not excessive force.

Second, Coates's pragmatist position on war suggests that persons have already judged or accepted as given a set of interests to be more important than the interest of others and so decisions are justified on the basis of one group having a greater need than others. While political outcomes are important, all political objectives and goals are shaped by a good philosophy or a bad philosophy of social living. The cultural question as to what constitutes

14. Ibid., 23.
15. Ibid., 32.
16. Lee, *Ethics and War*, 16–18.

the good life for human living reveals a set of value judgments that help us work out whether the common good and the interest of a community are being served or not. If the good life is founded simply on security, comfort, and self-preservation, then too easily property accumulation becomes the measure of success for a country and self-interest translated into a materially prosperous life becomes the standard for assessing right from wrong.

Girard's work contains an important warning about the pragmatist position. He argues that Carl von Clausewitz's treatise *On War* in the modern period is both a comprehensive strategy for engagement in modern war and implicitly a demonstration of how modern war is potentially bound up by mimetic rivalry founded in the desire for comfort and security.[17] In the modern secular state, freed by the constraints of religious society, Girard warns that "our civilization is the most creative and powerful ever known, but also the most fragile and threatened because it no longer has the safety rails of archaic religion. Without sacrifice in the broader sense, it could destroy itself if it does not take care."[18] Implicit in Girard's comments is a warning on the dangers of the pragmatist mindset, which evaluates the engagement in modern warfare primarily according to understandings about the most practical strategies and objectives for deploying one's army so as to win battles. This mindset does not take account of mimetic fascination, where both parties reach a point of mimetic doubling, flowing from their hatred of one another. For Girard, these extreme positions are evident in the involvement of whole populations of countries or partisan groups in war, giving rise to high levels of civilian casualties, pronounced as "collateral damage," reaching down in mass killings, contempt for the law, and lack of respect for prisoners. Thus, this mindset diminishes the importance of a moral evaluation on what truly constitutes the good life and the importance of virtue and conversion, and, instead, elevates the concerns of the political interests of one group above a fuller sense of human dignity and justice for all.

In contrast to the pragmatist horizon, Lonergan asserts that there are norms to be discovered in human consciousness that guide the formation of values or interests. The values that underpin the pragmatist mindset are often merely utilitarian in nature and put aside a full consideration of human authenticity. Following Lonergan's account in chapter 3, there is a normative requirement to do the truth, having come to know the truth. Yet, knowing the truth cannot be taken for granted in any political society, and what may be needed is a dialectical engagement with the truth and values of one group over against those of another. When warfare as simply

---

17. Girard, "On War and Apocalypse," 1; Clausewitz, *On War*.

18. Girard, "On War and Apocalypse," 5.

a balancing of mere power becomes the dominant mindset of the political system, the shift from what is merely satisfying to what is truly valuable can come about only through moral conversion. In this case the achieving of power over others so as to secure one's own interests is radically different to a cessation of hostilities, the achievement of peace, mutual cooperation, and the promotion of the common good. Since moral conversion sublates intellectual conversion, knowing the truth may require moving out of the omnicompetence of practicality into the realm of interiority, facilitating a distinction between practical knowledge, universal moral knowledge, and the converted or unconverted stance of the subject.

## Militarism

Coates states that the "hallmark of the militarist is the lust for war . . . an enthusiast for war, a 'happy warrior' who shares none of the moral anxiety rightly associated with the just recourse to war."[19] Militarism "abolishes the moral threshold of war" and "establishes a predisposition to war or a moral bias in favor of war."[20] The cause for war may or may not arise out of the perpetration of an injury for, even before such an event, there exists for the militarist "the general threat posed by the existence of the other."[21] To overcome the threat of the existence of the other, a group must achieve supremacy, whether through the elimination of internal enemies (militarist states), or of external enemies, or even of whole peoples and cultures (militaristic empires). In this way, war and mere power over others is intrinsic to human living, creating communities whose economic and political institutions are marked by extreme expenditures toward the technology of war.

I argue that the militarist position, too, contains weaknesses. First, similar to the pragmatist position, the militarist takes political interests as given, so that decisions are justified on the basis of one group's power being more important than the interest of others. The distorted conclusion: there is no need to work out whether each group's interests promote the common good. Since the common good is not even considered, then the nature of community as a set of cooperative schemes to deliver recurrent goods is easily repudiated.[22] Second, once all the enemies have been subdued and there is a relatively long period marked by the absence of conflict, what happens to the horizon of the militarist? Militarism would suggest that fear

19. Coates, *Ethics of War*, 43.
20. Ibid., 45.
21. Ibid., 45.
22. See the section "Lonergan and Human World Processes" in chapter 4.

of a threat to human life is a significant component of the affective life of the militarist. The militarist's horizon betrays an inclination to an ethic of control and a state of fear. In terms of addressing fear, religious conversion as unrestricted love overcomes fear, providing the possibility for a new moral horizon, characterized by care, and not simply a defensive appeasing of fear and mistrust.

## Pacifism

Pacifism stands for the "moral renunciation of war."[23] Pacifists have a moral opposition to war, and yet when "the renunciation of war rests on moral grounds, the nature and extent of that renunciation allows a number of important distinctions to be drawn."[24] These distinctions range from the absolute moral prohibition of war to prohibiting war in some circumstances, or "contingent" pacifism.[25] A contingency-based approach notes that the modern conduct of warfare, while technologically more precise, in fact results often in a massive destruction of nonmilitary infrastructure and a massive indirect death toll to noncombatants, giving rise to a moral skepticism over our ability to limit war. The conduct of war becomes morally corrupting to the participants, desensitizing them toward the humanity of their victims. In the latter, there is a presupposition that while just wars remain possible, generally speaking, *particular* wars are often unjust. The absolute refusal to engage in warfare may cause people opposed to pacifism to discover its positive side, that is, a policy of nonviolence that leads to the possibility of resolving conflict peacefully before conflicts escalate to war.

I argue, however, that the pacifist position has weaknesses when it takes an absolute stance. The rightful moral opposition to war on the basis of distaste for bloodlust, political opportunism, or utility must be matched with the duties and rights of the community to resist evil, protect innocent life, and defend the cause of justice against an unjust aggressor. Individuals may choose the pacifist stance and rightly understand such a stance as identifying warfare as the last resort, with the priority of peace obtained through justice. The pacifist must come to terms with the responsibility of political communities to serve the common good, sometimes through the use of force prudentially considered, especially when individual desires

23. Ibid., 77.

24. Ibid., 78.

25. Ibid. See also Allman, *Who Would Jesus Kill?*, 63–67. Allman describes seven kinds of pacifism: absolute, universal, principled, classical, strategic, separatist, and politically engaged.

and the social systems of those communities truly are focused on what is worthwhile.

## Just War

The image of just war upholds the moral limitations of war through a set of principles based in natural law, insisting on "the moral determination of war where it is possible and on the moral renunciation of war where it is not."[26] We will consider just war further in the next chapter.

## Religious Apocalyptic Consciousness

The horizon of some religious agents is also shaped by religious apocalyptic literature that envisages a final transformation of existence and history, through the direct intervention of God or God's agents, often involving imaginative scenes of warfare.[27] Drawing from the writings of Eric Voegelin and Lonergan, Hughes describes religious apocalyptic consciousness as the awareness of an ontological divide between this world and divine perfection, with the felt conviction that history is a field of disorder and beyond repair by human action alone.[28] Subjects reach a high level of anxiety over social disorder and seek a resolution of this disorder through actions that seek to establish a perfected order of existence. This resolution is initiated by God, either directly or by the agents of God who act on God's behalf. Positively, religious apocalyptic texts usually heighten the centrality of God to address the problem of evil, directing the believer not to underestimate the power of evil and its ability to affect all of creation adversely.

Apocalyptic literature is common in communities that have been influenced by soteriological truth. Believers point to signs on earth and in heaven that symbolize the interrelationship between the material and the spiritual in an imaginative and symbolically dense narrative that demonstrates how and why history might be shaped in times of intense conflict. From my account of Jones's work in chapter 2, the designation of the mindset of religious agents motivated to violence as possessing apocalyptic overtones, serves to accentuate the belief that there is a war being waged against demonic and secular forces, whether mediated by a secular government or by the wider public. Appleby and others also note a litany of groups who

---

26. Coates, *Ethics of War*, 97.

27. Jones, "Eternal Warfare," 94.

28. Hughes, *Transcendence and History*, 85; Voegelin, *Ecumenic Age*.

draw upon religious apocalyptic texts to justify acts of violence against their enemies: Heradi or Ultra-Orthodox Jews; the Shiite Muslims of Iran who await deliverance by the hidden Imam;[29] and premillennialist Christians who anticipate the rapture, the coming of the Antichrist, and a great cosmic battle.[30] These religious agents often turn to this form of religious imagination to excite the faith of believers, to arrest the erosion of religious identity, to fortify the boundaries of their communities, and to create alternatives to secular behavior.

All this raises the question of what distinguishes the horizon of religious agents who have an apocalyptic consciousness that has become distorted? Apocalyptic consciousness is shaped by a particular tradition of apocalyptic texts, which are not always interpreted accurately. James Alison argues that there is a relationship between a distorted, dualist thinking and an inaccurate interpretation of religious apocalyptic texts.[31] There is the possibility of a strict separation between this world and the beyond, shaped by a dialectic of sin and grace, tending to a cosmic dualism, which I explored in the previous chapter. What follows is a temporal dualism, mirroring the cosmic dualism, symbolized through a utopian society brought down to earth by God and controlled by a doctrinal dogmatism.[32] Within community relationships, there is a strict division between the righteous and the unrighteous, the pure and the impure, which manifests itself in structures that marginalize certain groups and elevate others.[33]

There are a number of oversights in the horizon of persons who resort to a distorted religious apocalyptic consciousness. First, such religious agents can too readily assume that they know the end of human history and the cosmos, what precise form such an end will take, and how it will come about, often underpinned by a desire for absolute certitude in place of religious hope. For them, there is a direct correspondence between apocalyptic visions and the events of actual history, guided by a nonhistorical propositional approach to religious texts, and in contradiction to an understanding

---

29. In 2010, there had been reports that the then President of Iran, Muhammad Ahmadinejad, had publicly communicated a renewed commitment to the doctrine of the Hidden Imam. This doctrine speculates that the Hidden Imam will reappear at the end of history to lead an era of Islamic justice. The prefigured signs for the return of the Imam will be the general invasion of the earth by evil and the victory of the forces of evil over those of good. Ahmadinejad correlated evil with American policy and the state of Israel. Diba, "Hidden Imam."

30. Appleby, "Apocalyptic Imagination," 1–8.

31. Alison, *Raising Abel*, 124–25.

32. Hughes, *Transcendence and History*, 85.

33. Alison, *Raising Abel*, 124.

of history as a mystery unfolding in which the future is unknown.[34] In this scenario, human living, usually punctuated by only moments of conversion, shifts to an understanding of time completely filled with crisis, where every event in time is read as a sign from God pointing to a disastrous end.[35]

Second, where the transformation takes a particular religious, cultural, and social form, the line running from time into eternity is brought to a particular historical endpoint. This yields to the illusion that there is no more need for growth or discovery, and that renewal requires simply real-izing an ideal religious society or golden age. This is simply the projection of perfection onto a future community idealized around a transcendent no-tion of God and, as such, fails to adequately take into account the problem of evil and to distinguish historical time from eternity.[36] While religious communities that live according to such an illusion may serve in part as a correction and protection to the chaos of the present, they cannot possibly answer all future questions.

Third, apocalyptic consciousness becomes distorted when it is influ-enced by a nihilistic pessimism in which religious agents decide to actively bring about the end time through violence. Such religious agents then uti-lize violence as a means to bring about a new beginning by imagining them-selves to be heroic servants of the end time and of the judgment of God. An image of collective death dominates the religious and moral horizon.[37] The day of destruction may be brought about either by active religious agents or by passive ones who stand by and let others or God do the destroying, and relinquish their own guilt and responsibility for impending destruction.

Fourth, in general, one of the consequences of a distorted religious apocalyptic perspective is the secular thinker's interpretation that apoca-lyptic literature is simply "biblical genocide with God acting" as "a divine terrorist."[38] This assessment of their image of God, for example, correlates with James W. Jones's account, which describes all such writings as the product of a religious mind, fixed on a wrathful, punitive deity or on an idealized leader. Consequently, the believer must find "a way to relate to an omnipotent being [that] appears to will the destruction of the world. The believer must humiliate himself before this demanding figure, feeling him-self profoundly unworthy and deeply guilty [and] the punitive, omnipotent

---

34. Hughes, *Transcendence and History*, 86.

35. Strozier and Boyd, "Apocalyptic," 30.

36. Hughes, *Transcendence and History*, 86.

37. Strozier and Body, "Apocalyptic," 31.

38. Strozier, "Apocalyptic Other," 68.

being must be appeased, placated. A blood sacrifice must be offered."[39] Given these distortions in interpretation and performance by religious agents, I can understand why authors are very skeptical about the helpfulness of religious apocalyptic literature as a means to imaginatively inspire religious people to live authentically.[40]

I have argued that apocalyptic religious narratives used to promote violence are the product of a distorted religious imagination, while, following Lonergan, an authentic religious imagination begins in the power of unconditional love and the gift of hope. It is only in the context of religious and moral conversion that apocalyptic texts can be read correctly and acted on with integrity. Moreover, intellectual conversion is needed to develop a critical hermeneutics to explore the meaning of inerrancy and of the texts. I believe there is a place for religious imagination and, in chapter 6, I will explore an authentic understanding of apocalyptic narrative from a Christian perspective grounded in an experience of transcendent love.

## Warfare and Political Organizations

The concrete religious agent is also part of a political community and joins with others to enact warfare to bring about political change. From my account of Lonergan I proposed that, within the scale of values, the political dimension of social values is a higher organizing principle compared to vital values as it tries to obtain social consensus so that the practical intelligence of the economy and technology may deliver goods in a recurrent manner. There are diverse forms of political organization that may conceivably use aspects of religious tradition explicitly or implicitly to justify decisions for war. Juergensmeyer and others narrowly confine their treatment of religiously justified violence to those individuals, groups, or communities that privilege a theocratic state, leading them to the conclusion that warfare and religion intermingle to achieve political ends. I will demonstrate specifically that a secular political form has used implicit religious justifications, namely, the democratic secular nation-state of the United States of America in its decision to prosecute the war in Iraq (March 2003 to December 2011).

39. Jones, "Eternal Warfare," 94.

40. Strozier, "Seven Seals of Fundamentalism." See also Lewis, "Apocalyptic Imagination," 37–45.

## Warfare and Secular States

A nation can be characterized as a group of people who share a common language, culture, and historical experience. The state is the political dimension of the nation. In Western secular countries, there has been a separation of church and state, in which Christianity has become one movement within a wider social and cultural milieu.[41] Generally, the historical realization of the state raises cultural questions about the nature of political community and about the dialectic between community and empire, and ethical questions about legitimate pluralism as a value and about the rightful use of power.[42] Some forms of political community claim that common principles between diverse groups are agreed upon by extrinsically imposing them uniformly over the whole, either through the voluntary will of the majority or through elites whose knowledge is used as a source of power over others.[43] In the latter case, the problem of pluralism is settled through the processes of domination, and the political realm is reduced to the mere exercise of power. This is one of the central characteristics of empire.

"Anarchical" forms of political community settle the problem of pluralism by professing that there are no criteria for evaluating differences in ideas and actions about the human good and there are no common or universal principles governing free choice, engendering the utopian ideal that particular groups will form their own values separate from one another and mutually coexist.[44]

Beyond these various ways of dealing with pluralism, there is a way of conceiving of political community that argues that universal principles and values are intrinsic to freedom yet these can be worked out only by means of freedom. Freedom does not mean simply the ability to make choices, but the ability to orient oneself toward what is truly good through a process of self-determination. Political forms such as these respect human living conditioned by social and cultural factors, while they seek to enhance such living through meaningful truth and responsible freedom. The standard of genuine universality respects particularity according to a "transformation . . . not extrinsically imposed but [one that] invites change from within by appealing to the self-correcting processes of learning and acting intrinsic to pluralist human freedom."[45]

---

41. Lovett, *Dragon*, 45–46. Lovett gives a brief history of this cultural change.
42. Lamb, "Christianity," 75–89.
43. Ibid., 82.
44. Ibid., 75, 82.
45. Ibid., 82.

Within this perspective, Matthew Lamb argues that community and empire are dialectical contradictories. Inherent in the idea of community is a set of relationships that begin in concrete and particular desires that seek fulfillment recurrently, that reach up to a higher integration through common understandings, judgments, commitments, and decisions, and that rest on the power of "free and conscious cooperation and consensus," mediated by political community and informed by what is truly valuable.[46] By contrast, inherent in the idea of empire is a lack of genuine freedom and pluralism, with a tendency to sustain systems that have a narrow under-standing of freedom and justice.[47] Empire-oriented systems often use the specter of anarchy and annihilation to justify domination while neglecting to attend to human suffering occasioned by the intervention of war. For example, the United States was able to justify its ongoing occupation of Iraq on the basis of having overcome a brutal dictator and of progressively es-tablishing democracy in which the will of the people was paramount. These justifications gave less concrete consideration to civilian deaths, which were estimated to number between 108,000 and 109,000 people; the creation of conditions that allowed massive violent divisions to take hold; and the de-struction of important infrastructure.[48]

## Religious Expression and the Justification of War

Within this broader discussion of the role of political community, and not-ing the difference between community and empire, I want to particularly focus on the United States post-9/11 to offer a critique to some of the reli-gious meanings and values that implicitly underpinned the justification for the war in Iraq.

T. Walter Herbert characterizes American self-understanding prior to 9/11 as "the myth of American invulnerability." Joined to "the myth of American virtue," this has created a blindspot in the post-9/11 era.[49] Three days after the 9/11 attacks, President Bush defined the "war on terror"[50] as a monumental struggle between good and evil.[51] He led a prayer service

46. Ibid., 90.

47. Ibid., 87.

48. Hicks et al., "Casualties."

49. Herbert, *Faith-Based War*, 17.

50. The "states of terror" sponsoring terrorist acts (also called states of acquies-cence) referred to by President Bush in his post-9/11 speech were contrasted to "states of consent." See Bobbit, *Terror and Consent*, 182.

51. Singer, *President*, 2. Singer notes that Bush spoke about evil in 319 separate

in which the attacks were couched in terms of a hatred of American virtue in the same way that Satan hates the goodness of God simply because it is goodness.[52] This attitude toward the nation is captured by Michael Northcott in the widespread term "American Exceptionalism."[53] This rhetoric opened up the possibility of a sociocultural divide between "them and us," transmuting an authentic desire to right the wrongs done to American citizens by subsequent scapegoating.

Two religious songs were sung at this prayer service. The lyrics of *America the Beautiful*,[54] written by Katherine Lee Bates in 1893, picture the United States as an alabaster city, symbol of a transcendent ideal, shrouded in virtue, where the good of national wealth cannot be achieved until there is brotherhood.[55] Ironically, Bates's moral admonitions address the neighborly manner by which Anglo-Americans are to treat one another, yet mask the systematic injustices toward other peoples, such as the Indigenous population, in the conquest of land from sea to sea.[56] Herbert states that, in part, this "blindspot that rendered otherwise morally alert Americans incapable of imagining why other nations harbor resentments against American projects" has formed part of its foreign policy in the post-9/11 context.[57] The lyrics of *Onward Christian Soldiers*[58] sung at the national cathedral celebrated Christian warrior saints prevailing in an apocalyptic crusade. In this song, Americans were espousing a nation ordained by God as a showcase for the virtues of God's chosen people.

Herbert argues that America's religious self-understanding is in part founded on the Puritan story of the seventeenth century as a fulfillment of the Old Testament biblical promise in which God chose a nation to be

---

speeches between taking office and June 16, 2003, using evil as a noun far more than as an adjective.

52. Ibid., 21.

53. Northcott, *Angel Directs the Storm*, 17. The idea of American "exceptionalism" is based on the myth of nationhood by which the United States of America is understood to be the first true exception in the quest of humanity for the good of society.

54. In the sixth verse of "America the Beautiful," Bates writes: "O beautiful for pilgrim's feet,/ Whose stem impassioned stress/ A thoroughfare for freedom beat/ Across the wilderness!/ America! America!/ God shed his grace on thee/ Till paths be wrought through/ Wilds of thought/ By pilgrim foot and knee!"

55. Herbert, *Faith-Based War*, 23.

56. Ibid., 24.

57. Ibid., 25

58. In verse two of "Onward Christian Soldiers," the apocalyptic triumph is echoed in the words: "At the sign of triumph Satan's host doth flee;/ on then, Christian soldiers, on to victory!/; Hell's foundations quiver at the shout of praise;/ Brothers, lift your voices loud, your anthems raise."

God's nation from all the earth.[59] Yet this story of divine election is found in two contrasting accounts of American religious myth-making. One version, typified by Edward Johnson (1654), known as the Massachusetts Bay version, depicts the Puritans as the Army of God, with a right to appropriate economic resources possessed by others, through the use of military power.[60] The group bias within this version is that a god who promises exclusive title of land to one group (the chosen) must equip the children of god with the means to remove rival claimants (the not-chosen) by force, whether by preemptive force or in response to attack. This links divine authority to justified killing.[61]

The contrasting religious myth of divine election was articulated by Roger Williams.[62] In the aftermath of the Puritan destruction of the Pequot tribes in the seventeenth century, Williams interpreted such action, not as demonstrating God's goodness toward God's people, but rather as the Puritan abandonment of God for material prosperity. Williams's positive vision of America was that of a city "exerting influence on other communities because its way of living is visible at a distance" and "sometimes requiring the use of military power, but never as God's wrath visiting divine punishment on behalf of his chosen," certainly with God's judgment applied to both groups and with "virtue and wickedness" found on both sides.[63] The religious myth implicit in this contrasting version invited the people to repent, and to be be moral and ever-vigilant of ungodly motivations.

For Herbert, these two rival traditions bequeath to American pietistic religious culture a sharp contrast: "the variant originating in Massachusetts Bay [which] grants Americans the God-given pre-emptive right to resources controlled by other peoples; [while] the rival tradition recognises that others [also] possess inherent rights and demand respect."[64] The view that Americans are a "chosen people" entitled *de novo* to the resources of a "promised land" estimates the character of other peoples in accordance with their conformity to the American standard. Those who resist American claims are defined by that resistance as enemies of the divine promise. By contrast, the tradition from Roger Williams holds that coming to know others cannot happen if a self-centered ideology takes precedence.

59. Herbert, *Faith-Based War*, 30.

60. Ibid., 35, 41.

61. Ibid., 33.

62. Ibid., 38.

63. Ibid., 40–41.

64. Ibid., 58.

Herbert argues that the invasion of Iraq was, in part, shaped by a distorted Puritan Christian piety, noticeably taking form within the earlier Reagan Government of the 1980s, in which the sinfulness of America lay in the refusal of Americans to offer their country unconditional worship.[65] According to Herbert, "Reagan believed that American freedom is the un-hindered pursuit of wealth, and his 'shining city' had the pre-emptive right to [attain] whatever resources can be applied to increasing its wealth and power."[66] Reagan drew on the Puritan, John Winthrop, and his model of Christian charity (1630) by which the new Puritan community was to be likened to "a city on a hill."[67] This city was to be a paradise of creativity and commerce. The Reagan Government's and, later, the Bush Administration's vision, were grounded in a particular conception of freedom and a pragma-tist position on warfare: America's unencumbered quest for limitlessly ex-panding wealth that will ultimately somehow enrich all other nations, with any power that posed a threat to America's wealth creation considered evil.[68]

In Herbert's estimation, President Bush's vision of his presidential duty was shaped by these particular pietistic threads. This piety was "at work in the lives of Massachusetts Bay Puritans, in which God's explosive wrath plays a dual role. It menaces faithful souls who fail to comply with the divine commands but if the faithful are obedient it will fall upon the evil doers, who threaten them. Bush must discharge the duties of the presidency in keeping with the requirements of an eternal drama, in which divine ven-geance is provoked by ceaseless recurring offences."[69]

Consequently, the regime change in Iraq was seen as a victory for free-dom and the establishing of a new and different "city on a hill" in Iraq.[70] From the USS *Lincoln* flight deck, Bush declared in 2011 that the mission in Iraq had been accomplished. This had been achieved due to the American military fulfilling the biblical promise of divine deliverance and liberation through self-sacrifice.[71] For Herbert, the location and content of Bush's speech drew to mind a central theme concerning the justification of war-fare: soldiers die so that others may live. The image of the fighting man preferred by the Bush Administration was the image of "the man of excel-

65. Ibid., 63.
66. Ibid., 63.
67. Ibid., 28–29, 60.
68. Ibid., 76.
69. Ibid., 74.
70. Ibid., 77. Both in President Bush's Inaugural Address, on January 20, 2001, and the State of the Union Address on 29 January, 2002, the themes of American freedom versus the hatred of freedom are given considerable mention.
71. Herbert, *Faith-Based War*, 97. See also Denton-Borhaug, "Language," 1–20.

lent health, invincible and triumphant, who exults in a victory achieved not through blood and agony but through the power of fabulous technology, here eloquently represented by the great carrier with its attendant planes and missile launchers."[72] Meanwhile, the administration had a firm policy against public ceremonies surrounding the return of the dead from Iraq by which the print media were forbidden to record arrivals in case it should dampen public opinion toward the war.

I have examined elements of religious meanings around the US decision for war in Iraq to demonstrate that warfare is accompanied by distorted religious as well as nonreligious justifications by secular states. Cultural justifications are often delivered to the public as a set of commonsense and popular symbolic meanings, carrying an emotive power—in this case, through reinforcing the myth of nationhood. Each of these symbols draws emotive force from distorted images of a national identity that lead to an idolatry of nationhood: a chosen people; notions of freedom wedded to choice and unlimited prosperity; political community shaped by empire building; and idealized images of America as a "city on a hill," a reference to Matthew 5:14.

These religious justifications for warfare gave increased legitimization to Bush's foreign policy, which consisted of pursuing the opening of borders to American investment and trade, as a means to spreading American values, in particular, the value of freedom.[73] This freedom was linked to markets in such a way that the "expectation of freedom is fed by free markets and expanded by free markets, and carried across borders by the internet."[74] Northcott argues that American foreign policy under Bush and his predecessor was determined by American diplomacy and military prowess, which was linked to corporate interests; these had been central to foreign policy since the end of the Cold War.[75] Rosemary Reuther argues that the rhetoric used by Bush was designed to appeal to two audiences: those who believed America to be an army raised by God to defeat evil, and those who couched the political freedom of the Iraqis in terms of a neoliberal ideology of free markets.[76] Reuther states that "what neoliberals meant by the free market is the right of mega-corporations to batter down any restrictions on their ability to monopolize the world's markets, preventing small nations from protecting their national production and subsidizing

---

72. Herbert, *Faith-Based War*, 102.
73. Northcott, "Angel Directs the Storm," 137–39.
74. Bush, "To the Joint Session of Congress."
75. Northcott, *Angel Directs the Storm*, 78–80.
76. Reuther, "American Empire," 7.

health care, education and basic commodities for the poorer classes," which, in Iraq, meant "a wholesale sell-off of Iraqi resources to favoured American corporations such as Halliburton."[77] In such a situation, the dominance of economic interests distorts the scale of values, ultimately disabling political leaders from meeting the recurrent needs of the population.

## Warfare and Nonstate Terrorist Groups

Many of the examples of religiously motivated violence and terrorism used by Juergensmeyer, Jones, and others are drawn from Islamic societies. While it is important to seek to interpret what is happening in all particular Islamic societies, such a project is beyond the scope of this work. Instead, I will examine the broad understanding of warfare when it is designated as jihad. However, since jihad is often associated with terrorist acts by the West, it is important to first understand the nature of terrorism.

Broadly, I argue that terrorism is the use or threat of violence, aimed at inducing fear in a way that draws maximum attention to the cause of the perpetrators, often for political ends, founded on cultural meanings and values that may or may not be religious. The difference between terrorism and guerrilla warfare is that terrorism targets noncombatants, while guerrilla warriors see themselves as fighting in the name of a people and often draw support from the civilian population.[78] Terrorism gains its advantage not simply from the fact of maiming but from the timing, performative intent, and random nature of attacks that cripple societies. It aims to create a high level of chaos. Paul Daponte cites Baur, who notes that terrorist acts are "bi-focal" in intent, that is, terrorists directly target those people who are killed and indirectly target those who observe the violence and who receive a message of fear.[79] Often terrorist groups are, by comparison to the resources of states, the poor person's response to modern warfare since it only takes only a small-scale outbreak of violence to bring about a large-scale response of fear—fear that is aimed at influencing popular opinion and government policy in a manner that serves such groups' objectives.

Charles notes that terrorist acts are an indirect form of engaging the enemy, allowing the death of innocent noncombatants in order to achieve the terrorizing objective.[80] Generally speaking, for the nonstate terrorist, there are no innocents, nor is there immunity through diplomatic protocols

77. Ibid.

78. Allman, *Who Would Jesus Kill?*, 217–20.

79. Daponte, *Hope*, 119; Baur, "Terrorism," 3–22.

80. Charles, *Pacifism and Jihad*, 153.

since the usual rules for engagement are put aside. As Charles states, the key notion that unifies all terrorists is "the conviction that they are engaged in a form of vigilante justice. All who represent this battle are guilty, even the innocent bystanders, since all are representative of the enemy."[81] The targeting of people is primarily instrumental, that is, the objective is not so much to reveal the personality of the agent, or to draw attention to the moral "rightness" of killing both the soldier and the innocent bystander. Its primary objective is to shock or terrify the intended audience.[82] Since the terrorist does not abide by the normal rules of armed conflict, a refusal to recognize the possibility of a truce is set in place. This demonstrates that the "terrorist *qua* terrorist is implicitly committed to the principle of uncontained and perpetual war, that is to the kind of war that we can never end through mutual recognition or a negotiated truce, but only by the ongoing suppressing or complete obliteration of the adversary."[83] As Juergensmeyer suggests, terrorists' performative and symbolic acts are meant more to provoke a reaction in their enemy than to achieve a victory. These characteristics suggest that the defeat of terrorism requires more than military means.

Coates argues that the terrorist mindset is more aligned to militarism, and identifies Islamic fundamentalism as an example.[84] I argue that while there are differences among various terrorist groups, the stance of the nonstate terrorist is more a pragmatist position to warfare that tries to achieve political and social interests through a balance of power. The actions of such nonstate terrorists are a violent reaction to perceived or even real attacks on their cultural heritage and to the sociopolitical disempowerment of their people. If these tactics do not achieve their desired outcomes, then terrorist anger degenerates into a spiral of warfare that assumes a more militarist form.

## Jihad and Islam

Barry Cooper observes that, prior to the nineteenth century, religion provided both a motivation and a limitation for terrorist conduct.[85] Thugs, assassins, and zealots were all linked to religiously inspired ritual killings.[86] A great deal of terrorism in more recent times, though, has been associated

---

81. Ibid., 154.
82. Cooper, *New Political Religions*, 40.
83. Daponte, *Hope*, 119.
84. Coates, *Ethics of War*, 46.
85. Cooper, *New Political Religions*, 35.
86. Ibid., 35–36.

with militant Islamic organizations, including military wings of the state, such as Iran, who sponsors *Hezbollah*; the terrorist group *al-Qaeda*; Hamas's armed militant wing, *Izz ad-Din al-Qassam*; and most recently, the Sunni based Islamic State or IS fighters in Iraq. These groups claim to follow Islam, and combine religious ideological purity, contempt for compromise, and a keen urgency to fight states that in their eyes embody ignorance of God (*jahiliyya*).[87]

Therefore I argue that it is important to engage with the Islamic idea of jihad. For some groups, the justification for warfare comes out of a particular interpretation of the religious tradition concerning jihad.[88] In chapter 7, I will argue how a distorted understanding of Islamic martyrdom and a distorted understanding of jihad mutually influence one another to promote wrongful actions. The distorted understanding of jihad has been influenced by a mindset in relation to warfare that moves between Coates's pragmatist and militarist types. A more constructive understanding of warfare within Islam must be able to argue an ethical recourse to, and conduct within, warfare grounded in religious love. Yet such a position within Islam will more likely come about through a more authentic understanding of jihad and a greater control of meaning around the idea and practice of religious martyrdom.

While the commonsense understanding of jihad in the West since the 1970s has been linked to terrorist armed conflict, it must also be noted that the words *holy* and *war* (*al-hard al muqaddasah*) do not occur together in the Koran or in any authoritative tradition of Islam.[89] The justification for violence by terrorists has rested on the assertion that since the West has been engaged in a Crusade against Islam, the combatant/noncombatant distinction is void, even though noncombatants would not normally take part in war.

The diverse meanings of jihad rest, in part, on two considerations: first, while there are a number of universal elements linking various Islamic communities, there are also many different interpretations of the Islamic tradition since Islam does not have a central authority to judge on matters of doctrine; second, a justification of jihad based on an approach to sacred texts that amounts to the prooftexting of preformed moral opinions.

In chronological terms, the first reference to jihad in the Koran is to be found in the context of the Prophet's being instructed by God not to compromise with the polytheistic ways of the elders of Quraysh, the main

87. Karawan, "Islamist Impasse," 16.

88. Sonn, "Irregular Warfare," 140.

89. Kung, *Islam*, 597.

tribe in Mecca in 570 CE. The Prophet was ordered to perform *jihadan kabrian* (struggle with the utmost strenuousness) against the polytheists with the truth of the Koran (Q25:52). Similarly, the reference to jihad in the Surat al-Hajj exhorts the believer to "strive" in Allah's cause (Q22:78) and is encapsulated in the requirement to resist oppression and struggle against it by *al-amr bi'l-maruf wa al-naby 'an al-munkar* (enjoining the good and forbidding the evil). In the verses of the Surat al-Ankabut, the observance of patience and self-restraint in the face of persecution is hailed as a noble act and believers had been told that those who act in this way would be led along God's path (Q29:1–6, 69). Jihad at this time of Islam's history involved no fighting (*qital*). In the medieval period, several scholars such as al-Ghazali and al-Khatib spoke about jihad in terms of the lesser and greater jihad, pointing to a developing tradition. There emerged a hadith that depicts the Prophet returning from a raiding party and exhorting his followers that "we have now returned from the lesser *jihad* to the greater *jihad* . . . to the *jihad* against oneself."[90] In this hadith, the distinction between the greater jihad (interior struggle or striving against evil) and lesser jihad (armed fighting for the cause of God) emerged and has been accepted by Muslims till our time.

According to A. Rashied Omar, contemporary Muslim scholars such as Mohammad Abu Zahra and Louay Safi contend that the classical doctrine of jihad as linked to war was forged by Muslim jurists, primarily in response to conflicts between the Abbasid caliphate and the Byzantine Empire.[91] The Muslim conquerors of the seventh century CE (the Umayyad dynasty) and scholars of the eighth and ninth centuries CE (the Abbasid dynasty) began to use the term "jihad" in the context of Islamic expansionism and empire consolidation to describe the relation of Muslims to non-Muslims. This early evolution of jihad was a way for jurists to give legal instruction on the recourse to war and the conduct of war within the political domain of empire. According to John Esposito, the consequence was that "the religious scholars who enjoyed royal patronage repaid their patrons by providing them with a rationale for pursing their imperial dreams and expanding the boundaries of their empires."[92]

I contend that the specific meaning of "jihad," which today is often referred to as the lesser jihad or armed struggle in the cause of God, was

90. There is much dispute among Muslims as to whether this is a true hadith of the Prophet or a weak hadith originating from the eleventh-century book, *The History of Baghdad*, by the Islamic scholar al-Khatib al-Baghdadiis, by way of Yahya ibn al 'Ala'. See Marranci, *Jihad Beyond Islam*, 20–21.

91. Omar, "Islam and Violence," 1–9.

92. Esposito, *Future of Islam*, 49–50.

solidified in a cultural context of empire building, and grounded in the belief that Islam was the one true religion that God desired all people to follow.
The Islamic revelation represented disillusionment with the cosmological
order of polytheism that dominated the cultural life of the Quraysh tribes
and the Arabian Peninsula. Through the discovery of the One God who
transcended the natural world and the importance given to the individual's
pursuit of goodness and avoidance of evil, Islam was opened to the possibility of an anthropological cultural breakthrough. However, following the
revelations to the Prophet and his death, historical Islam became marked
politically by Islamic expansionism among the Arabic tribes, socially by
problems over leadership, and culturally by a lack of differentiation between
social and religious values.

While the notion of jihad as striving for purity of life gave legitimacy
to the individual's obligation to seek goodness and avoid evil, the military
connotation of jihad reassured the believer that fighting for the cause of
God in the context of a battle contrasted greatly to the dominant mindset of
fighting for the honor of one's kinship group.[93] During the Abbasid caliphate in the ninth century CE, the world of classical Islam matured with the
development of Islamic law and theology. However, the revelation of Islam
did not lead to a break with the cosmological form of empire. Rather, the
authorities of the day used the oneness of God as a bureaucratic support for
empire. The ideal society become one in which the political and religious
realms were oriented to the same goals. The anthropological cultural type
could not gain a sufficient foothold during the classical period, when the
notion of jihad was being pondered, so preventing a new set of insights
from emerging.

Modern Islamic militants have taken this latter idea of jihad out of its
historical, cultural, and social setting and inserted it into a modern context,
arguing that fighting for God's cause legitimately grounds their violent actions. The problem with the modern interpretation of jihad as fighting for
the cause of God is the same problem as when the notion first emerged: that
is, there is the danger of political and religious realms working toward the
same goals. The religious level has the potential to be manipulated by the
political realm, and the image of God can easily be distorted by warrior-like
elements. Terrorist groups who make the connection between God's cause
and terrorist acts end up repressing important moral criteria for warfare
such as noncombatant immunity, the aim of peace, and proportionality,
each of which apply to the conduct of warfare.

---

93. Allman, *Who Would Jesus Kill?*, 291.

By contrast, Anthony T. Sullivan suggests that the widely accepted distinction between the greater jihad (spiritual struggle against evil) and the lesser jihad (defensive war) among Muslims today invites the revival of an alternative traditional Islamic term for terrorist acts that are examples of neither greater nor lesser jihad, namely, the term *hirabah*, which, translated from the Arabic, means to be furious or enraged.[94] *Hirabah* has traditionally been understood to be both an abominable form of murder, a method used to intimidate an entire civilian population, and the attempt to spread a sense of fear and helplessness in society. Those involved in brands of violence that are strategically offensive, amounting to suicide and mass murder, promoting hatred among races, and unholy *hirabah* are against the ways of genuine Islam.

## Jihad: An Alternative Viewpoint

Despite the correlation between jihad and fighting in the cause of God, there has been, in the minds of many, an alternative understanding in Islam that indicates a developing tradition. This alternative idea represents the healing vector in human history as believers recover lost aspects of the jihad tradition within a wider context of religious Islam founded in transcendent love. In Lonergan's terms, this represents a development that requires religious and moral conversion from a distorted heritage that has placed fighting jihad in the foreground to the retrieval of other aspects of the heritage that put peace and nonviolence as the higher purpose of Islam.

The classical tradition of jihad is founded upon the premise that there is an interconnection between a just and equitable social order and the will of God within a religious tradition that accepts the interdependence between religion and politics. In this setting, jihad is understood to be an instrument in the fulfillment of a divine promise to bring all people under submission to the one God. Such a submission of faith is never to be forced. While the language of military activity is *qital* (fighting), *sira'at* (combat), *ma'arakat* (battle), and *harb* (war), jihad or striving could be reserved for the religious and moral struggle of individual purification and its consequences for an Islamic social order, suggesting that the task of personal purification is within the higher order of personal value within the scale of values.[95]

94. Sullivan, "Conservative Ecumenism," 179–88. *Hirabah* is also associated with *fitnah*, which designates the disruption of the established political and social order and has long been considered by Islamic jurists to be among the most serious of crimes.

95. Sachedina, "Development of *Jihad*," 37. Note that the words *jihad* (striving), *qital* (fighting), and *harb* (war) are rarely, if at all, found in the early Meccan verses (610–622 CE).

This developing tradition identifies Islam primarily as a spiritual and social means to peace, and jihad as a means to accomplishing that peace through personal transformation.[96] This form of jihad has its origins in a renewed intellectualist approach to reforms in the nineteenth century CE that were scripturally based, yet opposed to both authoritarianism and apolitical quietism. The proponents of this movement recommend a return to the sources of their sacred texts so as to bring about a reformation or reawakening to social and political change. The Koran is centrally understood as a document that speaks of peace, while the "sword verses" are interpreted as a temporary circumstance in Islamic history.

In this interpretation, the proper response of the Muslims to each other and to other persons is a "just mercy" since God's justice is merciful.[97] While a post-Enlightenment view of justice is based in human actions and compromises, Islamic justice is a gift of God and reveals God's will. It is not easy to conform to the will of God and so the greater jihad requires sacrifice, effort, and the willingness to allow God to rule lives. Two religious principles are key elements for putting justice into practice. The first is the principle of *tawhid*, which attests to the absolute oneness of God. *Tawhid* expresses the truth that God is "the first Principle, Creator of all, eternally present in history and at every moment, He is the most High, beyond all that is, infinitely near, closer to each of us than (our) jugular vein. He is the One, the Only One, the Absolute, Justice, Truth and Light."[98] Accordingly, this oneness leads to a number of religious truths including: God cannot have conflicting wills or desires; God is merciful yet not indulgent; in God there is light and not darkness; and all creatures participate in the being of the Creator. From *tawhid* follows the principle of the unity and harmony of all creation so that morality grounded in God's will unifies all things.[99]

The second principle for putting justice into practice is the importance of human freedom and responsibility. *Taqwah* is the inner light ingrained in the souls of people to discern right from wrong, good from evil; while the basis of all freedom is doing the will of God.[100] Therefore, jihad founded in obedience to God's will is the greater struggle (*akbar*). Doing God's will is an integrating principle within Islam that gives greater clarity to concepts such as salvation, wholeness, justice, human development, perfection, and harmony.

96. I have taken this insight on jihad from the thought of the Turkish theologian and philosopher, Fethullah Gulen, "Lesser and Greater Jihad."

97. Wagner, *Opening the Qur'an*, 351.

98. Ramadan, *Western Muslims*, 12.

99. Ali, *Islamic Revivalism*, 37–39. *Tawhid* is a doctrine of belief that leads to a certain kind of religious and moral practice.

100. Wagner, *Opening the Qur'an*, 354–59.

One scholarly interpretation of doing God's will and undertaking the jihad of personal purification is found in the writings of Jawdat Said, who privileges the Koranic text, "The Way of Adam's Son."[101] This text describes the first brother's refusal to defend himself against the violence of his brother, preferring to accept death rather than retaliate. Said's moral horizon could be characterized as pacifist. In his judgment, the text Q5:27–28 elevates human consciousness above the urge to survive and becomes a pivotal moment for the moral structure of the Koran, in a similar manner, as I shall argue, to how the Suffering Servant figure of the Hebrew and Christian Scriptures becomes a pivotal moment in Christian religious consciousness. Adam is prototypical in Islam for all prophets, and "The Way of Adam's Son" declines self-defense, preferring patience (*sabr*), stillness in the face of harm, and commitment to speaking the truth. This passage and other parallel ones (Q2:28, 32) proscribe force and privilege forgiveness as the norm, a position that escaped the collective triumphalist Muslim imagination that turned its back on the texts of the Meccan phase and its orientation of peace. This dialectical engagement with the Islamic tradition demonstrates the possible textual foundations for an alternative view of jihad that holds to nonviolence as foundational for social change.

An alternative view of jihad in Islamic tradition would then see warfare as the last resort in a sinful world enacted out of a defensive posture, and motivated by a just cause and against oppression. Muslims would be encouraged to fight in a way that does not unduly provoke hostility from the enemy so as to arrive at a peaceful coexistence. In this approach, the dominant moral idea is the belief that the use of violence would be permitted under certain circumstances, especially in the case of defending the faith and of defending the land against an unjust aggressor.[102]

This interpretation of jihad aligns closely with the religious and moral dimensions, except that it conflates openness to God and the act of discerning what is good and avoiding what is evil in all one's practical moral decisions. However, jihad relates also to the circumstances of warfare, seeking to establish that fighting in war may not be sinful when the recourse to war and the conduct of war are just. However, I suggest it could also relate to other moral arenas such as family, employment, the economy, and political life.[103]

---

101. Burrell, *Jewish-Christian-Muslim Theology*, 148–50; Said, *Adam's Son*.

102. Esposito, *Future of Islam*, 49.

103. The jihad of personal purification bears some similarity to the Christian idea of holy warfare, which, according to Aelred Squire, prioritizes getting our values right through prayer and spiritual discernment so that these values may be given a practical recognition in the vastly different circumstances of our lives. See Squire, *Asking the Fathers*, 101–16.

With regard to the practical judgments of warfare, jihad as personal purification is the higher moral principle, and jihad applied to war highlights the importance of moral conversion in discerning whether to engage in warfare. When moral discernment occurs around questions of warfare, we can distinguish two approaches. First, there are those who argue that the means and ends must be based on ethical grounds such that if war is permissible, it must be limited and proportionate. For those with this mindset, there is a presupposition that Islam is primarily a religion of peace and opposed to war until it becomes a last resort, and then the conduct of war must follow ethical guidelines. As I will show in the next chapter, this position is similar to a just war approach. Second, there are those who argue that although Islam permits war under certain moral conditions, such as oppression and unjust aggression, it also allows Muslims to adopt all means to win once the end is justified. This position aligns more with the pragmatist mindset and fails to note that both recourse to war and conduct in war need to be morally acceptable.

## Conclusion

In this chapter and the previous one on the notions of cosmos and warfare in the symbol of cosmic war, we have seen that this symbol goes some way toward explaining the actions of the diverse groups who engage in violence underpinned by a religious justification: it does not go the whole way. Nor can we say that the use of violence to shift power relations provides a sufficient set of conditions to establish human flourishing. What is needed is a promotion of conditions that make possible peace, not victory; community, not empire; loving mutuality, not division; legitimate plurality, not a monocultural attitude; and leadership achieving freedom by freedom, not dominative power. Therefore, the decision for absolute war cannot be central to a religious understanding of our place in the world. Against Juergensmeyer's claim that warfare is the business of religion, I have argued that authentic religion is concerned to form the consciences of people in the paths of justice. Coates's pragmatist type forms the horizon of subjects who promote the primacy of power relationships and national interest, such as might be found in either nation-states or terrorist groups, with a capacity to lead to militarism. To move beyond such biased thinking requires a new cultural understanding of justice within the scale of values.

I have also argued in previous chapters from a Christian perspective that genuine religion privileges redemptive love founded on religious conversion as the integrating principle within religion. This is an example of the healing vector within human history. Within Islam, the notion of jihad founded in doing God's will guides the believer toward personal and social transformation, where God's will is known from the words of the Koran. On the other hand, religious distortions are perpetuated when decisions are married to distorted understandings of the will of God, to justice as simply revenge, and to the blind obedience of followers following inauthentic religious leaders.

In the next chapter I will argue that, among other things, the recovery of the just war tradition has the potential to guide the deliberations of leaders and authorities, but only when legitimate authority, justice, and right intention are dialectically engaged.

# 6

# A Constructive Engagement
# with Warfare

AUTHORS SUCH AS JUERGENSMEYER and Jones do not sufficiently attend to
the distinction between genuine and false religion, nor do they explore the
different moral horizons that inform religious agents' reasons for warfare.
There can be no doubt that the sacred texts of religious traditions also influence the moral horizons of believers, whether or not those texts have
been communicated and received after critical and responsible interpretation. Judeo-Christian and Islamic religious texts, uncritically examined, can
lead one to conclude that religious traditions present a preoccupation with
warfare and an image of a warrior God. The Old Testament Scriptures give
many examples that connect warfare and religion, prompting people outside and inside faith communities to judge such texts as evidence of the link
between violence and religion.

   In the context of the Judeo-Christian religion, there is however a religious development from the Old Testament to the New Testament that
points to the way of suffering self-sacrificing love as the central motivation
for Christian moral decisions. This integrating principle stands in opposition to moral trajectories driven by the desire for mere power or warfare
as the means of establishing the reign of God on earth. I will demonstrate
that the way of suffering and self-sacrificing love within the Christian religious tradition founded on religious and moral conversion gives rise to
a set of principles called the "just war" tradition. By means of these principles political agents can assess a moral recourse to war that is just and
a conduct within war that is humane. These principles extend also to the
postwar period, where there is a responsibility to work toward the reconciliation of parties, the restoration of war-torn areas, and the administering

of punishment to those who have participated in war crimes. However, since just war criteria are used to guide decisions in particular and specific historical circumstances, it is important to critically engage not only the criteria themselves but also the methodological thinking that shapes the criteria, otherwise decisions based on the criteria alone may only exacerbate the problem of violence.

## Warfare in the Judeo-Christian Tradition

In the Judeo-Christian religious tradition, there is religious development from the Hebrew Scriptures (Christian Old Testament) to the specifically Christian tradition (New Testament) that calls for peace, moving away from the notion that religion promotes war toward the notion that war is a last resort to counter injustice in a sinful world.

Exploring the trajectories of war in the Hebrew Bible, Susan Niditch describes the history of war in ancient Israel as "a complex one involving multiplicity, overlap and fragmentation," with "several war ideologies" as "neither self-contained nor related to one another in simply chronological sequences in the social, religious and intellectual history of Israel."[1] Niditch explores seven trajectories, from which I choose three as particularly relevant to this work: the "ban" as God's portion, the "ban" as God's justice, and the ideology of nonparticipation.

## The Ban as God's Portion

This practice refers to those texts that speak of *herem* or ban (Num 21:2–3, 23–24; Deut 2:30–35; 7:2–6; Josh 6:17, 21; 8:24–29; 10:28, 30, 31–32, 35, 37, 39, 40; 1 Sam 15:3), in which captured members of an opposing army are set apart by the victors for destruction through sacrifice and are promised to God in exchange for God's support for the victors' military campaigns.[2] This particular practice required "a wider view of God who appreciates human sacrifice, so those who partake in the ideology of the ban would presumably have something in common with those who had something in common with child sacrifice."[3] Girard captures the underlying sociocultural assumption for this practice in his insight around the scapegoat mechanism, religion, and social order. In this case, the enemy is not part of

1. Niditch, *War*, 154.
2. Ibid., 28.
3. Ibid., 50.

the community but the scapegoat whose destruction is the promised sacrifice to God in exchange for victory.

## The Ban as God's Justice

This practice represents a trajectory promoted by the Deuteronomic writers, who considered the ban as "a means of rooting out what they believe to be impure, sinful forces damaging to the solid and pure relationship between Israel and God."[4] The overwhelming presumption is that enemies deserve punishment based upon an absolute distinction between friend and enemy, the pure of heart and the evil ones, and those worthy of salvation and those deserving of death, thus encouraging an acceptance of the idea of killing humans through demonizing and dehumanizing them.[5] This trajectory highlights what happens when the religious agent's horizon is shaped existentially by the grace–sin dialectic. The subject has a distorted understanding of the world characterized as a battleground between their own identity and the identity of the other whom they consider to be evil.

W. M. Slattery argues that both the ban as God's portion and the ban as God's justice capture the Israelite fear and loathing of what is culturally, politically, ethnically, and religiously unknown, which lead to xenophobic attitudes that thwart any rational interrelationship or dialogue.[6] The bans, however, were also challenged by writers of the Old Testament, especially the prophets, and the writers of the first and second books of the Chronicles, who "appear to be conscious of unwanted and tyrannical violence [involved] in slaying all under the ban, eliminating Israel's enemies so that they will not have to be reencountered," and who were bothered by "cruel, vengeful and rapacious killing of physically and socially weak members of society."

## The Ideology of Nonparticipation

In Niditch's account of the ideology of nonparticipation, she describes a trajectory within Israelite thinking that dialectically opposes domination and reconciliation, and seeks to eliminate war and establish peace.[7] In the cosmologically oriented culture of ancient Israel, the saving revelation of the God of Israel was the beginning of a long development that moved from

4. Ibid., 56.
5. Ibid., 77.
6. Slattery, *Jesus the Warrior?*, 47.
7. Niditch, *War*, 134.

understanding God as a warrior to God as the Suffering Servant–Redeemer. I argue that this particular trajectory within the Hebrew and Christian biblical revelation of God provides an example of the healing vector in history, by which a new revelation brings about personal transformation, a new cultural attitude about warfare, and a new sociopolitical situation.

## The Suffering Servant in the Old Testament

According to Millard Lind, the Suffering Servant trajectory represents a significant development in the religious thought of the exilic prophets, who proclaimed a second exodus and return to Zion by the hand of God.[8] The Songs of the Servant in Second Isaiah especially focus attention on the Suffering Servant of God, the vision of a sole just one who wins healing, not by the processes of warfare backed by political and technological might, but by taking on the iniquities of all. Citing the work of Eric Voegelin, Doran asserts that the Servant Songs of Second Isaiah represent a "culmination of Old Testament revelation and the completion of the transimperial form of existence that this revelation introduces into history."[9]

The Suffering Servant symbolizes for Israel a new order away from warfare and the cult of empire. The symbol represented the means to bring about change in human history and a movement from a "cosmological imperial civilization to society in history under God."[10] Most importantly, salvation and suffering are no longer alternatives in this new order since, as Doran states, salvation "is not with the order of life under the covenant of the Law, but with the order under the Redeemer God. The servant embodies that order, and so is the covenant to the people, the light to the nations. Redemption is revealed as the fruit of suffering, right here and now," and, by implication, salvation and redemption are not the fruit of actual warfare.[11]

---

8. Lind, *Yahweh Is a Warrior*, 168–74. Lind traces a developing understanding of warfare from the patriarchal period to the period of kingship and the Deuteronomist tradition before and after the exile. By the latter period, the message was that Israel's power base was not military might but trust in God, obedience to God's word, and loyalty to the covenant.

9. Doran, "Suffering Servant," 45–46. See Voegelin, *Israel and Revelation*, 501.

10. Doran, "Suffering Servant," 48.

11. Ibid., 48–49.

## Jesus the Suffering Servant and the Church

The Suffering Servant is a key christological theme in the Christian Gospels.[12] Doran states: "The New Testament acknowledges Jesus as the fulfilment of the Suffering Servant. It is not through ritual and cultic action, but through his suffering in history, that the sole Just One opens access to God."[13] By extension, Doran argues that the church is summoned to be the Community of the Servant of God, for, as redemptive suffering is so central to Jesus so "the principal catalytic agency of the community called and empowered to do as Jesus did will lie in its participation in the redemptive suffering and death through which he did in fact mediate a transition from a situation of sin to a situation of grace in history."[14] Here, the role of the church as servant is "to be understood quite strictly in terms of the Deutero-Isaian servant of God *in* the world, and not primarily as servant *of* the world."[15] The Christian is thus invited to acknowledge Jesus' suffering and death as one's own path to redemption and is "invited as well to have some share in the historical catalytic agency of that suffering and death as its power mediates," a situation of grace in history.[16]

This religious tradition reveals a development, in religious understanding, from warfare as a means to salvation through imposing God's retributive justice, to an alternative trajectory characterized by reliance on God in the midst of suffering and conflict. As Matthew Lamb asserts: "The empire of God as proclaimed by Christ is a free gift and call to enter into communities of expectation, faith and love with the poor, the hungry, the sorrowful, the untold victims of sinful histories of domination and oppression."[17] The community of the church is to be the catalytic agent that brings about change in human history through suffering and self-sacrificing love, forming the consciences of political leaders and individuals in the ways of justice and truth. The danger for the church, however, is that of succumbing to the kind of betrayal where the reign of God is pressed into the service of dominative cultural meanings and values that found oppressive symbols and institutions.

---

12. Kereszty, *Jesus Christ*, 152–54; Bourbonnais, *Behold My Servant*, 84–157; Burke, "Crucified People"; Wright, "Servant and Jesus," 281–97.

13. Doran, "Suffering Servant," 46.

14. Doran, *Dialectics of History*, 120.

15. Ibid., 121.

16. Ibid., 122.

17. Lamb, "Christianity," 92.

## Christian Apocalyptic Imagination

We saw in chapter 5 that apocalyptic literature is a form of religious text that is filled with images of warfare in which God is depicted as a warrior. In my critique of apocalyptic consciousness, I highlighted the potential for apocalyptic texts to be inauthentically interpreted. The religious truth of Christian apocalyptic texts that uses the imagery of warfare, however, is an example of the healing vector within history addressing believers who are facing suffering and evil, exhorting believers not only to tell the truth but to live the truth, where doing so requires courage and perseverance.[18] The Christian is encouraged to endure undeserved suffering in the way Christ endured through hope, imitating the Suffering Servant by returning goodness for evil and thus transforming evil into good by making it an occasion of love. "Apocalypse," after all, is the English rendering of a Greek word meaning "revelation" or "unveiling," and is characterized by "a narrative framework in which a revelatory vision is accorded to a human being, most often through the intervention of an otherworldly being, e.g. by an angel who takes him to a heavenly vantage point to show him the vision and/or to explain it to him. The secrets revealed involve a cosmic transformation that will result in the transition of this world to a world or era to come and a divine judgement on all."[19]

As we saw in chapter 3, Doran argues that the integrity of the cultural dialectic is maintained through soteriological meanings and values. Christian eschatological consciousness begins in the belief that God is the source and goal of human history. Therefore, an authentic religious apocalyptic imagination, while recognizing disorder and not underestimating the power of evil, discourages a purely human ability to change this disorder.

Following the overview of Lonergan's account in chapter 3, we can see that social order is proximately related to cultural values, and cultural values are proximately related to personal transformation. Proximately, authentic religious apocalyptic consciousness orients the person, not only toward a hope-filled anticipation of the *eschaton*, but also remotely toward the end of the present disorder and the destabilizing of a good of order through intelligence, patience, and commitment. Here, violence and terror are not defeated by violence but rather through redemptive love that changes the moral horizon of the believer toward new cultural directions and social institutions and away from the infliction of a reciprocal violence and terror.

18. Griffith, *War on Terrorism*, 205.

19. Brown, *Introduction*, 775.

The responsibility of the Christian is to provide the conditions in which others may be open to this love.

From the Christian perspective, the book of Revelation remains one of the most significant sources for apocalyptic narrative in the New Testament. However, there are many misleading interpretations of this literature. One example is the *Left Behind* series, a popular fiction and television series, in which the text of Revelation 19:11–21 is interpreted as an historical period and where there occurs the destruction of countless unbelievers at the command of a stern and merciless Christ figure.[20] Yet Revelation was written when the Roman Empire was the dominant political and religious system of the known world, where the social circumstances among the majority were characterized by the relative calm and prosperity of *pax Romana*; the book offered a message of hope for Christians who, in a context of suffering and crisis, were to resist the persecutions of the empire with patient endurance.[21] If a holy war were to be fought, it was to be fought within the human heart and fought against the inclinations to violence in oneself, rather than by the bloody conflict of actual physical war.

Certainly, the mythic narrative of the book of Revelation presents us with some unnerving scenes, such as the scene found in chapter 12. There is a war in heaven and Satan is unmasked (Rev 12:7–9) and cast down to earth, where Satan makes war on the woman about to give birth. But the weapon for defeating Satan is not some instrument of warfare; rather, it is the blood of the Lamb, a reference to the salvific action of Christ through his death and resurrection.[22] The Lamb does not cling to physical life in the face of death but hands over his life to the heavenly Father out of love for the Father and for humankind. The blood of the Lamb becomes the site of purification for all believers, indicating the site of vindication of all who suffer for the sake of their faith, reminding believers that their suffering is never forgotten by God and that no service in love is ever without fruit. The Sword of God is always and only the Word of God and the truth that it proclaims (Heb 4:12).

---

20. The "Left Behind" series is a set of twelve novels by Tim LaHaye and Jerry B. Jenkins, told from an apocalyptic and premillennialist perspective that has achieved sales of over 50 million copies. It focuses on an underground Christian resistance movement that confronts the Antichrist, Nicolae Carpathia, who, as a charismatic political leader, seeks world domination. See http://www.leftbehind.com. Authors such as Harvey Cox and Barbara Rossing are concerned with the series' tendency to resacralize violence. See also Bergen, "New Apocalyptic," 1–16.

21. Brown, *Introduction*, 774–79. Lamoureux and Wadell, *Christian Moral Life*, 213: "Patient endurance in the midst of suffering or 'bearing wrongs patiently' . . . does not mean passively accepting a bad situation . . . Properly understood neither patience nor endurance is passive in nature for both are active responses to suffering."

22. Brown, *Introduction*, 790–91.

So, while the book of Revelation is an unflinching portrait of the judgment of God over evil in the world, bloodshed is never attributed to God but only to empire. The distorted schemes of recurrence characterized by irrationality, distorted values, and systemic injustice can be exposed for what they are only through a new way of dismantling evil, namely, by forgiveness, sharing, fellowship, and truth.

## The Development of the Just War Tradition

Returning now to the just war image referred to in the previous chapter as one of Coates's four images of war, we recall that it is a fourth horizon of expectations and values that influences a moral response to war. I offer it as a foundation for a constructive engagement with warfare. Just war thinking has developed in a religious culture shaped by the command to love God and love one's neighbor, yet with the obligation to defend the citizenry against unjust aggression. However, I am convinced it is important to examine the just war tradition from an Islamic perspective, too, since, as John Kelsay cogently argues, similar principles can be found in Islamic moral thinking on warfare.[23] While Juergensmeyer provides many examples of religious believers linking violence, religious justification, and militarism, I believe that it is important to argue an alternative moral perspective that may facilitate more constructive decisions on warfare.

Since the Constantinian era, engagement in war has prompted theologians such as St. Augustine of Hippo (in an unsystematic manner) and, much later, Thomas Aquinas (in a thoroughly systematic manner) to theologize on the nature of war and what constitutes responsible action on the part of Christians in war.[24] Most notably Aquinas presented three criteria for a just war: just cause, sovereign authority, and right intention. Following Aquinas's systemic approach, these criteria were to be interpreted under the guidance of the theological virtues of faith, hope, and love. This tradition provides overarching principles to rulers on the practice of statecraft, guidance to commanders in battle, and help for individuals in the formation of their consciences.

23. Kelsay, *Just War in Islam*, 97–124. Kelsay explores the historical deposit of thinkers—such as the Iraqi Mohammad Al-Shaybani (750–805), who wrote extensively on Islamic ethics and military jurisprudence and Al-Mawardi of Basra (d. 1058)—to indicate a rudimentary examination of criteria within Islam that would guide recourse to war, such as legitimate authority, just cause, and righteous intention.

24. Charles, *Pacifism and Jihad*, 123; Aquinas, *Summa Theologiae*, II–II q.40a. Ic, q.83 a.8 ad.3; Finnis, *Aquinas*, 284–91.

## The Just War Tradition: Methodological Issues

The accounts of Girard and Taylor in chapter 2 show how authentic Christian belief unmasks the destructive violence of warfare used mistakenly by power groups to transcend personal and social sin. In the Christian tradition, destructive conflict has always been understood as the inevitable consequence of a sinful world. However, Christian hope leads the believer to affirm that warfare is not inevitable and can even be avoided. When warfare is enacted, the harmful consequences are great, and therefore the violence of warfare ought to be subject to moral restraint and seen as a last resort from the very beginning of a discernment process that seeks to resolve a war-threatening crisis.[25] A moral decision to engage in war ought to be couched within a context of statecraft and the moral responsibility of political leaders who try to discern the common good.

Yet one of the most significant challenges for the twenty-first century is to take a tradition that has evolved out of a unified vision of life, which included belief in God and a discerning community of religious faith, and to dialectically engage with it in a setting that is often secular, sympathetic to liberal ideas (and rather different from the way in which the tradition had been understood in previous centuries), and that sees international agreements principally in legal rather than ethical terms.

A hermeneutic of recovery toward an ethical approach to war must begin by addressing certain methodological issues pertaining to the just war tradition. The first methodological issue pertains to the proposed grounding of the tradition in natural law, if the tradition is to provide a basis for a universal ethic and a global moral discourse for governments and other groups. Fuchs suggests that natural law ethics pivots on two ideas: "law" and "nature."[26] The idea of "law" prompts us to think of morality in terms of commands or rules, yet with the challenge of showing how such laws bind humanity in a genuine common good that is interiorly founded and not simply externally imposed. The idea of "nature" claims that we can justify binding obligations on free persons based on the essence of what it means to be human, by which, as Fuchs notes, reason therefore must ask "nature" about the ethical and legal order that derives from *it* in order to discover what is correct in the total context of the human person.[27]

Two points follow. First, natural law ethics may be effective from a pedagogical point of view to dictate a clear set of rules that help verify where

---

25. Himes, "War," 977.

26. Fuchs, "Natural Law," 669–75.

27. Ibid., 671.

there is compliance, where there is noncompliance, and how to avoid the error of relativism. Nevertheless, this ethical approach contains a number of problems. For example, it may miss the interior elements of intention, motive, conscience, and personal freedom. No observance of the law can do away with the need for the self-appropriation of one's attentiveness, intelligence, reasonableness, responsibility, prudence and goodness exercised by persons in any particular context. Second, associated with the legal idiom of "natural law," is the presupposition that decisions are made within an ideal "moral situation without any acknowledgement of the evils that affect the human condition," prompting the objection that if natural law is to be conceived, it must acknowledge a history of decline "in the victimisation of the other, in social dynamics of envy, and in the totalitarian use of violence."[28]

Therefore a universally applicable natural law, according to Lonergan's intentionality analysis, must include the subject's openness to conversion and a shared orientation with others to self-transcendence. Kelly states that "the more these self-transcending imperatives are heeded, the more attuned we are to the inner law of our being—without which natural law can be nothing more than external imposition."[29] To achieve this level of self-transcendence, a shift in consciousness is required where the subject moves from theory to interiority, helping the subject identify the norms immanent and operative in consciousness, thus allowing the subject to understand conflicting moral viewpoints and the kind of questions that generate their starting points. Interiority then becomes the common foundation moving ethics from a closed system to an open system, from a system dominated by logic to one guided by considerations around method, and from a conceptual system imposed from without to an ethics founded on personal authenticity and conscience properly understood.

The second methodological issue pertaining to the just war tradition concerns the irreducibly social dimension of moral knowledge and evaluation, as identified by Kenneth Melchin.[30] The just war tradition is a set of principles to guide decision making, hopefully directing people along a path of progress and goodness. Melchin argues that such prescriptive notions "are essentially dynamic notions pertaining to patterns of changes in human living."[31] Since moral knowing is concerned to direct human action toward the future from a past and present state of living, "the content of moral knowledge pertains to the development, maintenance, and ongoing transformation

28. Kelly, "Natural Law," 11.
29. Ibid., 18.
30. Melchin, "Moral Knowledge."
31. Ibid., 523.

of the cooperative systems of social relations which condition the emergence and satisfaction of a wide range of individual desires and feelings."[32]

Therefore, moral evaluation toward a course of action prescribing war must be attuned to the effect of decisions on social schemes of recurrence, the flow of goods whose delivery they condition, and the manner by which social schemes can influence individuals in their desires.[33] Melchin argues that "citizens in any society come to understand their welfare as implicated in the wider fabric of social relations."[34] Individual desires become inseparable from wider social concerns. But, equally, it is very possible that people locked into any scheme of social order may not easily appreciate the need to change even when the system becomes destructive.[35] In this case, fundamental heuristic notions such as justice, political freedom, right intention, leadership, and democracy remain important cultural meanings and values for deliberations, orienting our moral enquiry in a specific direction.[36] The commitment to these values highlights the importance of the social structure and its ability to deliver goods toward progress through an elimination of biases and the quest for authenticity. To ascertain moral truth, Melchin argues that we must analyze concrete situations carefully, armed with questions and criteria from both the level of social structures and the level of cultural meanings and values.[37]

## The Criteria for *Ius ad Bellum:* A Critique

As a moral reflection on the action of war, the just war tradition distinguishes between *ius ad bellum* (recourse to war), *ius in bello* (conduct in war), and *ius post bellum* (conduct upon the termination of hostilities).[38] While stating that all three dimensions are important, Mark Allman and Tobias Winright argue that insufficient attention has been given to how just peacemaking as a postwar justice matter relates to the just war tradition.[39] I would like to focus on the first of these dimensions, *ius ad bellum*, although I would agree that there exists an interrelationship between all three in any

32. Ibid., 501.
33. Ibid., 521.
34. Melchin, *Living with Other People*, 57.
35. Ibid., 58.
36. Ibid., 59.
37. Ibid., 60.
38. Flynn, *War on Terror*, 19–22; Charles and Demy, *War, Peace and Christianity*, 159–66, 205–8.
39. Allman and Winright, *After the Smoke*, 55–56.

process of moral evaluation concerning warfare. With *ius ad bellum*, the tradition identifies three major and five minor criteria for a moral recourse to war. The major criteria are just cause (*iusta causa*), legitimate authority (*legitima auctoritas*), and proper or right intention (*recta intentio*). The minor criteria are last resort, reasonable chance of success, proportionality, the aim of peace, and comparative justice.[40] Primarily focusing on the major criteria for *ius ad bellum*, I wish to show the importance of a dialectical engagement with each of them.

The major criterion of just cause relates to the imperative by a state to be able to identify an injury inflicted by another group as truly unjust, while enacting a response motivated by the concern to rectify or prevent injustice, which may include not only a defensive but also a punitive dimension.[41] This criterion proceeds on the assumption that human beings are equipped to understand the difference between justice and injustice, genuine wrong and mere harm. At present, when the term "war on terror" has some currency among secular Western countries, just cause is being evaluated in response to the threat of or actual terrorist attacks, where the attack constitutes an offense against the equilibrium of a just order. It could be argued that restoring balance requires both a defensive and a punitive dimension to help restore or rebuild the equilibrium that has been so severely damaged by terrorist acts.[42] As a moral criterion, just cause represents a necessary but not a sufficient reason to justify having recourse to war.

Within the criterion of just cause, however, there are various challenges. The first is the relationship between religious and moral dimensions in the evaluation of justice. According to Kenneth Melchin, the challenge is for Christian faith to help us name the prethematic expectations that structure our way of thinking about and evaluating a just order.[43] Security and psychological anxiety can shape the expectations about the whole of our lives and the notion of the good can shrink to simply what is comfortable and physically secure. Melchin states that faith "calls us to cultivate these expectations in a specific direction, a direction that bears upon the question of ultimate justice. Christian faith makes a claim about God's justice. It acknowledges massive structural decline but does not allow this evil to have the last word. This is because faith is the expectation of the encounter with

---

40. Charles, *Pacifism and Jihad*, 123–35.

41. Ibid., 132–33. It should be noted that the *Catechism of the Catholic Church* (par. 2309) defines just war as being solely defensive and not punitive, a moral position possibility borne from the sad history of warfare in the twentieth century.

42. Mooney, "Old Wine," 216.

43. Melchin, *Living with Other People*, 109.

God's liberating grace in the midst of our experience of sin and evil."[44] This stands in contrast to the mindset of pragmatism, an ethic of control, and *realpolitik* that have people convinced of their own ability to eliminate evil for the sake of balancing power through the imposition of force.

The second challenge within the criterion of just cause is to work out the relationship between just cause and the other criteria for recourse to war. There is a difference between recourse to war based on a presumption against injustice and recourse based on a presumption against war.[45] The presumption against injustice prioritizes restoring a just order and treats the other criteria as less important. The presumption against war would give weight to the other criteria, especially last resort, in which war would be initiated only when there is no other choice.

Lonergan argues that appropriating our own self-transcendence inherently leads to respecting the self-transcending existence of others. All our efforts to be just require that we take into consideration a threefold structure of human living when it comes to selecting or rejecting data that bear upon moral knowledge: the needs of individuals; recurrent schemes to deliver goods; and, importantly, values. The Christian ideal of self-sacrificing love challenges us toward a form of justice that leaves behind egoism and a strict calculation of what is owed. Therefore, just cause grounded in a presumption against war would emphasize a number of elements: limiting war to a defensive approach; recognizing a propensity to exceed moral limits in war; valorizing reconciliation over punishment; being healthily skeptical about the provisional nature of judgments made by leaders; and recognizing comparative justice, that is, that both sides may have some perceived sense of just cause, with one side having a more actual just cause.[46]

The third challenge within the criterion of just cause is the relationship between *ius ad bellum* and *ius in bello*. If the criteria of recourse to war have been established, but a war is prosecuted with multiple acts of injustice, do these actions render the decision to go to war also unjust? It could be argued that a decision to go to war cannot possibly predict the unforeseeable future. However, for such a decision there must be a reasonable expectation that it be fought in substantial accord with *ius in bello* principles.[47]

The second major criterion for *ius ad bellum*, which is legitimate authority, identifies the ability to declare war as a legal and political process made by political authorities. The burden of waging war morally requires,

---

44. Ibid., 110.

45. Lee, *Ethics and War*, 107.

46. Ibid., 107.

47. Ibid., 101.

therefore, that legitimate authority act for the common good, exercising a moral responsibility toward peace among those governed.[48] At present, proper authority includes yet goes beyond ideas of democratic elections by the people, proper representation for the people, valid forms of government, and the separation of powers. Proper authorities need to be attuned to a host of moral considerations that include the economic interests of a nation. However, given the increasing transnational and international interdependence of countries, legitimate authorities need to work in cooperation with international bodies, such as the United Nations, and according to international law and shared conventions. Even in the case of nations opposing terrorism, it seems important that restraints be placed on unilateral action to more effectively avoid the presence of bias.

As I noted in my account of Lonergan in chapter 3, the political order is a higher integration of economy and technology. However, legitimate authority is grounded in a movement from inauthenticity to authenticity through a self-transcending process of inquiry.[49] Human authenticity is a constant journey of conversion—religious, moral, and intellectual. A sustained commitment to the desire to know and intend the good is conditional upon being in love in an unrestricted manner (religious conversion). The criteria for responsible choices in political life are the norms discovered through the process of moral enquiry (moral conversion). The criteria for affirming reality require a shift from appearances to insight and properly grounded judgments (intellectual conversion). The effort to recognize and identify with those norms in human consciousness requires a shift to an interiorly differentiated consciousness.

Yet, leadership with authenticity is very difficult to realize where cultural and social processes work against authenticity. When there is distortion of the social dialectic toward the pole of practical intelligence, authorities under the sway of limited and instrumental reasoning are likely to disregard far-reaching solutions in their desire to focus on practical short-term economic and political considerations. Political authorities are likely to diminish, abolish, or simply be blind to genuine values when they avoid symbols that speak to the human heart and the drama of living as flourishing human beings.[50] In this case, the common good is no longer a good of order to deliver goods underpinned by concretely prioritized values but, rather, merely the satisfaction of particular needs and desires. In this case

48. Charles, *Pacifism and Jihad*, 133–34.

49. Lonergan, *Third Collection*, 5–6.

50. Lonergan, *Insight*, 238. Lonergan warns that political authorities often may use feelings and symbols to evoke an intersubjectivity that is primarily focused on ideological justification.

the purpose of government too easily reduces to the ability to protect civil rights to property, and liberty shrinks narrowly to the freedom to create institutions that will assure security.

The third major criterion of *ius ad bellum*, which is right intention, is also crucial to any moral evaluation. Evoking the notion of interiorly differentiated consciousness, Kelly notes the many registers of human consciousness by which right intention is all too easily not realized: the "impulsive" who hurry past all the relevant data; the "obtuse," who refuse to raise all the relevant questions; the "immature," who make judgments of fact based on mere impressions; and the "vicious," who cannot see beyond the limits of their own selfishness or group interest.[51] Right intention signals that a just response is founded on four interrelated aspects: first, the greater good of a just peace that goes beyond the sentiments of hatred, vengeance, sovereign pride, reputation, national aggrandizement, blood thirst, or territorial expansionism; second, the moral understanding that the goal of war is not so much killing but rather stopping the aggressor;[52] third, a cultural critique that recognizes that unjustly invading another country for the sake of profit or gain causes deterioration in human living in both the country invaded and the country invading;[53] and fourth, the leader's attention to the social consequences of entering on a war footing. Therefore, when one is dealing with terrorist groups within a country, a central feature must be the winning over of hearts and minds and doing so by seeking to fully address the social conditions that may have motivated or prepared the ground for the actualization of the terrorist threat.[54]

## Conclusion

Juergensmeyer presents two positions on warfare. The first position is the horizon of the religious agent motivated to violence who envisages war as primarily a religious matter by which the agent would achieve victory over antireligion. I have argued that Christian religious experience founded in transcendent love privileges self-sacrificing love in the manner of Jesus. Yet the Christian tradition does not negate legitimate self-defense, especially defense of the innocent. A careful investigation demonstrates that the just war tradition is a means to control violence, while also humanizing its conduct during a conflict and in the postwar reconstruction stage. Juergensmeyer's

51. Kelly, "Natural Law," 19.
52. Charles, *Pacifism and Jihad*, 134–35.
53. Melchin, *Living with Other People*, 39–40.
54. Mooney, "Old Wine," 218.

second position on warfare is the horizon of secular leaders who envisage war primarily as a matter of political and economic power. Following on from the previous chapter on warfare, I have argued that it is possible for secular leaders to implicitly draw upon religious images to justify political goals and these religious traditions require dialectal engagement.

However, we have seen that there are complex methodological issues around the ethical basis of the just war tradition, as founded in natural law, presenting problems for those who would argue that only a natural law basis can provide a cross-cultural or global reflection on the morality of war. We have also seen that through a dialectical engagement with the three major criteria of *ius ad bellum* that decisions regarding recourse to war cannot be separated from specific cultural frameworks for understanding just cause, legitimate authority, and right intention.

In the next chapter, we will examine Juergensmeyer's second symbol for understanding the link between violence and religion, namely, heroic martyrdom.

# 7

# A Dialectical Engagement with Martyrdom

IN THIS CHAPTER I engage dialectically with the idea of martyrdom, the second of Juergensmeyer's symbols for understanding the link between violence and religion. I critique his claim that religious martyrdom and self-sacrifice are simply ritualized rites of destruction that in the eyes of religious agents leave the impression of a religious heroism that transforms history. Since martyrs are also called heroes, I hypothesize that true heroism is marked by a particular kind of courage, hope, and an ethic of risk. I assume that true heroism is a necessary, though not a sufficient, condition for true religious martyrdom, and I argue that the Christian idea of martyrdom, which sublates true heroism within a context of transcendent love, provides an authentic understanding of martyrdom.

Since many of Juergensmeyer's examples of martyrdom are taken from the context of Islam, I believe that it is important to examine Islamic martyrdom in particular. After a short historical overview of martyrdom within Islam, we will see how the meaning of the term "martyrdom" lacks control within the Islamic tradition. This lack of control of meaning facilitates multiple narratives and leads to a history of reception of both authentic and inauthentic understandings about martyrdom. Hence I will argue that radicalized martyrdom as promoted in some forms of Islam is an example of false heroism.

For Juergensmeyer, there is a symbiotic relationship between cosmic war and martyrdom, especially through an emphasis on religious warfare as entailing sacrifice.[1] Leaders present their struggle in terms of a spiritual battle that will give rise to heroes, martyrs, and heroic sacrifice. While in

---

1. Juergensmeyer, *Terror*, 167.

most cases religious communities exercise spiritual resistance against aggression, sublimating physical violence by spiritual exercises, some religious groups counter violence with violence to the point of death. From the perspective of groups who counter violence with violence, their actions witness to the heroic defense of religious and political identities that constitutes a sacred duty. While believers are persuaded that they can never lose the struggle, their historical "failure" in death is transformed into a "victory."[2] For Juergensmeyer, death through sacrifice is both "a rite of destruction that is found, remarkably, virtually in every religious tradition in the world"[3] and an act that has economic, political, and cultural consequences.[4]

Juergensmeyer notes that religious traditions present the idea of transforming death through multiple symbols, such as purgatory, heaven, and hell, Christian resurrection, and the Buddhist levels of consciousness and cycles of reincarnation. Yet each of these symbols instance occasions "of avoiding what humans know to be a fact: eventually they will die."[5] Informed by Ernest Becker's thesis on religion's denial of death, Juergensmeyer assesses the religious agent's general preoccupation with order and the specific defeating of chaos through self-sacrifice as a denial of death.[6] In particular, Juergensmeyer examines the Christian Eucharist, stating that "Christ died in order for death to be destroyed and his blood was sacrificed so that his followers could be rescued from a punishment as gruesome as that which he suffered."[7]

For Juergensmeyer, the Christian Eucharist ritualizes a religious control of disorder through violent means. In this case, the violent death of Jesus proves that religious acts even for the good of others may require a rite of physical destruction. Yet when someone's death happens in a religious context, the act is thought by many to be ennobled, leading Juergensmeyer to the conclusion that the idea of religious sacrifice finds a fitting context within the practice of war. According to Juergensmeyer, since both war and religion are traditions that focus on bringing order from chaos, it follows that those who give themselves to warfare for the sake of religious motives regard themselves as chosen martyrs.[8] He supports this contention with

2. Ibid., 169.
3. Ibid., 170.
4. Ibid., 175.
5. Ibid., 161.
6. Ibid., 162.
7. Ibid., 163.
8. Ibid., 173–74.

data from a number of personal interviews by believers prior to attacks that have resulted in their deaths.[9]

While Juergensmeyer takes an empirical approach in his assessment of religious martyrdom, there are indications in some of his other writings that the differences between inauthentic and authentic understandings of God, of heroism, and of martyrdom clearly exist for him.[10] I will argue that martyrdom primarily founded on a direct intention to die or to kill others is a distortion of both heroism and martyrdom, and we will see that there exists a distinction between true heroism and false heroism that centrally is about the manner by which each person authentically faces suffering and crisis. True heroism in the face of suffering and crisis is founded in courage, hope, and an ethic of risk. Semblances of courage and an ethic of control lead to false heroism, so that even if communities may call such people courageous or heroic, their actions are the fruit of false heroism.

I will argue there is a difference between false martyrdom and a true religious martyrdom that sublates heroism for a higher religious purpose. This religious purpose cannot be equated with the political goals of any group or empire. At times the state's appeal to nationalistic fervor to justify taking up arms and dying for one's country must be called into question. From the perspective of Christian theology, I argue that a genuine religious purpose is grounded in a religious culture that encourages the believer to live an authentically heroic life to the point of living and dying for Christ's sake. Such a life is an invitation to practice suffering through self-sacrificing love, to expose the depth of sin through one's death, and to show the need for God's redemption so as to overcome sin.

## An Hypothesis Concerning Heroism

One way to approach the problem of martyrdom's authentic meaning is to examine the idea of "heroism." We imitate heroes so as to make progress in our own psychological, social, and moral formation. In monotheistic communities, religious martyrs are memorialized as heroes and worthy of imitation. In Western secular societies, citizens who have died during war in order to defend the freedoms of their nation against an unjust aggressor are memorialized as heroes. From my account of Girard in chapter 2, mimetic theory highlights the importance of imitation within an intersubjective

9. Ibid., 70–80. One example is of a videotape interview of a young "smiling boy" who is preparing for a suicide bombing.

10. Juergensmeyer, "Gandhi vs. Terrorism." This article extols a Gandhian approach to violence, which includes active resistance without violence or terror.

field. The mimesis of true heroes revolves around the imitation of a good model, one that receives desire well from the model, and then desires the good of the model and others. The goodness of the model/hero moves in accord with the dynamics of mimesis, seeking more being through the model's reception of self and gift of self to others. Distortion of mimesis occurs when the model seeks to grasp the object of desire and control that desire in opposition to the other.

However, it is important to engage dialectically with the idea of heroism. As I noted in chapter 3, the incomprehensibility of God presents its most powerful challenge to us in the face of insurmountable suffering and crisis. I argue that an authentic understanding of martyrdom begins with an examination of heroism centrally grasped in the subject's existential response to danger, suffering, and crisis. While the circumstances of danger provide for the possible emergence of heroism, one critical question is: How may we determine whether persons who face danger and personal dread are truly heroic?

I will now present a particular hypothesis about heroism, arguing that there are differences between true and false expressions of heroism, by examining several elements that relate to either expression: first, affective responses to danger and crisis, namely, fear, horror, terror, and dread; second, true courage, and semblances or simulacra of courage in the face of danger; third, hope, as distinct from despair or nihilism; and fourth, an ethic of risk, and an ethic of control in the face of danger.

## Affective Responses to Crisis

Since heroism and martyrdom are moral responses in situations of crisis, it is important to explore our affective responses to crisis. In the normal course of life, suffering and crisis have the potential to severely curtail our autonomy, rupturing our sense of belonging to communities, and our living reasonably within our world. According to Jerome Miller, in the face of crisis, people potentially react to protect themselves from suffering through a will to control that permeates the subject's relative horizon.[11] The will to control becomes the routine psychic mode by which the subject deals with the difficult events of life through suppression and, at times, repression of suffering that inhabits the mind and heart. Often this may result in a set of closed frames of meaning, either as a set of closed cultural meanings or personally by means of various forms of bias. Yet, crisis has the potential to

---

11. Miller, *Throes of Wonder*, 98–100. Miller's idea of the everyday ordinary corresponds to an ethic of control and instrumental reason.

make us keenly aware that we are not in control and that we cannot be fully protected by constructing a closed system.

Beginning with the experience of crisis, Miller draws attention to all those experiences in life that could potentially destructure and shatter our accepted understandings of ourselves, our attitudes, values, and worldview, providing a set of conditions that might lead to a change in our horizon.[12] The experiences of fear, horror, terror, and dread are all found within the experience of crisis.[13] Fear springs on the subject with immediacy, is essentially self-protective, and motivates or is motivated by the desire to prevent injury and establish safety. Horror is the subject's recoil from an unbearable reality, the sight of which has already started to devastate the subject affectively—the first stage of the end of the subject's world and the subject's reaction to "protect its world of meaning from what has the capacity to shatter it."[14] Horror has the potential to reveal that we cannot completely protect ourselves from suffering.[15] Terror originates in our desperate desire to remain in control of our existence and amounts to a refusal to be vulnerable.

Dread is "the heart's trembling consent to undergo what is horrifying, to suffer the end of its world, to surrender itself to the very truth from which it would like to recoil in terror."[16] Thomas McPartland cites a set of notes from Lonergan's lecturing on existentialism in 1957 in which Lonergan understands dread, on the one hand, as a fear within consciousness that prefers not to move beyond settled routines, and on the other hand, as a resource within the human psyche impelling the subject toward moral self-transcendence.[17] If dread is the heart's consent to surrender itself to truth no matter how difficult that may be, then, according to Elizabeth Morelli, the object of dread is the possibility of freedom, that is, "the freedom to become what one is not yet, the freedom to transcend one's present horizon to arrive in the strangeness of a new horizon."[18] The true hero feels a tension within human consciousness between the possibility of greater inner freedom and the security of established routines.[19] As soon as one notices

12. Ibid., 124, 130.

13. Miller, *Way of Suffering*, 68–69.

14. Ibid., 68.

15. Ibid., 75.

16. Ibid., 69.

17. McPartland, *Philosophy of Historical Existence*, 183–84; Lonergan, *Phenomenology and Logic*, 284–97.

18. Morelli, "Appropriation of Existential Consciousness", 54. Morelli equates dread with the affective state of anxiety that qualifies existential decision making so that one's actions conform to one's reason to achieve what is truly good.

19. Ibid., 55.

this dialectic within moral consciousness, the subject's stance will either be challenged to self-transcendence and toward true heroism, or be one of flight from self-understanding.[20]

While dread affects us at the core of our being when we consent to undergo its wound, it is not the fragility of the heart that terrifies us but the piercing truth that suffering makes us face.[21] Lonergan's understanding of conversion consisting in a radical change to our horizon would suggest that suffering and crisis can be part of our growth in authenticity. Far from being simply an undermining of one's particular horizon, suffering enables one to discover a possible, new horizon, revealing that our avoidances have come to nothing in our progress as moral agents.[22] Miller notes that crisis can be appropriated "not as a terminal event but as a radical beginning, not as an interruption to be avoided but as an opening to be discovered."[23] The hero's or the heroine's consent to undergo something dreadful and to suffer the end of his or her world often requires love through religious conversion, which grounds the moral virtue of courage.[24]

By contrast, self-sufficient persons held by the will to control will always seek to gain control over their lives, choosing when to exclude that which is uncontrollable, even to the point of choosing when to end their own life in suicide. The will to control, or willfulness, is always motivated by the fear of vulnerability.[25] Vulnerability may take many forms: physical, psychological, social, and spiritual. We practice the will to control when we cannot bear to expose ourselves to weakness experienced through an encounter with another who might wound us. It precludes other questions emerging into consciousness and leads to the tyranny of being trapped solely in a biased commonsense mode of thinking. In the face of harm perpetrated or threatened, vengeance and anger further establish the will to control.

## The Virtue of Courage

A second element that relates to true heroism is the virtue of courage. Heroes are known for their courageous deeds and character in the pursuit of human excellence. Yearley describes courage as "an intelligent disposition that allows people to respect but control the effects [that] perceptions of

20. Ibid., 56.
21. Miller, *Way of Suffering*, 31.
22. Ibid., 67.
23. Ibid., 77.
24. Ibid., 48.
25. Ibid., 20.

danger produce. Courage, then, consists in having a character that lets neither fear nor confidence unduly change behaviour."[26] Persons draw on the
virtue of courage when they are in danger, knowing that desirable goods
must be sacrificed, yet they are prepared to forgo those goods for other
goods that they believe are worthy of pursuing. Since courage deals with
significant dangers as well as the imperative to weigh up real but conflicting
goods, our decision to act will always consist in evaluating a situation.[27]
Since courage is exercised in times of crisis, the cultivation of a disposition for courage will require one's ability to surrender desirable goods and
to engage in acts of self-giving in times when dangers are not present.[28]
Similarly, the practical skill to deal with otherwise frightening situations
and an ability to distinguish real from false dangers will be important in the
development of courage. However, what makes an act courageous depends
primarily on the end for which the agent endures threats. Therefore, traditions that privilege warfare as the proper place to find courageous deeds,
through the channeling of one's passions in order to strike out against the
enemy with extraordinary force and effectiveness, are putting the emphasis
mistakenly on outward results rather than on an inward orientation toward
a good end.

Yearley examines the insights of Aquinas regarding the virtue of courage, noting that he uses Aristotle's structure for exploring ethics: the idea of
the mean between the two extremes of excess and deficiency.[29] According to
Yearley, critical to Aquinas's understanding of courage is his analysis of the
affective roles of fear (of primary importance to courage) and confidence or
daring (of secondary importance to courage). Normal courage is then a virtue with two closely related affective aspects. The mean state of fear is brav-
ery; its deficiency is cowardliness; its excess is daring or being overly bold.
The mean state of confidence is caution; its deficiency is timidity; its excess
is insensitivity to fear.[30] However, for Aquinas, courage in its expanded religious form involves a third emotion, that is, sadness or sorrow through
which the believer comes to notice how much the world is mired in suffering and hate and how far people are separated from God.[31] Furthermore,

---

26. Yearley, *Menius and Aquinas*, 113. Most of Yearley's examination of Aquinas
comes from his *Summa Theologiae*: II–II, q.123, a.1–12; q.124, a.1–5; q.125, a.1–4;
q.126, a.1–2; q.127, a.1–2; q.128, a.1; q.129, a.1–8; q.134, a.1–4; q.139, a.1–2.

27. Yearley, *Menius and Aquinas*, 116.

28. Ibid., 117.

29. Ibid., 120.

30. Ibid., 120.

31. Ibid., 121.

persons who deal courageously with danger draw upon the expertise of the other cardinal virtues, that is, prudence, justice, and temperance.

Yearley explores Aquinas's treatment of the semblances or falsely understood ideas of natural courage.[32] These semblances are: perceived advantage, simple ignorance, tempered optimism, acquired skills, and spiritedness. Those who act in accord with perceived advantage calculate between commensurable goals and choose those goods that preserve safety, as distinct from the truly courageous who choose to endure a fearful option for the sake of a higher good.[33] Simple ignorance is attributed to people who act without full knowledge of, or even with a naivety toward, the dangers involved.[34] Tempered optimism acknowledges that people can fail to evaluate both the situation faced and their own history. They act on the basis of the memory of winning in the past; therefore, their actions are founded in a false confidence as distinct from intelligent and responsible reflection on the current context.[35] Acquired skills such as those formed in military establishments may be part of developing a courageous attitude, but if such skills lead people to feel no fear, then these acquired skills may lead people to miscalculate their capability to deal with the dangers faced. Spiritedness acknowledges that people may be moved to action because of powerful emotions, such as anger, without being directed by intelligent and responsible choices. While simple anger arises from our passions, there is a place for the motivating influence of appropriate anger, especially in a situation that has harmed or could do harm to someone, but not without reasonable reflection.

These semblances of courage that stand in contrast to true courage highlight the importance of practical wisdom's "astute judgements about situations, personal capacities and justifiable goals, as well as [on] its ability to make those judgements [to] inform emotional responses" and a comprehensive view of the kind of life that generates human flourishing.[36] Yearley also notes that for Aquinas any pursuit of a life plan that fails to correctly understand God's plans and actions is inadequate, highlighting the primacy of spiritual goods over physical security, so that the courageous person's major fear should be the fear of not possessing fully the spiritual goods of the Gospels.[37] The centrality of God and our willingness to die for our faith point to the importance of courage under the form of martyrdom. I will

32. Ibid., 124.
33. Ibid., 125.
34. Ibid., 125–26.
35. Ibid., 126.
36. Ibid., 127.
37. Ibid., 128.

examine this more fully later when we explore the meaning of Christian martyrdom.

## False Heroism and True Heroism

At this point, I propose what true heroism might be demonstrated by persons who are religiously and morally converted. Earlier I alluded to the fact that Juergensmeyer's research placed before us the actions of religious agents whose self-understanding led them to believe that they were engaged in the "heroic" transformation of history. Yet we need to be aware that modern imaginations have been shaped by distorted notions of heroism. To discover the difference between false and true heroism in modern Western societies, we need to begin with a hermeneutic of suspicion. For example, there is a need in the West to exercise a measure of suspicion toward social and cultural assumptions about heroism projected either by the state or by the pop culture ideologies of Hollywood images.[38]

Miller asserts that there is a distinction between the falsely heroic and the truly heroic. At the personal level, false heroism often conveys an air of control and coolness[39] and continues through the guises of nihilism and despair.[40] The guise of nihilism longs for a final catharsis that will consume the whole of creation.[41] The nihilistic subject, who wills nothing but the purity of his or her violence, proves that he or she has failed completely to transcend ordinary existence and the will to control.[42] Caught by feelings of helplessness before the events of life, such a person cannot understand that there is more to life than the attitude of willfulness. The tragic outcome is "heroic" rage that is "at the same time, the paroxysm of a will too pathetically weak to be able to suffer without seeking in violence both a purified form of suffering and a final antidote for its wounds."[43] The nihilist displays an excess of fearlessness, coupled with a failure to see the goods that may be lost and therefore an inability to love properly the goods of this world.

---

38. Long and Holdsclaw, "Anything Worth Dying For?," 171–74.

39. Miller, *Way of Suffering*, 85.

40. Ibid., 81.

41. Ibid., 82.

42. Ibid., 8. Miller states: "Ordinary existence is the opposite of letting be what is. It is my attempt to subdue the totality of what is to the plans I have made for it. It is the will to repress anything that tries to interrupt the flow of my routines. The essence of the ordinary is control, the essence of control is the will to dominate."

43. Ibid., 82.

The person of despair prides him- or herself on an honesty to think the worst about any situation and closes him- or herself off from asking any other relevant questions—a stance that becomes another form of control.[44] The certainty that no future will ever be hopeful shows implicitly that such persons are motivated by the need to be infallible, terrified of exposing themselves to any hope that casts suspicion on a verdict already made. Courage as patient endurance will prevent a person falling into despair or spiritual apathy. In this way, dread as opening the possibility of freedom is very different from despair since in dread the subject is open to further suffering and the possible questions arising from it.

I argue that the true hero is someone who faces danger and crisis with courage. Miller names as the true *hero* that person who has broken away from the will to control, with its strategies and avoidances, so that he or she is open to the way of suffering and the disruption produced by crisis.[45] The true hero has "the will to greatness that would welcome crisis, the belittling of its radical disruption which crisis requires one to suffer, the kind of will that seeks to do justice to the radical demands that crisis makes on the individual."[46] The truly heroic person understands that crisis becomes an opportunity to achieve a kind of greatness that is not accessible in any other way, even if greatness cannot be imagined in such circumstances, and to discover that greatness is its own reward. The truly heroic person hopes that he or she will be able to prove worthy of any crisis. The main task is to be equipped for this heroic ordeal.[47] Miller states that the hero "enters the abyss not just without regret, without self-pity, without looking backward, but with a sense of having hungered all his life for precisely this kind of radical suffering. That is why the heroic individual sometimes seems to us to belong to a different species: the hero seeks out, with the eagerness of a born warrior, exactly those crises which we avoid at all costs."[48]

Such a person has no pretensions to immortality and does not believe that entering the darkness makes him or her invulnerable. For this reason we can say that there is a form of sadness or sorrow that accompanies entering the darkness: goods will be lost—but others will be gained. Miller states that the process of destructuring and restructuring of one's thinking "requires that the one engaged in it follow his line of thought no matter how demanding the ordeal into which it leads; it requires him to call into

44. Ibid., 83.
45. Ibid., 84.
46. Ibid., 78.
47. Ibid., 84.
48. Ibid., 85.

question those basic assumptions on which his world as a whole depends. The crucible of radical questioning, the travail of dialectic, upsets every thesis, however secure and irrefutable it seems."[49]

To my mind, Miller's process of destructuring and restructuring complements Lonergan's notion of conversion. Implicit in Miller's account but explicit in Lonergan's account is the assertion that without religious, moral, and intellectual conversion we may end up committed to a cause—either knowingly or unknowingly—that is unintelligent, unreasonable, irresponsible, unloving, and not worth dying for.

## True Heroism: Risk, Gratitude, and Love

In my account of Lonergan in chapter 3, I proposed that an ethic of control is founded on the mistaken assumption that moral agents can "fix" evil by violence, force, and coercion. Cynthia Crysdale argues that, contrary to the ethic of control, authenticity gives rise to an ethic of risk, an ethic of gratitude, and an ethic of love.[50] Moreover, in the context of heroism, there are four characteristics that make up the ethic of risk.

First, the true hero as moral agent is involved in a restructuring of moral meaning brought about by some crisis. Crysdale argues that risk and conditions of possibility are inherent in all moral judgments, since in judgments of value one determines what *might* be the case through weighing up projected courses of action and their outcomes.[51] Predictions about the outcomes of acting in accord with particular moral judgments involve risk and the uncertainty of not knowing exactly what all the repercussions of one's actions will be. Crysdale asserts that "judgements of value and decisions go beyond mere determination of the current facts to a determination of the probable outcomes of various courses of action. This latter determination involves calculating probabilities and such probabilities, by their very nature, involve risk."[52] Additionally, Lonergan notes that the moral agent may need to weigh the relative values between various courses of action and his or her commitment to such values.[53] There are many situations in which heroes find themselves where circumstances cannot be changed since they involve the decisions of other people. The best that one can do is work

---

49. Ibid., 95.

50. Crysdale, *Embracing Travail*, 42.

51. Crysdale, "Risk, Gratitude, and Love," 155.

52. Ibid., 156.

53. Lonergan, *Insight*, 633.

toward creating the right conditions so that there is a possibility for personal and social change.

Second, while the ethic of risk serves as an antidote to the ethic of control, Crysdale asserts that an ethic of gratitude needs to be added to an ethic of risk. An ethic of gratitude comes from realizing that, while all of us are originators or creators of value, we are primarily discovers of value, that is, "as we engage in moral deliberation and action, we need to acknowledge the *givenness* of the Good, and the concrete goods by which we know and participate in the good."[54] In other words, some value judgments lead us to the conclusion that we need to stay with and enjoy existing values and honor the already valuable, rather than think that we need to make something new in the world. As Crysdale notes, "an ethic of risk grounded in an ethic of gratitude becomes a humble discernment combined with courageous action."[55]

Third, true heroes living from an ethic of risk and gratitude take responsibility for their contribution, if any, to the suffering of others.[56] This painful acceptance of their responsibility in personal and social breakdown reaches down to the point of allowing themselves to be shamed for their acts of omission or commission. Miller adds that the true hero is able to acknowledge his or her own fallibility and, through a process of mortification, to give up the one prize that might mean more to him or her than anything else, the stature of being heroic.[57]

Fourth, true heroes need a community of meaning that supports their efforts to live an ethic of risk and gratitude, to discern authentic surrender to crisis, and to assess authentic resistance.[58] This insight highlights that the hero is not a solitary individual living outside a tradition of values and meanings, but rather lives within a tradition with its entire matrix of political, economic, cultural, and religious meanings that may be authentic or inauthentic. The task of helping people move from inauthenticity to authenticity is not easy and requires a community of love.

## Martyrdom in Christian Tradition

I have been arguing for a distinction between false heroism and true heroism, highlighting the moral and psychological horizon of true heroism,

54. Crysdale, "Risk, Gratitude, and Love," 164.

55. Ibid., 165.

56. Crysdale, *Embracing Travail*, 48.

57. Miller, *Way of Suffering*, 97.

58. Crysdale, *Embracing Travail*, 49.

which is aided by the virtue of courage and morally structured by an ethic of risk and gratitude. When we come to speak of religious martyrdom, we are considering heroism constituted by a courage where the believer is willing to die for the sake of doing God's will, the knowledge of which is grounded in the experience of transcendent love. The goodness that the martyr embraces is not primarily his or her own excellence as a human but the truth revealed by God about the world. Further, the martyr grounds an ethic of risk and gratitude in an ethic of love.

As we saw in chapter 3, Lonergan notes that religious experience is falling in love with God, who first loved us. This religious love situates all our quests within a larger horizon and shifts the ground of moral deliberation to the quest for an encounter with holiness.[59] When the believer abides in the presence of God, he or she is able to acknowledge all the concrete goods in the world that point to God, who is all goodness. When believers are overcome with concern for the world, their sense of moral responsibility projects them toward new values and invites them to listen and discover God's will. Given the uncertainty of moral judgments and deliberations, Crysdale notes that religious love grounds hope, "the trust that our limited choices, and the ambiguity of merely creating conditions of possibility without sure knowledge of all the consequences will nevertheless become part of a larger work of God's meaning and value."[60] Specifically in the case of the martyr, an ethic of risk becomes an ethic of sacrifice, that is, new values can be created or distorted values overcome only by accepting a set of consequences that may be against our physical well-being.[61]

Within the context of Christian faith, the word "martyr" comes from the Greek *martyros* meaning "witness," indicating that the believer's suffering and death had borne striking testimony to the witness of Christ.[62] Jesus was the preeminent witness whose words, deeds, and relationships gave rise to the truth of the reign of God. The martyr witnessed to the power and truth about God, in situations where the lack of truth would bring about personal, cultural and social distortions. The primary impulse of the martyr was *witnessing to God* and not *dying for God*, since death was not deliberately or recklessly chosen, even though death might have been a foreseeable outcome of the martyr's actions. The witness of the martyr had been directed to all people, including the martyr's enemy, revealing the possibility that the enemy might be transformed. The early Christian martyrs were privileged,

59. Crysdale, "Risk, Gratitude, and Love," 167.

60. Ibid., 167.

61. Ibid., 167–68.

62. Cunningham, "Martyr," 628.

therefore, to imitate the death of Christ in a dramatic way. In this way they imitated the law of the Cross, an idea that I will develop more extensively in chapter 8, whereby the martyr returned good for evil, loved the enemy, and thus transformed evil from within. In the thought of Girard, the martyr's death became a self-giving mimesis in Christ, passed on through the Spirit to the Christian community.

By the time of Clement of Alexandria in the third century CE, the difference between a confessor of the faith who may have undergone persecution and the martyr had been established in the Christian community. The critical difference was that the martyr was both persecuted and killed.[63] By the early 300s CE, due to the savage brutality of the Roman military, Christians began to speak of martyrdom as bearing witness to the faith and enduring death due to a hatred of the faith at the hands of Christian persecutors.[64]

Later, in medieval times, Thomas Aquinas underscored the priority of the theological virtue of charity that commands the act of martyrdom toward upholding truth, doing good works, and defending justice, out of love for Christ and God's kingdom.[65] The love of God for us and our love of God and neighbor provide the foundation on which to bear the cost of martyrdom while courage aids us to face death specifically with patient endurance. Only a grace-inspired courage helps Christians to hold fast to their faith as they face the horror of persecution and walk a middle path between paralyzing fear and false heroics, between cowardice and recklessness.

Linked to an authentic act of martyrdom is the gift of hope. The gift of theological hope inspires and heals the believer to long for the supreme good of God, despite the setbacks and limitations of human being and doing.[66] The gift of hope tells us that human existence is something that is beyond our control where we are invited to accept our vulnerability. The energies of hope nourish the self-transcending dynamism of the human spirit, refusing to settle for anything that is not truly worthwhile and genuine. Hope focuses on what will truly bring self-fulfillment and inspire a sense of vocation. It moves the believer to desire the supreme good of God, experienced through

63. Schubeck, "Salvadoran Martyrs," 10.

64. Pope Benedict XVI makes a distinction between direct and indirect hatred of the faith. The martyr is killed by people who hate the faith (*in odium fidei*). Yet there are also those killed by persons who hate the way of love (*in odium caritatis*). See Cunningham, "Martyrs Named and Nameless," 10–13.

65. Schubeck, "Salvadoran Martyrs," 11. See footnote 12 on Thomas Aquinas and charity.

66. The theological virtues work together: faith reveals knowledge of the end, charity unites one to God, and hope causes one to move toward God.

a graced participation in divine life, so that "with hope we do not lower our expectations for our lives; rather, we steadfastly cling to God, confident that God accompanies us and assists us, and will provide what we need to reach the greatest possibilities of our lives, the unsurpassable good of everlasting beatitude with God."[67] Theological hope is a future good, dealing with a possible and difficult good, sustained by an enduring courage that necessarily relies on God alone for the fulfillment of the divine promise.[68]

Further, Aquinas argues that the gift of hope enables a form of courage linked to the major virtues of perseverance, patience, magnificence, and magnanimity.[69] While courage as firmness undergirds the kind of continuity of response that is required for all virtues, courage inspired by the theological virtue of hope appears especially when people face the kinds of danger that come from doing the will of God.[70] Ordinarily, since every fearful situation evokes our fear about death and reinforces our natural inclination for life, every courageous act has its roots in a preparedness to die for a higher good.[71]

The link between courage and the martyr's preparedness for death leads Aquinas to conclude that the chief activity of courage inspired by the gift of hope is not attack but endurance.[72] Endurance highlights an important point, namely, that acts of courage finally are evaluated only in terms of the agent's intentions, dispositions, and emotional states. The exact character of these components normally becomes clear (either to the agent or to an outsider) only if they can be studied in a variety of different manifestations extended over a long period of time.[73] Endurance also can be more finely described through perseverance and forbearance: perseverance focuses more on endurance characterized by a concentration on the good sought; forbearance concentrates more on the pain and difficulty encountered.[74]

According to Yearley, for Aquinas the Christian in exercising patient endurance manifests a form of courage that is inspired by the gift of hope,

---

67. Lamoureux and Wadell, *Christian Moral Life*, 138–39.

68. Kelly, *Eschatology and Hope*, 18.

69. Yearley, *Menius and Aquinas*, 130. Magnificence "concerns the planning and performance of great deeds that display spirited resolution and constancy and therefore manifests a person's grandeur" (ibid.). Magnanimity "concerns those actions that rest in a justified trust in the self" (ibid.). Perseverance and patience refer to those qualities needed to endure in the pursuit of a good over a long period of time.

70. Ibid., 131.

71. Ibid., 131–32.

72. Ibid., 133. *Summa Theologiae* II–II, q.124, a.1–3.

73. Yearley, *Menius and Aquinas*, 133–34.

74. Ibid., 134.

which preserves an intelligent and responsible good while not allowing despair or sorrow to overwhelm him or her.[75] Patience will allow the believer to feel sorrow at the state of the world, how far the world is from God, and sadness at their own fragility, in view of the suffering present in the world and his or her inability to change it.[76] Endurance, on the other hand, mediates a graced joy, holding believers firm in the pursuit of valuable goals with a confidence that God alone will "reveal the evidence of love at work in every moment of history" in a promised future.[77]

According to Schubeck, Aquinas understands the martyr as not only committed to truth and goodness, but also to the specific truths of the faith.[78] Aquinas uses the example of John the Baptist, showing that John suffered martyrdom not because he refused to deny what he believed to be the truth before Herod but because he refused to deny that the practice of adultery was sinful and was a violation of justice. Aquinas's example of martyrdom widened the material object of faith, calling one to bear witness against unjust practices and immoral public policy.

More recently, the Catholic Church has been experiencing a shift in its understanding of martyrdom from simply enduring suffering and death at the hands of those who have a hatred of religious truth, to enduring death at the hands of those who have a hatred of love in the service of neighbor.[79] In the writings of Pope John Paul II, the idea of martyrdom through an act of love in the service of our neighbor was given a specifically moral direction.[80] Witnessing to moral truth goes to the heart of defending human dignity and to opposing immorality, which may undermine dignity through acts that include genocide, euthanasia, subhuman living conditions, arbitrary imprisonment, deportation, slavery, prostitution, and selling women and children. In this way, social, bioethical, and sexual moral teaching as well as doctrinal truths are defended by the martyr.

## Christian Martyrdom and Self-Sacrifice

By exploring heroism through interiority, I have argued that the true hero is prepared to enter crisis courageously, allowing a destructuring and

---

75. Ibid., 136. *Summa Theologiae* II–II, q.136, a.1–5.

76. Yearley, *Menius and Aquinas*, 137. We recall the beatitude, "Blessed are they that mourn; they shall be comforted" (Matt 5:5), and the Pauline exhortation to bear our sorrows (2 Cor 5:8).

77. Kelly, *Eschatology and Hope*, 54.

78. Schubeck, "Salvadoran Martyrs," 12.

79. Ibid., 14. This kind of martyrdom was reflected in the life of Maximilian Kolbe.

80. *Veritatis Splendor*, pars. 90–93. Martyrdom is a witness to the moral law.

restructuring of his or her world, while experiencing dread as a possibility of freedom. The true hero is willing to accept his or her own vulnerability, is prepared to give up the social status of hero and, if necessary, to claim his or her own contribution to the suffering of others with contrition. I have argued that the love of God and neighbor is foundational for a truly heroic martyrdom.

One of the key categories used to describe the act of martyrdom is self-sacrifice. As I showed earlier, Juergensmeyer, Jones, Girard, and Taylor share a concern that we should be saved from a narrow rhetoric of sacrifice that has become synonymous with distorted self-immolation, false purification, scapegoating of others, and deprivation. For Juergensmeyer, the focus of martyrdom is physical sacrifice or simply a rite of destruction. His understanding of the sacrificial aspect of the Christian Eucharist seems both to emphasize sacrifice as a rite of destruction, and to interpret the death of Jesus as the means for others to avoid punishment for their sins.[81] I will now dialectically engage the idea of "sacrifice," arguing that the term "sacrifice" from a Christian perspective is best understood in terms of effective love.

Neil Ormerod argues that Christian sacrifice should be understood through the category of effective love, acknowledging the presence of two discourses of sacrifice in the Christian biblical tradition, in an effort to positively critique Girard's negative concerns about sacrifice.[82] The first discourse of sacrifice is the darker side of sacrifice, of which Girard is most suspicious. Taking an historical-critical account of the Gospels, Ormerod shows that Jesus represented the stage of final purification for the religious society of Israel through his mission to the poor.[83] The poor were those who were the objects of sacrifice, treated as sinners and social outcasts, and judged to be far from the traditional customs and laws. Jesus appeared as a subversive force to question the distorted practices of the community toward sinners and outcasts. From the beginning of his public ministry Jesus sought out the victims of the social structures of sacrifice, and aimed to restore the original charter of justice to the society of Israel.[84] Jesus' identification with victims became the context for society's compulsive need to kill him. For the sake of its own survival and social cohesion, this community turned their attention toward destroying him, making him the victim, the perfect victim since there was every reason for eliminating him. Yet, he was the most innocent

---

81. A secular approach to sacrifice analyzes a number of perspectives to ritual sacrifice; however, the secular approach is often silent on the interior disposition. See Daly, *Sacrifice Unveiled*, 9.

82. Ormerod, "Eucharist as Sacrifice," 46.

83. Ormerod, *Grace and Disgrace*, 167–68.

84. Ibid., 168.

of victims, the scapegoat victim. On the Cross, the identification became complete and total as Jesus became the Victim, the pure sacrifice, who uncovered the scapegoat mechanism for what it really was.

According to Ormerod, such a reading of the sacrifice of Jesus fits well with the Passion narrative: a sacrifice by unjust men for an evil purpose masked by a religious ideology. In the words of Caiaphas: "It is better that one man die for the nation than for the whole nation to be destroyed" (John 11:50).[85] Scapegoating, which survives on being hidden from view, falls into its own trap, and, according to Girard, violence reveals its own game in such a way that its workings are compromised and exposed to the light. Rather than being an act to save the community, the violence toward the innocent victim is revealed as an act of evil and distorted self-preservation. The interests of some are being protected over the good of the whole for all the wrong reasons. Ormerod states that, inasmuch as we take hold of this insight, we can recognize the countless ways that others become violently sacrificed on the altars of our disesteem, felt self-hatred, malice, anger, and apathy.[86]

However, there is a second discourse to sacrifice in the Christian Gospels: the true sacrifice of praise and thanksgiving. Positively, Girard argues that Christianity is about exposing the scapegoat mechanism and putting an end to violent sacrifice.[87] There is a form of sacrifice that is not violent but rather an obedient handing over of one's life in love and service to God. Genuine obedience sacrifices the lower good for the sake of some higher good. We recognize this in the field of battle and in acts of martyrdom. We also recognize it in the events of Jesus' Passion.[88] Contrary to the understanding of the Eucharist given by Juergensmeyer, Jesus summed up in the Eucharist his whole mission to the lost sheep of Israel, the mission of healing and forgiveness and the mission of loving and praying for one's enemies. Both at the Last Supper and on Calvary, Jesus embraced his victimhood and offered it to God as a living sacrifice of praise, exposing sacrificial necessity as a sinful mechanism leading to victimization.

In this way, Jesus, the first witness, becomes the divinely ordained solution to the problem of evil rather than the instrument used by God so that humankind can avoid punishment. Jesus does not use violence to promote his cause, either by fighting evil or by fleeing it. He chooses to enter the darkness freely and, while not dispelling it, shows his disciples that we can wrestle with our conscience in the darkest moments of our lives, trusting in

85. Ormerod, "Eucharist as Sacrifice," 47.
86. Ormerod, *Grace and Disgrace*, 171.
87. Ormerod, "Eucharist as Sacrifice," 46.
88. Ibid., 48.

God and confident that our identity continues.[89] Evil is not destroyed or overcome through greater violence but by taking evil to oneself and returning good. Evil is transformed through suffering and self-sacrificing love into a generous moment of conversion and forgiveness. On the one hand, Jesus' death denounces all sacrifice that amounts to a victimization of others and self.[90] On the other hand, the sacrifice of Jesus affirms that the life and action of God, who is love, is the source and end for discerning God's will.[91]

Following Jesus, the witness of the martyr is to act in such a way as to transform the evil of the world by means of a graced and hopeful intelligence. The life of grace for the martyr has affective, intellectual, moral, and religious dimensions. Affectively, the martyr decides on the path of suffering self-sacrificing love and solidarity with victims. The martyr's witness is not simply meant to be for the martyr and martyr's community but for the whole human family. Intellectually, the martyr's thinking is manifested in an intelligent, reasonable, and responsible grasp of reality, truth, and value through the eyes of love. Morally, the martyr's actions are not so much an act of defiance as an act of courage and patient endurance. Religiously, the martyr's experience is measured by the standard of God's love for all and God's presence in our lives, creating in the martyr both sadness and joy: sadness over what opposes our life with God, and joy in recognizing the life of God in him- or herself and in the neighbor. The martyr's act of self-sacrifice is meant to persuade all, even the hearts and minds of those who kill the martyr, so that the gift of grace offered and responded to, leads each person toward reality and truth.

## Martyrdom in Islam

Let us turn now to Islam, since the prime focus of much negative criticism in the West about martyrdom is against its radicalized form within Islamic communities. While the critique offered by Juergensmeyer, Jones, and others often focuses on these distorted expressions, it is also important to demonstrate that Islamic beliefs have the potential to provide the basis for a more authentic tradition of martyrdom. I will explore the broad scope of Islamic martyrdom, with particular reference to the Middle East, without intending to cover the whole range of Islamic expressions conditioned by diverse cultures, histories, and geographical locations. I acknowledge that

89. Crysdale, *Embracing Travail*, 54–55.

90. Ormerod, "Eucharist as Sacrifice," 49. In this sense, the sacrifice of Jesus is a once and for all sacrifice.

91. Ormerod, *Grace and Disgrace*, 170.

differences exist in the understanding of martyrdom between the various traditions within Islam.[92] The differences between various Islamic traditions, especially those between the Shiite and Sunni traditions, are poorly understood by Westerners.

Further, Charlotte Boyer argues that too great a connection is made in the West between violent jihad and martyrdom, often presenting martyrdom as a subsidiary concept within the notion of jihad.[93] I will demonstrate that the meaning of the Islamic notion of martyrdom lacks control of meaning and that unless this issue is addressed the difference between authentic religious martyrdom and dying for a cause, even if the cause is interpreted as doing God's will, can never be discovered. Further I argue that the narratives grounding radicalized martyrdom are not in accord with normative Islamic beliefs.

## Classical Islamic Martyrdom

Within classical Arabic Islamic thought, the term *shahid*, which literally translates to "witness," was used when reference was made to the Prophet, because he was considered the primary witness to the truth of God before all people through his deeds and thoughts.[94] By contrast, the actual verses of the Koran that speak of dying for the faith or the cause of God are few and are usually conveyed through phrases such as "those slain in the path of Allah."[95] The designation of the word *shahid* to mean "martyr" or one who witnesses to his faith through the sacrifice of his or her life generates some controversy due to its earliest association with jihad, though it must be said that contemporary Koranic commentary reads "witness" as "martyr" in many verses.[96] Classically, Muslims in the generation following the death of Mohammad came to equate witnessing to the truth of Allah (*shuhada*) with being noble warriors for the cause of God, so that dying in battle established the jihad to the death as the initial context for martyrdom.[97] Both

92. Howard, "Differently Crucified," 83–92. Sufism, as a distinct branch of Islam, has a different view of martyrdom but this will not be explored in this book.

93. Boyer, "If You Can, Kill," 6.

94. Ibrahim. "Al Shahada," 112. See also Koran 16:84, where Mohammad is a witness against the unbeliever.

95. See Koran 2:154; 3:169.

96. Goldziher, *Muslim Studies*, 350. There is evidence to show that the connection between witnessing and death is a post-Koranic construction and derives from the Syriac Christian notion of the concept of martyrdom.

97. Boyer, "If You Can, Kill," 19. See Koran 3:140, where *shahid* (witness) became associated with martyrdom to the point of death when it was linked to the idea of

on the field of battle during a period of expansion and simply in defense of
Muslim territory, holy warriors (*mujahid*) who threw themselves into battle
with or without expectation of surviving were called *shahada al maruka*
or "battlefield martyrs."[98] Yet, diverging from the idea of battlefield martyrs, the hadiths also record a saying by Mohammad on the conduct of Ibn
Rawaha in a battle around 629 CE. In this hadith Mohammad asserts that
the martyr-warrior did not have to intend death for him to be designated
a believer who fights for the cause of Allah, that is, it is not the intention
to die that accords the warrior the designation of martyr but the believer's
involvement in battle with courage.[99]

## The Shiite Tradition

With the separation of the Shiite communities, Shiite jurists from the beginning of the tradition modeled martyrdom on the person of Imam Hussein,
asserting legitimate leadership within Islam to those who stood in the blood
line of the Prophet. Hussein is known popularly as the Lord of Martyrs in
Shiite tradition since he rode up against a superior Islamic force with no
chance of victory, as a witness to the faith—in this case over the question
of succession. According to Shiites, Hussein sacrificed himself for justice
to revive the religion of the Prophet by standing up to the corrupted Sunni
Caliph Yazid.[100] This emphasis also had the potential to propel into center
stage a form of martyrdom in which the believer intends their own death.
Again diverging from this idealized time, other elements of the Shiite martyr tradition would recall scholars who had become a threat to the Sunni
leadership through their writings, and who were subsequently killed for
their outspoken comments against Sunni authorities.[101]

---

following a just cause. This *sura* probably dates back to the period after the battle of
Uhud in 625, when the followers of Mohammad endured a great numerical defeat. It
became important to develop a martyrology in the face of this defeat and a possible
interpretation of the events that saw God withdrawing God's favor.

98. Nasr, *Shia Revival*, 57.

99. Boyer, "If You Can, Kill," 22.

100. Ibid., 30. This was a struggle for political control between two contenders. The
Shiites understand the Battle of Karbala as centrally concerned with political legitimacy.
The history of Shiite Muslims is one of martyrdom, starting with the revered Twelvers,
who all died through persecution, mostly at the hands of other Muslims.

101. Ibid., 28–29.

## The Sunni Tradition

While accepting the classical position on martyrdom in battle, the Sunni jurists took an approach to martyrdom that attempted to dissociate them from the Kharijites,[102] as well as from possible Shiite nuances. Sunnis banned suicide (*intihar*) as an act of self-murder (*qatal al-nafs*), leaving moral judgments as to whether an act was suicide or martyrdom to be determined by intention (*niyyah*). This paved the way for the emergence of a range of expressions of nonfighting martyrdom exemplified in those who were killed in defense of the faith or of property, honor, or money; in those who died while performing a religious duty such as pilgrimage (*hajj*) or fasting; and in women dying in childbirth.[103] This position, according to Lewinstein, reflected both the conflict and eventual triumph of scholars over more militant religious agents in coming to understand martyrdom.[104] It was no longer death in battle that was the central factor to being a martyr but rather the act of living as a pious Muslim that may occasion persecution and death.

## Radicalized Islamic Martyrdom[105]

The modern period has witnessed some extremist expressions of martyrdom. Scholars diagnose the multivalent context of this radicalization in terms of a reaction against colonialism,[106] modernity,[107] the politico-historical relationship between Islam and the West,[108] and the sociopolitical milieu of pan-Arabic and nationalist calls for unity against Western imperialism.[109] One example of a defining historical moment that has fueled the rise of radicalized martyrdom is the establishment of the state of Israel (1948) and the continuing conflict between Israel and Palestinians, especially the Six Day War in 1967, in which the Israeli Army was able to acquire the occu-

102. The Kharijites broke away from the main body of Islam in the seventh century with the motto, "God and God's Book."

103. Cook, *Martyrdom in Islam*, 34–36.

104. Lewinstein, "Revaluation of Martyrdom," 86.

105. There is some debate as to whether the term "extremist" is more precise than the term "radicalized," which often denotes going to the root, or what is more authentic about a tradition. I am using the words "radical" and "extremist" interchangeably while acknowledging this debate.

106. Ali, *Islamic Revivalism*, 25–29.

107. Ibid., 45–49.

108. Kung, *Islam*, 540.

109. Cook, *Martyrdom in Islam*, 135.

pied territories, an act that has been an ongoing source of violent dispute to the present.[110] Further, David Johnston argues that Western foreign policy married to the promotion of Western corporations, Western consumerism, and anti-Muslim global media also provided the conditions for the rise of greater extremism.[111]

## Radicalized Shiite Martyrdom

The modern radicalized Shiite approach to martyrdom specifically evolved out of a distrust of Western influence in both Iraq and Iran. Both countries are among the few with a majority Shiite base. In Iraq, for example, when the dictatorial leader Kassem was deposed, Shiite leaders of southern Iraq began in 1963, around the town of Najaf, to reinterpret Shiite religious traditions. They took up the writings of the Iranian Shiite cleric, the Ayatollah Khomeini, as a way of reviving their faith against the new Sunni-based Ba'ath party of Baghdad. This desire for revival was partly fueled by the failure of Sunni-based political policies to socially integrate the southern Shiites, leading to adverse social conditions among the Shiite people.[112]

The Iranian scholar, Ali Shari'ati (1933–1977), who studied revolutionary Marxism and existentialism in Western schools, shifted the emphasis of martyrdom from waging a battle for the cause of God with some hope of victory, to violent actions designed to create a symbol of the people's determination for the cause of the oppressed and poor.[113] In this way, Ali Shari'ati helped reposition Shiitism from a devotional religion to a religion of activism and revivalism.[114] Influenced by the Marxist class dialectic, Shari'ati argued that, at any point in history, humanity is in the throes of a struggle between God and Satan, poor and rich, good and evil, truth and falsehood, oppressed and oppressor. The danger with such categories is dualistic thinking (which I explored in chapter 4), stereotypical demonization, and the psychic phenomenon of *ressentiment* (which I will explore in the

110. The events of Israel's political victory in the Six Day War not only affected the morale of the Israeli people but also led to a change in the political leadership of those countries opposed to Israel, for example, Sadat came to power in Egypt and Assad in Syria. Both leaders had a more "open door" policy to Israel and other countries. Choueiri, *Islamic Fundamentalism*, 93.

111. Johnston, "Islamic Critique of Globalization," 1–24. Johnston asserts that the political hegemony of US foreign policy strengthened the Egyptian authoritarian regimes while at the same time doing the bidding of the United States.

112. Boyer, "If You Can, Kill," 41.

113. Ibid., 48.

114. Ibrahim, "Al Shahada," 114.

next chapter), leading to groups being locked into the dialectic of oppressed and oppressor.

Due to Ali Shari'ati's influence, and in the context of Iran, Khomeini's ideas around the oppressed were given an important boost, joining the idea of fighting for the cause of God to actively overcoming the oppressor. By the early 1960s, and over many years, Khomeini had protested against the ruling Shah and the Pahlavi regime in Iran and it was in his utilizing of the two words *mostazafin* (oppressed) and *shadid* (martyr) that he was able to transform the idea of martyrdom: the martyr is the one who fights for the oppressed, guided by faith in God, and gives his life to overcome the oppressor. Boyer notes that by the 1960s, Khomeini gave elevated status to those killed by the "tyrant" regime of the Shah so that their death took on the title of *bicharehha* (unfortunate ones).[115] Later, those who died in the Iranian Revolution of 1979 were understood to be martyrs since they helped overcome the oppression of the Shah.[116] When Saddam Hussein invaded Iran in September 1980, Khomeini advocated Ali Shari'ati's interpretation of Imam Hussein's martyrdom, casting Saddam in the role of the usurper Yazid, Imam Hussein's nemesis so many centuries before.

One example of a distorted form of radicalized martyrdom from this period, which was meant to symbolize a message of determination against the oppressor, came during the Iran–Iraq War in the 1980s. Christopher Reuter, a journalist who reported on the conflict, states that ten thousand Iranian children "volunteers" died with a plastic "key to Paradise" around their necks, many with clenched fists and others holding Kalashnikovs with difficulty, as they were sent into the line of Iraqi gunfire and across minefields in what he called the "human wave attacks."[117] According to Khomeini, the people of Iran saw themselves as the oppressed, while Saddam's forces were the oppressors, and so for this reason both the soldiers and the child "volunteers" who died on the battlefield were to be called martyrs. Boyer

115. Boyer, "If You Can, Kill," 44.

116. Note that the Khomenian-led revolution of 1979 mercilessly suppressed violent attempts by the Marxist people's *mujahidin* to seize power. While Khomeini used the language of oppressed and oppressor, he was oppressive toward communism and Marxism.

117. Reuter, *My Life*, 34–35; Farzaneh, "Shia Ideology." These children were part of a paramilitary volunteer militia known as the *Basij*, ordered to be formed by Khomeini in 1979. During the Iran–Iraq War volunteers from the *Basij*, including children as young as twelve and unemployed old men, some in their eighties, swept along by a Shiite love of martyrdom and patriotism, were mobilized for war through intensive media campaigns.

interprets the intention of political authorities as "choosing to *die* is the tool and the *death* is the condition" for being a martyr.[118]

## Radicalized Sunni Martyrdom

The modern radicalized Sunni tradition of martyrdom has been influenced by three prominent Sunni intellectual figures: Sayyid Abu Mawdudi (Pakistan), Hassan al-Banna (Egypt), and Sayyid Qutb (Egypt). I will explore the thoughts of Qutb in the next chapter as an example of the phenomenon of *ressentiment*. However, in the context of secular Egypt, it is worth noting that Qutb taught that offensive jihad was the obligation of every Muslim, an obligation that included a willingness to die, if death was required to gain victory.[119] Boyer argues that the Shiite radicalization of martyrdom demonstrated by *Hezbollah* in Lebanon during the 1980s, and the jihadist focus of Qutb and others, combined to help radicalize other offensive jihadist Sunni Islamic groups such as the military wing of *Hamas*.[120]

## Islamic Martyrdom and the Control of Meaning

This brief historical account of martyrdom within the broader Islamic community demonstrates that the term's meaning has not come under sufficient control. Universally, the designation of "martyr" in Islam is accorded to those believers who die for the cause of God, whether they intend to die or not. However, the context in which death is occasioned, the inner intentions of those who die, and the cause for which they stand varies greatly, including: those who die through reckless actions in battle to prove the nation's resolve; those who volunteer walking over landmines and toward bullets not knowing whether they will live or die (the human wave attack); those soldiers who fight, hoping for a political victory to defend their country against an unjust aggressor but who die in the process; those who intend to expand Muslim territory but who die in the process; those who intend to live their faith devoutly, raising a family and protecting property but who die unintentionally, such as in childbirth or by being a victim of crime or

---

118. Boyer, "If You Can, Kill," 55.

119. Ibid., 64.

120. Ibid., 67–74. Boyer explores the writings of Sheikh Fadlullah, the spiritual Shiite guide of Hezbollah who advocated that the only difference between the early battlefield martyrs that stormed into battle with a sword and the person strapping a bomb to their chest is simply timing and technology.

by being a victim of those who hate the faith; and those who intend to die and to kill others through suicide bombings for the sake of a political goal.

This demonstrates a lack of control over meaning, which is due to a number of factors. First, Islam today places great importance on a mimetic ethics, that is, ethics that places great importance on imitating the founder. Mohammad's role as a servant of God is summed up in the *Sunna* (or exemplary conduct) primarily derived from the hadith literature. Though the Koran does not use the term *Sunna* to refer to Mohammad as a behavioral example, nevertheless by the mid-ninth century religious scholars had begun to associate the term *Sunna* with the Koran verses that speak of Mohammad as a superb model.[121] Mohammad as the first witness to God for Islam was a prophet, a merchant, and a military general. He engaged in wars, primarily wars of defense against unjust aggression, though he did authorize raids on pilgrims to pagan shrines as a way of disrupting the worship of false gods.[122] Since he engaged in wars to protect the followers of Islam from those who sought to destroy them, the possibility of other believers being both martyrs for God and soldiers in battle emerged. However, I argue that simply being a battlefield soldier defending Islam or expanding Islamic territory cannot be the only criterion for assessing a righteousness of life that would ground martyrdom in a normative sense. The criteria for evaluating the righteousness of those who die in battle must be something like those criteria explained in chapter 6, on just war: just cause, right intention, legitimate authority, proportionality, last resort, and noncombatant immunity. As I demonstrated in chapter 6, according to Kelsay, the criteria of just war, legitimate authority, and right intention are implicit in Islamic thought on warfare.[123] If these criteria are not present then the soldier's witness in battle falls short of true martyrdom.

A second factor demonstrating a lack of control over the meaning of the term "martyrdom" relates to my argument that true heroism is a necessary, yet not a sufficient, condition for authentic martyrdom. One of the features of true heroism is true courage as distinct from the semblances of courage. Martyrs who display a direct intention to die make us question whether we are dealing with true courage. Here, we may be dealing with semblances of courage, such as spiritedness, where people throw themselves into battle without fear but with a determination to die; or simple ignorance, where people are manipulated by higher authorities, as in the case of human wave attacks. When all who have died in battle are called "martyrs," the

---

121. Renard, *Islam and Christianity*, 177–78.

122. Allman, *Who Would Jesus Kill?*, 287–88.

123. Kelsay, *Just War in Islam*, 97–124.

uniqueness of the each person's witness and its relationship to the virtue of courage is diminished. For this reason, establishing whether individuals are true martyrs is best dealt with through a process of investigation that has carefully thought-out criteria to judge the motives and intentions of each individual.

Third, while historians may assess the motivations of Mohammad in terms of the crude power politics of the time, such an assessment would disguise the larger theological issue of the relationship between the sacred and the secular, as discussed in chapter 4. I argue that in parts of the Islamic world today the distinction between sacred and secular is insufficiently differentiated, leading to a sacralizing of the political. This results in a political theology that can too easily link the cause of God to killing, and sacralize a direct intention to die, opening Islam to the possible distortion of "holy war."[124] This goes against what I argued in chapter 4, namely, that any form of sacralization using the name of God or the word of God or any sacral object to justify persecution, exclusion, and scapegoating, should be dropped.

A fourth factor demonstrating a lack of control over meaning consists in the correlation between the commonsense meaning of martyrdom and the examples of heroic deeds in battle, adherence to faith in times of danger, and ethical guidance in Islam that are drawn from the Koran and hadith literature. Islamic theology chooses to place the criterion for being a martyr on doing the will of God as recorded in the Koran. Two concerns arise from this perspective. First, an idealist religious ethic carries the same danger that all ethics based on assumptions about obeying the will of God carry, namely, the danger of banishing reason from moral evaluation, preferring to follow the inner logic of God's unquestioning supremacy.[125] Second, there is a danger in all religious traditions that exalt right living (orthopraxis) and diminish right thinking (orthodoxy). Right living must rank higher than right thinking. However, orthopraxis as a higher integration is dependent upon orthodoxy. What is needed in Islam is a more systematic approach through an interiorly differentiated consciousness that helps to move understanding and practice toward a new synthesis.

## Which Is It: Islamic Martyr or Suicide Bomber?[126]

One extreme form of martyrdom is the case of the suicide bomber. There is a larger debate in both secular and religious communities as to the motivations

---

124. Kung, *Islam*, 598.

125. Renard, *Islam and Christianity*, 182.

126. There is much debate about the term "suicide bomber." See Schweitzer, "Suicide Bombing."

that drive suicide bombers.[127] From the 788 suicide bombings conducted globally between December 1881 and March 2008, the vast majority who claimed responsibility for them were Islamic-based groups and individuals, with a majority subscribing to a Salafist Sunni Jihadist ideology (for example, *Hamas*) and a minority to Shiite ideology (for example, *Hezbollah*).[128] These events need to be placed in an Islamic context mindful of both the prohibition on suicide and the designation by some that these are acts of martyrdom.[129] Therefore, the critical moral question is: Are "martyrdom operations" a form of authentic martyrdom or simply acts of suicide?

There are a number of arguments against equating suicide bombers with true martyrdom. First, many Islamic scholars take a negative moral view toward suicide bombings generally, judging the context as critical to shaping the moral designation of such acts. One example is the political context of Israel and the lack of choice by the Palestinian people.[130] In this context, scholars have framed this conflict in the oppressed/oppressor dialectic and the moral intent of "martyrdom operations" is viewed not as suicides but as sacrifices that overcome oppression.[131] I would counter this reasoning by saying that this moral assessment wrongly privileges the hegemony of the political over the religious and moral argument, causing a distortion in the scale of values and an imbalance in the dialectic of community. Such a primacy of the political goal does not take into consideration that violent acts simply reinforce a cycle of violence.

Second, in terms of moral understanding, right intention (*niyyah*) is a common Islamic criterion for judging the morality of an action, inviting discussion on the nature of moral evaluation. A common argument among Muslim scholars is that "a fine thread may separate suicide from sacrifice, which is determined by the intention of the actor," that is, the

---

127. Moghadam, "Motives for Martyrdom," 46–78. According to Moghadam's data, between 1981 and 2008, 1857 suicide attacks were perpetrated worldwide (from which 20,603 people were killed and at least 49,209 people wounded): 1020 suicide missions took place in Iraq (54.9 percent); 235 (12.7 percent) in Afghanistan; 188 (10.1 percent) in Israel, including the West Bank and Gaza Strip; 107 (5.85 percent) in Sri Lanka; 88 (4.7 percent) in Pakistan; 41 (2.2 percent) in Lebanon; 37 (2 percent) in Russia; and 141 (7.5 percent) in twenty–nine other countries. He provides a list of groups and their ideological affiliations (65–69). According to Moghadam, when dealing with groups who are Salafist jihadist, religion plays a significant role in the motivation for suicide bombing (62–71).

128. Ibid., 65–69.

129. Malka, "Must the Innocent Die?," 1–8; Cook, "Implications."

130. Tamini, "Islamic Debate," 101.

131. Ibid., 102.

intended purpose of the action.[132] I argue that this statement is an example of commonsense moral knowing that has not come to a full theoretical differentiation of moral thinking. By contrast, Brian Cronin argues that moral intentions alone do not constitute an unqualifiedly good person.[133] The intention of the moral agent is one element in the moral evaluation of an action and is a response to the question: What goal was the person intending to achieve? If one's intention is, at least, to expel foreign forces from one's country and one does so through suicide bombing in which both innocent people and bomber are killed, the act will simply not bear the full meaning of a good act since the act perpetuates and widens the cycle of violence. Intention is not enough as a criterion for judging good moral character. To be an unqualifiedly good person, Cronin states "our actions must be wholly good, the intentions benevolent, the motives wholesome and the consequences good for all."[134]

One hermeneutical key for understanding the moral nature of actions is to examine moral intention from the perspective of Lonergan's intentionality analysis. Following my account of his analysis in chapter 3, I pointed to the relationship between the experience of moral conscience and the dynamics of human consciousness. Kelly states that conscience is, in the first place, "a consent to the self-transcending outreach implied in being attentive to new data, in asking questions that need to be asked, in deliberating over the evidence in order to judge the reality of the situation; and, in consequence, in being responsible in collaborative decision making."[135] He concludes that if any of these operations are denied, human beings are left with a gnawing sense of unease. Clearly, if one's deliberation on values is focused solely on intentions and occludes the deadly consequences for innocent noncombatants and self, the suicide bomber is an example of someone who is not asking all the relevant questions.

A third argument against equating suicide bombers with true martyrs relates to the actions of such bombers reflecting an ethic of control that often emerges from despair or nihilism, and fails to hope. By contrast, Muslims are encouraged to proceed in their decision making with *tawak-kul*, the practice of trusting in divine providence. This practice holds to the primacy of doing God's will through trusting God, often captured in the cautionary Islamic phrase, "God willing," before proceeding with any

132. Ibid., 100.

133. Cronin, "Value Ethics," 218.

134. Ibid. Cronin distinguishes moral intention, consequences, motivation, and moral reasoning in human actions.

135. Kelly, "Natural Law," 18.

action. This phrase has been incorrectly interpreted by non-Muslims as betraying a fatalistic attitude about one's actions and the events of life.[136] In fact, "God willing" points to a religious truth, namely, that an authentic human path aligns itself with God, aiming to return to God all that the believer has received from God, with the servant's freedom being realized when one responds to the divine call. For Islam, the personal destiny of the individual is preordained by God through our God-given natures, where freedom is exercised through accepting our God-given nature as part of the gift of creation, with no question of the person being independent of God.[137]

Fourth, while Islam does not forbid engagement in war, it must also be said that doing God's will is central to a genuine Islamic religious life. In chapter 5, on warfare, I argued that the integrating principle within Islam is doing the will of God as known from the Koran. Doing God's will for the Muslim is equivalent to doing what the Koran says. Since the Koran presents a number of verses that seem to contradict one another on what the will of God might be, a literalist application of the texts may not yield a correct interpretation on the will of God. For people who are nourished by the word of the Koran and who want to move beyond a narrow literalist interpretation, exegetical issues, such as the religious and moral horizon of the interpreter of the text and the authenticity or inauthenticity of the religious tradition, are crucial to a developing tradition.[138]

My own position on doing God's will comes out of a Christian context and corresponds to my account of Lonergan in chapter 3, that is, knowing the will of God derives from God's love moving the subject to discern truth and value in the concrete circumstances of his or her life. This highlights the importance of religious conversion sublating moral conversion. God's will is not a matter of the subject reaching a judgment about the state of God's mind, but rather a judgment of value motivated by being in love with God, who first loved us without reservation.[139] Similarly, when the subject is engaged in a process of deliberating on values, the goal is not primarily to discover the will of God, but rather to identify through an interior dialectic

136. Burrell, *Jewish-Christian-Muslim Theology*, 72. This interpretation of fatalism comes out of a distorted secular cultural perspective that understands creation "over against" the Creator and that mistakenly understands freedom as mere choice or doing what one wills.

137. Ibid., 42, 72.

138. For a fuller treatment of these questions, see McEvenue, *Interpretation and the Bible*, 40–46, 61–62, and 65–68. Scriptural texts (whether in the Bible or Koran) do not offer us a theology as such but rather a series of "normative foundational stances demanding various conversions of its readers" (62). McEvenue argues that we must enter into dialectical engagement with these stances.

139. Dunne, *Doing Better*, 275.

which of the several feelings and thoughts spring from the love of God carrying one's actions toward moral integrity.[140] The recent declaration, *A Common Word Between Us* (2007), signed by more than 300 Muslim signatories, opened a new vein of Christian-Muslim dialogue by grounding doing God's will in the love of God and love of neighbor.[141] If love of God and neighbor is central to being a good Muslim, then authentic deliberative and practical insights must be informed by love. The centrality of transcendent love invites all to a moral imagination that goes beyond pragmatic idealism and, in the context of conflict, enables the development of something like the just war principles as discussed in chapter 6.

The fifth argument against equating suicide bombers with true martyrs focuses on issues concerning the nature of hermeneutics and is especially relevant when we turn to a specific point in Islamic exegetical criticism, the practice of abrogation, or *naskh*.[142] Abrogation refers to the practice of adjudicating the priority in truth between one holy text and another by postulating that an earlier text is superseded by a later one. To my mind, the process of abrogation mistakenly asserts the priority of chronological order as more important than other considerations to do with the nature of hermeneutics, such as the converted horizon of the interpreter and the authenticity of the tradition.[143] In the case of radicalized martyrdom, the practice of abrogation has had a profound effect on the process of interpreting texts, whereby some have put aside earlier, more pacific verses in favor of more aggressive, later verses. There is a tendency among those who think this way to presume that the later Medina texts are more important than the nonviolent earlier Meccan texts, resulting in the "sword" verses abrogating the "peace" verses of the Koran.[144] This assertion discounts the earlier periods of Islamic revelation on the basis of a cunning and militarily weak leader in Mohammad, for the later period of revelation, when the military power of Mohammad had grown.[145]

---

140. Ibid., 276.

141. *A Common Word Between Us*, 1–29. The document asserts that the invitation to accept the truth "There is no god but God" (*tawhid*) leads to the command to love God above all else. See Shah-Kazemi, "God, the Loving."

142. Kirwan, "Girard, Religion, Violence," 918.

143. Ibid., 919.

144. Burrell, *Jewish-Christian-Muslim Theology*, 150. Interestingly, there is not a single reference to sword (*sayf*) in the Koran.

145. Ibid., 151.

## Conclusion

In this chapter, we have seen, first, that it is possible to speak about true and false heroism. Growth into true heroism is potentially put before us all when we face suffering, danger, and crisis. True heroes, morally structured in an ethic of risk, informed by natural courage, and strengthened by hope allow suffering to destructure and restructure their horizon even to the point of enabling them to give up their status as heroes. Religious conversion sublates true heroism into an ethic that prioritizes the centrality of suffering through self-sacrificing love. Authentic Christian martyrdom is the outcome of true heroism founded in a love of God and neighbor, seeking to overcome victimization and taking a courageous stance on matters of truth and justice. This requires the virtue of courage and the theological virtue of hope.

False heroism, by contrast, pushes away danger and crisis experiences through the will to control and therefore cannot face the possibility that one may have contributed and continues to contribute to the suffering of others. Suicide martyrdom that seeks to kill combatants and noncombatants is a form of false heroism. It portrays martyrdom as an overspiritualized reality while fueled by rage and mediated though reactive anger, lacking in charity as its commanding virtue, and contributing to the cycle of violence and further victimization. It stands in contrast to a stance of courage and hope, where one's endurance is filled with both sadness at the injustice of the world and a peaceful joy in God's providence.

Second, we have seen that there is a radical difference between a direct intention to die that creates victims and self-sacrifice that offers one's life to defend religious truth and justice. Religious traditions that assert that martyrdom involves taking one's life and the lives of others are distorted and do not come to terms with the responsibility that each of us has for choosing and protecting life without creating more victims. In the case of Islam, to address this distortion requires a reappropriation of the authentic Islamic tradition, which emphasizes doing God's will grounded in the experience of transcendent love, which, in turn, leads to the love of God and neighbor.

I have not specifically explored the Sufi tradition in my presentation of Islamic martyrdom. However, I concur with Burrell, who states that minority voices within a tradition can often help clarify distortions in the wider tradition, as was the case when the Sufi Muslim, Ibn Mansour al-Hallaj, of Baghdad in 922 was executed by religious and secular leaders after reminding "their Sunni and Shia companions in faith of the crippling effects of soul-less *sharia*."[146] While religious martyrdom may be justified by holding up goods such as the revival of the faith, social honor, and our desire to be in union with God,[147] such motivations must be critically and responsibly grounded in the higher purpose of loving God and neighbor.

In the next chapter I will explore the third of Juergensmeyer's symbols for understanding the link between violence and religion, namely, demonization.

---

146. Burrell, *Jewish-Christian-Muslim Theology*, 135.

147. Rahimi, "Dying a Martyr's Death," 1–5.

# 8

# A Dialectical Engagement
# with Demonization

THE THIRD SYMBOL PRESENTED by Juergensmeyer and others for understanding the link between violence and religion is the phenomenon of demonization. In this chapter, I will argue that without a heuristic account of
evil, people will be unable to discern why demonization continues the cycle
of violence. We will see that social exclusion and humiliation provide for the
emergence and survival of demonizing processes, while acts of dehumanization escalate those processes to the point where those demonized are robbed
of their subjectivity. Emerging out of situations where there is an imbalance
of power, I will demonstrate the role of *ressentiment* in fueling violence and
demonization. Demonization becomes even more entrenched where there
is a lack of response toward victims traumatized by evil. Concurrently, the
categories of "victim" and "perpetrator" may help to identify the difference
between evil done to persons and evil done by persons. However, such a
distinction may act as a barrier to healing when the victim is motivated by
retribution, revenge, and *ressentiment*. I will argue that distorted religious
symbols perpetuate demonization and the cycle of violence, while authentic
religious symbols help overcome demonization. The symbol of the Cross
in Christianity enables an affective healing beyond retribution, to the gift
of forgiveness.

Demonization is an aberrant and extreme form of stereotyping that
functions by reminding people to "maintain the enemy in the enemy role."[1]
Juergensmeyer argues that the process of demonization can be directed
toward people outside or inside one's social and religious groups, and he

---

1. Juergensmeyer, *Terror*, 174.

distinguishes between primary and secondary targets.[2] He notes that every struggle has its heroes and foes; therefore, putting people into the category of enemy has the effect of empowering people against the enemy over whom one hopes to triumph.[3] While it may be easy to demonize an opponent who has victimized innocent people through the use of "savage power," it is more difficult and requires greater creativity to demonize those who are relatively innocent.[4]

The process of satanization, a subset of demonization, is evident in religious communities where the source of evil intentions and actions is named a follower of Satan and where religious agents are empowered to defeat the power of Satan through some kind of violent struggle.[5] James W. Jones notes that one of the most widespread beliefs of violent religious movements is their self-belief characterized as the "struggle of the forces of the all good against the forces of the all evil."[6] In a Christian context, Reverend Paul Hill, who shot and killed a physician in front of an abortion clinic, wrote narratives, framing his actions in terms of choosing between the kingdom of God and the kingdom of Satan. In the Muslim context, Jones gives the example of the Ayatollah Khomeini, who, upon his elevation to leadership after the Iranian revolution of 1979, proclaimed the West as the "Great Satan."[7] Jones also notes that Osama bin Laden characterized the struggle between Al Qaeda and the West as "two adversaries: the Islamic nation, on the one hand, and the United States and its allies on the other," calling America the "Great Satan" and Israel the "Little Satan."[8]

In a secular setting and in the wake of the attacks of 9/11, President Bush's speeches divided the world into good and evil, those that love freedom against those that hate freedom, naming the campaign launched against terrorists "Campaign Infinite Justice" (later changed to "Enduring Freedom").[9] Bush viewed his response as grounded in justice and freedom so as to eliminate evil. The mainstream media of America responded by speaking of the attackers of the World Trade Center as the "many headed beasts whose tentacles were threatening to violate every secure space in the

2. Ibid., 180.

3. Ibid., 174.

4. Ibid., 175.

5. Ibid., 186.

6. Jones, "Eternal Warfare," 94.

7. Jones, *Blood that Cries Out*, 43.

8. Jones, "Eternal Warfare," 94.

9. Kearney, *Strangers*, 111. See also Tuman, *Communicating Terror*, 135–42. Tuman analyzes Bush's speech to the Congress, the nation, and the world on September 20, 2001, highlighting his rhetoric of good versus evil.

nation."[10] All these examples of dualistic thinking become a form of strategy to justify inflicting violence on others by "instilling the belief that we are dealing with a demon, someone less than human, and that this subhuman demon is a threat to us, which requires that we attack and even eliminate this enemy in self-defense."[11]

According to Juergensmeyer, demonization and, its subset, the process of "satanization", aim at the delegitimization of the enemy within a larger system of religious behavior, by which people desperately try to make sense of the world and maintain some control of it.[12] Any group moves toward delegitimation through a number of stages: a crisis of confidence in the dominant power, a conflict of legitimacy, and a crisis of legitimacy. Through delegitimation, the process of empowerment has a number of key moments. It begins in the awareness that the world has gone awry; it moves to the "foreclosure of ordinary options," where people see no possibility of improvement through ordinary channels; in cultures where religion names these forces as evil, a struggle to defeat evil is mandated; finally, the process moves to the enacting of a struggle through symbolic acts of power.[13] This struggle may include "perpetrating acts of terrorism . . . one of several ways to symbolically express power over oppressive forces and regain some nobility in the perpetrator's life," so that they may experience "the exuberance of the hope that the tide of victory will eventually turn their way."[14] Despite these insights into the process of satanization, Juergensmeyer does not identify how one might move beyond violence and demonization.

## Identifying Demonization: Critical Reflections

If we are to move beyond violence then it is important to identify both interiorly and externally what happens in the process of demonization. Those who demonize judge whole groups to be evil, opening themselves to the critique of social bias and, therefore, the inability to arrive at true judgments about people. The process of demonization presupposes that the demonizing group has an agreed understanding of moral evil, without having to engage in a mutual deliberation of values. Demonization acts effectively to shift the power relations of individuals and groups through a common conviction about who is the enemy (all against one); however, this shift may

10. Kearney, *Strangers*, 112.
11. Daponte, *Hope*, 69.
12. Juergensmeyer, *Terror*, 186.
13. Ibid., 188.
14. Ibid., 189.

serve only to legitimate a power over others. Demonization will not satis-
factorily address the trauma felt by those who have had evil done to them
nor does it necessarily provide a pathway for healing. If this is the case, then
we must distinguish the blanket stereotyping of people as the enemy from
the process of naming the demonic and responding to it. It must be said
that Juergensmeyer's social analysis of demonization does not deal with the
problem of evil and therefore can only identify the phenomenon empirically without providing an analysis to help people to determine critically a
better way of living.

According to my account of Girard in chapter 2, the process of demonization arises out of an acquisitive or appropriative mimesis mediated
internally, leading to covert or overt violence that infects the whole community, ultimately endangering the genuine humanity of the whole group.
All acquisitive desire runs the risk of distorting its desiring subject's perceptions of reality since the desirability of the object is not judged intelligently
on its own merits but by the designation given it by the model/rival. The
coveting of the model's desires reaches such a pitch that the subject desires
to take to him- or herself the being of the model, ultimately causing the subject to demonize the model/rival. Archaic religion was able to help prevent
this violence from destroying the whole community through the scapegoat
mechanism.

In anthropologically constituted societies, the kind of social hierarchy
present in archaic societies gives way to a more egalitarian social imagination shared across groups. According to Girard, this loss of difference and
social power between groups precipitates a "sacrificial crisis" through envy
for the same objects.[15] The crisis changes a situation of "all-against-all" to
a situation of "all-against-one." With the model and desiring subject on a
more level playing field, the potential for internal mediation is greater and
therefore a conflictual mimesis becomes more probable. This leads to a loss
of agreed meanings around distinctions such as good and evil, right and
wrong, rationality and irrationality, proper relations and distorted relations. For Girard, the meaning of demonization and the demonic is clear.
Demonization arises out of the process of naming those people "enemies"
who desire the objects that the subject desires and who are perceived as
models/rivals. Mimetic rivalry disguises distorted assessments of identity
and otherness.

Girard's insights help us explain the politics of difference within societies. The demonization of strangers or aliens seeks to create a wall of
separation between rival groups according to political, ethnic, and class

15. Girard, *Violence and the Sacred*, chap. 2.

identity. Such separation foments ideological tribalism, class struggle, and political antagonism in the demonizing group. The stranger is portrayed as dangerous, threatening, and even monstrous. From this assessment we can appreciate how demonization might be used as a manipulative process by political and religious leaders to attain certain ends. Those engaged in demonizing activity have already assigned distorted value to an enemy or outsider, naming the target of their rhetoric as a threat to the objectives of the group. Disinformation, embellishment, and erroneous judgments of fact concerning the threat are widely spread.[16] These erroneous judgments of value around social order must be called into question.

Girard also identifies the demonic. While one group may name another group demonic, Girard argues that the truly demonic is uncovered in the actions of the group who make the stranger a scapegoat or victim for the ills of the community, and expel or kill that victim for the sake of a social order. In the concrete, the "myth of pure evil"[17] acts as a narrative to facilitate dehumanization and murder. Ultimately, symbolizing others as monsters becomes a consequence of equating goodness with sameness in identity, and evil with otherness of identity. Again, these reveal a failure to discriminate between different kinds of otherness.

## Lonergan and Evil

The process of demonization often relies on commonsense symbols and ideas that presuppose an agreed understanding of good and evil. Therefore, any critique of demonization requires a heuristic notion of evil. My account of Lonergan in chapter 3 with regard to human knowing and valuing concludes that the unhindered normative operations within human consciousness are the basis for progress in human society and history. However, Lonergan also accepts that human history includes the possibility that biases block these sequences of operations, resulting in a world that manifests both the intelligible and unintelligible. Lonergan calls the unintelligible permeating society the "social surd".[18] The "un" in *un*intelligible not only signifies a lack of the intelligible but also a violation of the intelligible by unintelligent subjects.[19] If the social surd is left unchecked, it becomes part

16. Noor, "Islam and/in the West." This paper provides a critical assessment of the ways in which the West has engaged in a distorted memory of Islam.

17. Cliff, "Disinhibition and Terrorism," 43–45.

18. Lonergan, *Insight*, 255, 714.

19. Ibid., 690. Providing excuses and blaming extenuating circumstances for evil actions is not the same as producing intelligent reasons for actions.

of the everyday fabric of our social lives, normalized, elusive, and difficult to identify. Therefore, we should not be too hasty to reify evil, since reifying evil leads to the mistaken view that evil is understandable rather than being the opposite of intelligent.

Lonergan makes a threefold analysis of evil.[20] He distinguishes basic sin, moral evil, and physical evil. Basic sin is the failure of a person's will to grasp and choose a morally obligatory or responsible course of action. Basic sin is the fault of a bad will, bad intellect, and the refusal to follow the operations of human consciousness. It is not so much an event as the failure of an event to occur. Since the identification of the good takes its stand on the result of reasonable choice, so too an alignment with evil takes its stand on what is irrational, a nonintelligible order, and an unreasonable choice.[21]

Moral evils are the harmful consequences of basic sin further heightening the tension and temptation to participate in basic sin.[22] The consequences are social, cultural, and personal in such a way that social situations become distorted and limit our ability to be free. Structures of evil or systems of social and cultural domination take shape in our world: militarism, unjust wars, terrorist attacks, ethnic cleansing, and concentration camps, each of which brings about immeasurable human suffering.[23] Physical evils correspond to the shortcomings in the physical world that is evolving and such evils demand responsible action to overcome the harm and suffering that follows them.

Lonergan explored the effect of evil on the human good, defining evil as opposed to the human good, whether at the level of particular goods, the good of order, or the good of value.[24] Particular evils reflect the challenge of creating a good of order and a good of order reflects the challenge of reversing the negation of values through a cultural development conducive to human living. Particular evils are carried by numerous experiences of privations, sufferings, destruction, and harm. Evil schemes of recurrence emerge and survive in diverse ways, for example, international terrorist networks, the illegal trade of arms, human trafficking, and the system of repressive police states within repressive political systems. The demonic negation of values takes many forms: the devaluation of human life, torture, revenge, exclusion, and humiliation.

---

20. Ibid., 689. See also Dadosky, "Naming the Demon."
21. Lonergan, *Insight*, 690.
22. Lonergan, *Insight*, 689.
23. Wink, *Engaging the Powers*, 51–63.
24. Lonergan, *Method*, 43–48.

## From Demonization to the Demonic

There are three moments that encourage the emergence and survival of demonization toward actions that are fully demonic: exclusion, humiliation, and dehumanization.

## Exclusion

Demonization often manifests through the process of social exclusion. Miroslav Volf states that exclusion entails "taking oneself out of the pattern of interdependence and placing oneself in a position of sovereign independence."[25] Social exclusion emerges when moral evil becomes a cooperative scheme. Differences between groups usually invite the recognition of pluralism and, through dialogue, the possibility of mutual understanding and inclusion. Exclusion often comes out of an assessment of differences that goes on to construct barriers to mutual dialogue, often through a process of illegitimate demonization. Ultimately, it is a failure to take to oneself fully the intersubjective nature of human existence, preferring instead to be mired in group bias and a lack of critical judgment. The other emerges as an enemy who must be pushed away.

The problem with the logic of exclusion is that most ideas of identity have been socially constructed in relation to some notion of otherness. If the notion of otherness is distorted, then the sense of constructed identity will also be distorted. What is being forgotten through exclusion is that each distinct group has much in common with other groups. The challenge is to be able to discern different kinds of otherness, to accept those that are intelligent, and to reject those that are stupid and irresponsible. To move beyond the demonization of the stranger requires us to ask whether we can accommodate the experience of the *stranger as stranger*, without repudiating him or her or projecting onto him or her our fears, insecurities, and horror.[26]

## Humiliation

Acts of humiliation also provide the conditions for the survival of demonizing processes. Jones draws attention to forensic psychologists who cite numerous studies correlating violent acts to the conditions of shame and

25. Volf, *Exclusion and Embrace*, 67.

26. Miller, *Way of Suffering*, 35. Miller proposes a more authentic approach toward the stranger.

humiliation.[27] He notes that feelings of humiliation, on the part of Arab Islamic populations, have been one of the most cited causes for violence. He quotes a Palestinian bomber, speaking on the topic of motivation: "Much of the work is already done by the suffering these people have been subjected to. Only 10% comes from me. The suffering and living in exile away from their land has given the person 90% of the need to become a martyr."[28] In the context of American society, Jones, citing the work of Anatol Lieven, speaks of the perceived humiliation that White Americans felt during the difficult political and economic conditions of the 1960s, which fueled an apocalyptic thinking suffused with violence.[29]

## Dehumanization

The process of dehumanization moves demonization into the fully demonic by defacing the humanness of the victim, further extending the evildoer's full sense of power over their victim. Examples of dehumanizing schemes of recurrence include the Nazi death camps of World War II. This project required camp authorities to regard and depict their enemies as essentially subhuman. One of the SS pamphlets tells the story of dehumanization to- ward all who did not fit the Aryan profile: "From a biological view he seems completely normal. He has hands and feet and a sort of brain. He has eyes and a mouth. But, in fact, he is a completely different creature, a horror. He only looks human, with a human face, but his spirit is more powerful than that of an animal. A terrible chaos runs rampant in this creature, an awful urge for destruction, primitive desires, unparalleled evil, a monster, a subhuman."[30] In this context, dehumanization meant that the subjectivity of the victim was completely overlooked.[31] These people were known as *muselmanner* (literally, the man that looks like a Muslim) or the skin and bone one, the half-dead victim, the living corpse, the person who is dead yet still alive, and whose death is no longer a human death.[32] Paul Daponte states that the key stratagem of the dehumanizing processes of Auschwitz was to strip "victims of their integrity, dignity and identity through the

27. Jones, *Blood that Cries Out*, 36.
28. Ibid., 36.
29. Ibid., 137; Lieven, *America Right or Wrong*.
30. Segev, *Soldiers of Evil*, 80.
31. Daponte, *Hope*, 25.
32. Ibid., 24.

implementation of camp policies aimed at eliminating a semblance of a prisoner's humanity" so as to bring about an efficient killing operation.[33]

This same process of dehumanization can be identified in all instances of "ethnic cleansing." Mark Danner documents the horrors of Camp Omarska, where ethnic cleansing was carried out during the Balkan conflict of the late 1980s in which people were subjected to processes of dehumanization.[34] Volf characterizes the mindset of those who carried out ethnic cleansing as the "filth that must be washed away from the ethnic body, pollution that threatens the ecology of ethnic space. The others will be rounded up in concentration camps, killed and shoved into mass graves, or driven out; monuments of their cultural and religious identity will be destroyed, inscriptions of their collective memories erased; the places of their habitation will be plundered and then burned and bulldozed."[35]

## Victims, Perpetrators, and Moral Outrage

The various processes of demonization and the process of naming the demonic often distinguish between victims/violated and perpetrators/violators. The category of "victim" identifies someone who has been objectively wounded, harmed, and injured, who yet remains innocent and undeserving of the action committed against them. The category of "perpetrator" identifies someone who has inflicted harm on another person completely disproportionate to what the other deserves and against whom the victim has a legitimate cause for resistance. Such harm unveils the traumatic character of evil that has a profound impact on the victim.[36]

Exclusion, humiliation, and dehumanization point to processes that often have a progressive world-shattering effect on victims in human history. If the victim is to survive the ordeal and flourish as a person, the victim and perpetrator must first face evil as evil and recognize its horrific character. Naming the reality of the victim helps us understand the importance of moral outrage that "cries out to heaven" for justice. Moral outrage carries the element of love toward that which has been victimized yet deserves to be loved, signifying that evil has happened not only *in* the world but more importantly *to* the world.[37] This horrific past event has interrupted the moral narrative of order in the victim's life in such a way as to jeopardize the pos-

---

33. Ibid., 26.
34. Danner, "Camp Called Omarska," 1–17.
35. Volf, *Exclusion and Embrace*, 57.
36. Miller, "Trauma of Evil," 403.
37. Miller, "Wound Made Fountain," 534.

sibility of moving forward. One response that will not bring about healing is where moral outrage moves quickly to a form of forgiveness whose intent is to remove the trauma of evil in the mistaken idea that the conditions antecedent to the occurrence of evil can be restored.[38] True healing, by contrast, requires that any path forward, even into a problematic future, will be accompanied with the proviso that forgetting what has happened would involve a horrifying complicity in evil.[39]

## Retribution, Revenge, and Recovery

Moral outrage on the victim's side can be addressed in two ways. First, there is the victim's desire for retribution, and punishment for the perpetrator. The desire for retribution by the victim is understandable since, as Miller notes, for most, retribution is "the only modality of punishment that pays attention to, and attempts to respond to, the evil done to and suffered by the victim."[40] Objectively, the victim can seek to balance the scales of justice by the logic of equity, usually through compensation and some legal process.[41] Subjectively, the victim also seeks some sign from the perpetrator that he or she feels the same suffering as the victim, a process governed by the logic of vicarious suffering. The victim's desire insists that the guilty person must him- or herself undergo the same suffering that the perpetrator visited on the victim. Miller states that repentance is "to suffer in the place of the victim so that the suffering will be lifted from her [the victim] and borne by him [the perpetrator]," a process summoned by the victim's longing to be rescued from evil.[42] The victim's desire is threefold: for the perpetrator to experience an empathetic identification; for the perpetrator to be drawn to the wound of the victim; and for the perpetrator to desire the removal of the wound from the victim.

　　In the long run, Miller argues, the victim's desire for the perpetrator's vicarious identification is a form of retributive punishment. Further, the process sought is nostalgic, whether desired by the victim or the perpetrator and "longs to reverse history, to efface what has happened entirely, to retrieve

<hr>

38. Miller, "Trauma of Evil," 411.

39. Volf, *End of Memory*, 39–65. Volf explores the importance of truthfully remembering wrongdoing as an obligation of justice.

40. Miller, "Trauma of Evil," 411.

41. Ibid., 412. The establishing of International Criminal Courts to deal with crimes against humanity is an example.

42. Ibid., 412.

the condition antecedent to the trauma she has suffered."[43] Inasmuch as the desire to return to a past order represents the inner logic of retribution, moral outrage cannot be fully addressed since it does not fully recognize that the violation of evil has ruptured the moral accord that once existed between historical existence and the moral order. While there is benefit in the perpetrator's being punished and desiring repentance, on their own these elements do not justify the perpetrator. Later, we will see forgiveness coming from the Cross as that which alone justifies the perpetrator.

The second and more tragic form of retribution by the victim is one that engages in acts of revenge. Revenge is a form of reactive anger that goes beyond the moral outrage of the victim who feels victimized; often it is a form of anger disproportionate to the offense committed, with little practical benefit as a response to legitimate hurts. At the level of personal value, as explained in the previous chapter on martyrdom, revenge is a reactive response to suffering and horror through a horizon shaped by an ethic of control. Hannah Arendt describes the process of revenge as acting "in the form of reacting against an original trespassing, whereby far from putting an end to the consequences of the first misdeed, everybody remains bound to the process, permitting the chain reaction contained in every action to take its unhindered course, [thus] enclosing both doer and sufferer in the relentless automatism of the action process, which by itself need never come to an end."[44] Arendt alerts us to the "relentless automatism" of the revenge action, where there is something in the revenge process that lacks freedom and blocks creativity, a "drive which prevents the breakthrough of anything new or different."[45]

When conflicting parties engage in mutual revenge, they perceive their own reaction as morally justified, locking them into a spiral of violence. Girard calls this mimetic doubling, each part locked into a gravitational field of destructive rivalry. There emerges what Volf calls "the predicament of partiality" or the inability of parties locked in conflict to agree on the moral meaning of their actions and "the predicament of irreversibility," that is, a temporal condition that does not allow us to undo the physical wrong we have done.[46] Citing the work of Trudy Govier, Daponte also examines revenge by exploring the difference between the words "vindictive," that is, bearing a grudge, and "vindicative," that is, vindicating someone or oneself.[47]

43. Ibid., 411.
44. Arendt, *Human Condition*, 216.
45. Daponte, *Hope*, 77.
46. Volf, *Exclusion and Embrace*, 121.
47. Daponte, *Hope*, 80. Govier, *Forgiveness and Revenge*.

While vindicating means aiming for restoration after one has suffered a wrong, vindictiveness aims to damage, diminish, or put another down.

A responsible path beyond revenge, therefore, requires some "unthinking" since revenge is a condition of "being imprisoned."[48] To move beyond revenge invites us to validate the moral outrage by acknowledging that a wrong has been seriously done, while responding in such a way that does not perpetuate violence. Daponte argues that the victim "does not have to cultivate hatred against the victimizer. In fact, the victim may pursue . . . the restoration of dignity and honour through education, through the devotion of others, and through dedication to humanitarian causes. The victim may also achieve vindication by working to insure that further acts of the same injustice and wrongdoing never aggrieve future victims."[49]

Miller argues that if the victim traumatized by evil is to "right themselves," he or she cannot do so by a retrieval of the historical conditions antecedent to the rupture of evil nor by a form of forgetting that tries to move onto the future unclouded by the evil committed.[50] Any form of recovery would have to be conscious of the trauma of evil and "capable of moving the victim to a kind of generosity toward the evil-doer that would otherwise be inconceivable because there is nothing in the evil-doer that inspires it and no power in the victim that is capable of it. If it occurs in history, it occurs as an unprecedented possibility we cannot invent or create or bring into being."[51]

## The Anatomy of *Ressentiment*

Demonization can also give rise to and continue to foment revenge aided by the psychic condition of *ressentiment* in the victim. *Ressentiment* is an affective condition by which humiliated and conquered people reject the values of their conquerors, aided by the mechanism of psychic repression. Since it is a psychic repression, *ressentiment* permeates the whole of one's conscious intentionality, comprising an unobjectified propensity to select and obscure intentional objects, thus distorting one's ability to judge and deliberate objectively on good and evil.[52] Psychically, *ressentiment* is a good example of a mechanism that contributes to a repressed psychic censor in the dialectic of the subject as discussed in chapter 3. As such, *ressentiment*

---

48. Daponte, *Hope*, 77.

49. Ibid., 80–82. See Lerner, *Healing Israel/Palestine*.

50. Miller, "Trauma of Evil," 414.

51. Ibid., 417. There is some debate as to whether forgiveness can be a political act. See Shriver, *Ethic For Enemies*. Shriver argues that forgiveness can be a political act.

52. Morelli, "*Ressentiment* and Redemption," 200.

is a repressed feeling state that generates its own distorted values. Socially, it devolves into a state of mind within a powerless group that belittles the values of the more powerful group, eventually distorting the scale of values reflected in social practices, attitudes and ideologies, forms of religiosity, and ascetic practices.[53]

Following Lonergan, Morelli notes that the cyclical nature of Nietzsche's *ressentiment* operates like a scheme of recurrence. This scheme is contingent for its emergence and survival upon the distorted affectivity of free subjects and other social conditions. Morelli postulates that the scheme of recurrence of *ressentiment* operates as:

> a basic pride in oneself—a deep sense of self-esteem: a consequent sense of entitlement to pursue a certain kind of life and enjoy its fruits; the frustration by another of one's desire to pursue this kind of life; a consequent feeling of injustice; feelings of rage and hatred towards the other; a feeling of impotence to change the situation; a denial of the values of authority, positions, and wealth; repression of the desire for what was originally valued and of rage, hatred and desire for revenge; and a reconfirmed sense of superiority facilitated by this repression and grounded in the re-evaluation.[54]

Both Friedrich Nietzsche and Max Scheler recognized the potent effect of *ressentiment* within social living. The Nietzschean emphasis of *ressentiment* was primarily one that elicited revenge while Scheler's primary focus was envy. I will expound Nietzsche's position. While not advocating revenge as a response to wrongs, Nietzsche preferred revenge as a more healthy response to wrongs than the repression of *ressentiment*.[55] His genealogical approach led him to argue that the dichotomy between bad and good had two moments. The first moment was the differentiation between good and bad within the relative horizon of the powerful. "Good" in the powerful was a felt sense of being elevated above others, from which derived the values of power and physical strength.[56] "Bad" persons were those who displayed weakness of spirit. A second moment was generated in the antithesis between "good" and "evil" by the powerless group. The category of good derived from a felt sense of the evil other, where evil was an assessment

---

53. Morelli, "*Ressentiment* and Rationality," 1.

54. Morelli, "*Ressentiment* and Redemption," 201. According to Morelli, Scheler brings a different emphasis to this psychic phenomenon mirrored in social arrangements and focused on envy.

55. Ibid., 208.

56. Byrne, "*Ressentiment* and the Preferential Option," 216.

based on *ressentiment* by the powerless toward the powerful enemy and was substantially a reactive condition based on impotence.[57]

Nietzsche presented the example of the Palestinian rabbis of the ancient world, a noble class who believed their position to be special as mediators between God and humankind.[58] Their position and status conferred superiority on them. The Romans who conquered them had another set of values, forged through a warrior ethic: physical strength, power, and enslavement of people and lands. While the Romans, according to Nietzsche, did not resent the spiritual superiority of the rabbis, since such spiritual superiority did not interfere with their aspirations, the rabbis resented the Romans since the rabbis were powerless to change Roman rule. The rabbis felt that their authority had been unjustly usurped and that they were powerless to do anything about it. Thus, their own self-esteem and pride gave rise to a simmering hatred for their masters. According to Nietzsche, perversion and corruption entered the rabbinic social order neither with the ruthless conquerors, nor with the rage and hatred of the conquered, but primarily by the self-deception of the conquered toward their conquerors, a product of their repressed collective psyche.[59] Their repressed psyches caused the conquered to reaffirm spiritual values and deny the values of might, vitality, strength, political prestige, and worldly riches.

Nietzsche also postulated that this *ressentiment* gave rise to the slave revolt that is Christianity and a Christian rejection of human nature. For him, there was a wholesale devaluation by Christians of honor, political power, prestige, beauty, courage, and pride, which were all characteristics of the Roman nobility. The weakness of the oppressed was held up as a worthy goal while the original power of the nobility was considered evil. For Nietzsche, the process ended in revenge against the noble person, his or her way of life, and any persons who would want to follow that way of life. Christian invocations of self-denial and kenosis were nothing more than *ressentiment* at work, while the theological idea that a Christian God would redress all injustices was nothing more than revenge masked as love for the poor.[60]

I concur with Nietzsche's understanding of *ressentiment* as a possibility in any oppressed–oppressor relationship. For this reason I believe that couching martyrdom in terms of the direct intention to die so as to demonstrate one's resolve against the oppressor, as noted with Shiite martyrdom in the previous chapter, is problematic. However, I do not agree

---

57. Ibid., 215.

58. Morelli, "*Ressentiment* and Rationality," 2.

59. Ibid., 3.

60. Byrne, "*Ressentiment* and the Preferential Option," 219.

with Nietzsche's assessment of Christian love. His assessment does not adequately acknowledge that, while self-sacrifice and self-denial involve a negation of some good, they also involve the affirmation of a higher good, the command of Christian love, which is founded on our experience of God's love for us. For Lonergan, authenticity comes from living within the creative tension between body and spirit. When the tension is broken, the result is inauthenticity. The repressed affectivity of *ressentiment* represents a distortion in the dialectic of the subject as subject. This dramatic bias would affect intelligence and responsibility such that individuals and communities would be unable to reach up to practical solutions conducive to human living. Any reactive response can easily degenerate to revenge or envy through the maintaining of a false sense of superior values, ultimately distorting the scale of values. Lonergan states that "the attack [by the person of *ressentiment*] amounts to a continuous belittling of the value in question and it can extend to hatred and even violence against those that possess the value quality. But perhaps its worst feature is that its rejection of one value involves a distortion of the whole scale of values and that this distortion can spread through a whole society, social class, a whole people, a whole epoch."[61]

The question is: How can we be healed of *ressentiment*, with its often strident claims to superiority, and move toward dialogue? The issue at stake here is not a proper set of propositions or another bad philosophy, but rather a change to one's way of thinking and feeling so that it can be open to inquiry and different values. While good, intelligent philosophy may have a part to play by addressing the current situation, what is needed is effective love that will facilitate psychic healing and affective self-transcendence.

Girard's account of distortive rivalry also highlights the outworking of *ressentiment*. When the stronger model/rival blocks the subject's path from obtaining the desired object, the subject's immediate response of hatred can recoil back into *ressentiment*. The subject is left with an impotent yet continuing emotion that is felt each time the stronger rival is more physically powerful. Doran argues that Girard's mimetic theory accurately explains how the passive, yet extraordinarily complex, negotiation and reception of our affective intersubjective field can become distorted and lead to hatred.[62] As an illustration of basic sin, this distorted and repressed affectivity interferes negatively with our active desire for being and value, the pure

---

61. Lonergan, *Method*, 33.

62. Doran, "Essays in Systematic Theology 20," 24–25. Also see Doran, "Two Ways of Being Conscious," 20–23.

disinterested desire for being and what is good, and the unfolding of genuine attentiveness, intelligence, reasonableness, and responsibility.[63]

Doran further argues that Girard's account of mimetic rivalry gives
greater explanatory power to what is healed through psychic conversion.[64]
When psychic energy is blocked, driven by obsessions, and weighed down
by fear, people are unable to deal creatively with their tendencies toward
demonization and are therefore unable to arrive at needed insights, true
judgments, and loving action.[65] However, the psyche is not morally responsible for its own disorder. Distorted and victimized psyches are the product
of both "one's own self-destructiveness, that is, of the distorted dialectic of
the subject" and "one's social environment or from the cultural values of
one's milieu."[66] The psyche becomes victimized as the biases exercise their
distorting effect in various ways.[67] In each case this victimized dimension
of the self will be healed not by harsh judgment, but through a participation
in healing grace.[68] When we experience the satisfaction of being in love, we
are enabled to experience the moral satisfaction of choosing the good, and
the intellectual satisfaction of knowing truth. We will see later the importance of transformative religious symbols that communicate the gift of love,
enabling conversion and a fidelity to the imperatives of the human spirit.

### An Example of Ressentiment: Sayyid Qutb

One possible example of *ressentiment* is reflected in the life of the Egyptian thinker and activist, Sayyid Qutb (1906–1966). Qutb was an Egyptian
Muslim whose writings were to influence the development of militant Islam
within the Muslim Brotherhood and beyond. The imperialism and colonialism of Western governments in the nineteenth century shaped policies that
did not stem economic poverty in Egypt, but rather encouraged politically
weak institutions, a stagnant cultural life, and anti-Western sentiment.[69]
There is no doubt that the political conditions within Egypt from the 1919
revolution[70] up the Second World War created a fertile context for political

63. Doran, "Essays in Systematic Theology 20," 25.

64. Ibid., 28.

65. Doran, *Dialectics of History*, 229.

66. Ibid., 232.

67. Ibid., 233.

68. Ibid., 238.

69. Kung, *Islam*, 390.

70. The Egyptian Revolution of 1919 forced the British to begin a process of handing over political autonomy to the Egyptian peoples, with the recognition of political
independence by 1922 and a new constitution by 1923.

unrest. During that period, Great Britain continued to control foreign and domestic policy.

Qutb was raised as a secular Egyptian nationalist, believing Egypt to be part of a wider Arabic-speaking world. However, in the 1930s he committed himself to the religious piety of the Koran. By the early 1950s he started to solidify his ideas around social and economic reforms, pointing out the inadequacies of the patronage system and seeking to convince his readers of the applicability of Koranic law to complex problems in modern society.[71] In 1952, the Free Officers Corp, with populist support from the Muslim Brotherhood, overthrew King Farouk, and two years later Nasser became Egypt's president. Qutb joined the Brotherhood in 1953 and together with other Brotherhood members believed that Nasser would implement an Islamic state and Sharia law. Under President Nasser, the socioeconomic policies of land reform and increased industrialization, political tendencies toward socialism, and increased governmental control of religious institutions were instrumental in shifting Qutb's intellectual views from a reformist to a more radical agenda.[72] Qutb adopted an Islamist response and an anti-secularist reaction to the long-standing political problems in Egypt, which ultimately influenced authorities to imprison him. When a member of the Muslim Brotherhood attempted to assassinate Nasser, Qutb was caught in the dragnet and spent more than a decade in jail, where he wrote simply and directly about humanity standing on the brink of an abyss without Islam.[73] While in jail, Qutb was tortured and, in 1958, he witnessed the massacre of dozens of Brothers in Tora Prison.[74]

One of the least explored periods of Qutb's life is the time he spent in the United States, where he studied education-related topics from November 1948 to August 1950. What becomes noticeable, after examining his "letters home," is an increased dichotomy in his own mind between the civilization of the West as reflected in American society and Islamic Egypt.[75]

71. Choueiri, *Islamic Fundamentalism*, 124–25. Qutb laid at the feet of the patronage system such social defects as wastage, corruption, unemployment, exploitation, mounting poverty, widespread prostitution, and armies of wandering beggars.

72. Ibid., 89.

73. Ibid., 137.

74. Moussalli, *Radical Islamic Fundamentalism*, 36. There is a suggestion by Moussalli that a massacre in 1957 in the prison where Qutb was being held, and where almost a third of the Muslim Brotherhood population were either killed or wounded, had a profound impact on him. See also Moaddel, *Islamic Modernism*, 219. Moaddel quotes Hasan Hanafi, who points to the degrading and repressive conditions of incarceration, arguing that, under such conditions many believers would have felt a need to take revenge for what nationalism had done and a desire to destroy anything and everything connected to Nasser and the Ba'ath Party.

75. Calvert, "Sayyid Qutb in America," 1.

He judged that there existed a number of radical differences between the ideal Islamic society and Western secular societies, and characterized these differences in these terms: the spiritual nature of Islamic society versus the abject materialism of the West; the substantive issues of politics and religion discussed by Islamic people versus the preoccupation in America with talking about money, films, and cars; the rightful cry for justice of the Palestinians versus the distorted support of Americans for the state of Israel and Zionism; the modesty of Islamic women versus the base moral behaviors of American women, especially on the dance floor and through their overt assertiveness; the equality of Islam versus the American racist attitude toward African-American people.[76]

Qutb's long-standing concern for a unique Islamic Egyptian identity, separate from a Western otherness, was solidified by a mentality that became increasingly dualistic. This unique Islamic identity was to be grounded in the purity of the Koran. I argue that Qutb's assessment demonstrates *ressentiment*: his desire for Egyptians to follow the absolute purity of Islam, by contrasting this purity with the ills of American culture, masked a hatred for Americans and their way of life.[77] His assessment overlooked the good qualities of American society, for example, the moral rigor, temperance, and civil-mindedness that were hallmarks of the city of Greeley, Colorado, where he studied.[78]

*Ressentiment* does not work in isolation within the subject but is allowed to take root due to an incomplete hermeneutical approach to the sacred text. Qutb's desire for purity over and against what he saw as the impurity of American culture was made possible by a lack of a critical hermeneutics toward the text of the Koran. The conclusions arising from such a lack of criticality could not challenge *ressentiment*. Qutb's most read work, one that he wrote in jail, is titled *Milestones*.[79] In it, Qutb professed an exclusivist view of Islam in which salvation could come only from the Koran and

76. Jones, *Blood that Cries Out*, 29–30.

77. Sayyid Qutb, *Maalim fi al-Tariq* (Cairo: Maktabat Wahbah, 1964), 214–15, cited in Sivan, *Radical Islam*, 68. Qutb writes: "There is nothing in Islam for us to be ashamed of or defensive about . . . During my years in America, some of my fellow Muslims would have recourse to apologetics as though they were defendants on trials. Contrariwise, I took an offensive position, excoriating the Western jahiliyya, be it in its much acclaimed religious beliefs or its depraved and dissolute socioeconomic and moral conditions: this Christian idolatry of the Trinity and its notion of sin and redemption which makes no sense at all; this Capitalism . . . that animal freedom which is called permissiveness, that slave market dubbed 'women's liberation.' "

78. Calvert, "Sayyid Qutb in America," 1.

79. See the bibliography for publication details.

through the historical and superior community of Islam (*umma*).[80] Qutb held to the priority of the beginnings of this superior revelation of God's teaching over later teachings, which had been polluted by other sources.[81] This led to the basic principle that the truth of the Koran could not change or evolve historically, but rather remained constant and immutable (*thabit*) to historically engendered transformation. In Qutb's mind, Muslims must turn to the Koran and interpret its truth in an unmediated manner, and not allow themselves to be polluted by other currents of thought. Qutb believed that human reason was so flawed that for people to expound on matters to do with reform required them to have their reason subordinate to the unequivocal and literal meaning of the revealed text.[82] For Qutb, to equate reason with a degree of authenticity was to proceed from a false premise that reason could give us knowledge of God, a knowledge that only revelation could give.[83]

Qutb's conviction about the superiority and purity of the Koran justified the term *jahiliyya*, a word taken from classical Islamic discourse to characterize the historical pre-Islamic peoples who suffered an ignorance of God. The term was given a much wider meaning by Qutb, correlating this ignorance with all other non-Koran-based social, political, and religious doctrines of his day, including those of Western countries, and those of Muslims who did not interpret the Koran's truth as he did.[84] In order to hold fast to the superior quality and ethical practices of Islam, the believer was to acknowledge the divine sovereignty of God, or *hakimiyya*.[85] According to John Calvert, this term cannot be found in the Koran or classical political Islamic thought but rather gains its significance within the context of modern state sovereignty.[86] In this way "Qutb posits *hakimiyya* as the exclusive prerogative of God who alone is qualified to fashion principles appropriate to the proper functioning of a social, political and economic order. To submit to the supervision of secular authorities and humanly devised institutions is to surrender to the whims and selfish interest of imperfect worldly forces."[87]

---

80. Qutb, *Milestones*, chap. 1, page 2. Qutb states: "God . . . has ordained [Islam] as the religion for the whole of mankind . . . and made it to be a guide for all the inhabitants of this planet in all their affairs until the end of time."

81. Ibid., chap. 1, page 3.

82. Choueiri, *Islamic Fundamentalism*, 140.

83. Ibid., 141.

84. Qutb, *Milestones*, chap. 1, page 6. He states: "We are all surrounded by *jahiliyya* today which is of the same nature as it was during the first period of Islam."

85. Choueiri, *Islamic Fundamentalism*, 123.

86. Calvert, "Mythic Foundation," 36.

87. Ibid., 36–37.

More significantly, *Milestones* contains a whole chapter on the meaning of jihad, in a way that masks *ressentiment*. According to Qutb, jihad was
a method of conversion to be implemented by peaceful means toward fellow
Muslims and nonbelievers. However, given the right circumstances, jihad
was also a command to engage in violent struggle against all those who
live in ignorance and lack freedom, especially secularist governments.[88]
Qutb grounded the task of jihad in the mission of bringing God's freedom
especially to those in servitude to others. The lack of active faith in God
demonstrated by the West, as well as by Muslims who had succumbed to
Western ways, necessitated a violent jihad. Throughout *Milestones*, Qutb
often points out the error of those Muslims who interpret jihad as only a defensive measure, that is, one to defend one's country, people, and way of life
against those that would unjustly take it away by force. Since Qutb viewed
both Egypt and other non-Islamic societies as under religious and political
oppression, Qutb asserted that only jihad could establish God's authority,
abolish satanic forces, and bring about freedom from slavery.[89]

According to Luke Loboda, Qutb's assessment put oppression toward
the followers of Islam as a more heinous form of evil than the command not
to kill. Loboda interprets Qutb's position in this way: "If it is necessary to
kill innocent women or children to dismantle *jahili* society [then, for Qutb]
it is justified." Loboda adds that, although "such a blunt statement cannot
be found in Qutb's writings, it is the logical extension of his thinking. This
does not mean that jihad should be conducted without regard for ethical
guidelines. It does mean however that such violations are excusable if essential to the victory of Islam."[90] I argue that Qutb's framing of violent jihad in
the robes of universal freedom disguises a hatred for, and revenge toward, a
political system that imprisoned him, maltreated and repressed the Muslim
Brotherhood, and, in his mind, made pious faithful Muslims impotent to
bring about social and religious change. An example of the last-mentioned
is the political corruption of the 1945 elections, which returned not a single
candidate of the Muslim Brotherhood, even though they held majorities in
their constituencies.

88. Qutb, *Milestones*, chap. 3, "*Jihad* in the Cause of God," 31–49. Qutb states:
"This movement uses the methods of preaching and persuasion for reforming ideas
and beliefs and it uses physical power and *jihad* for abolishing the organisations and
authorities of the jahili system which prevents people from reforming their ideas and
beliefs but forces them to obey their erroneous ways and makes them serve human
lords instead of the Almighty Lord" (33).

89. Ibid., 44.

90. Loboda, "Thought of Sayyid Qutb," 21.

Due to the religious, social, and political circumstances of the time, Qutb was unable to carve a space for dialogue, instead advocating the path of *violent* jihad. Following Lonergan, Clifton and Ormerod note that the temptation to move directly from the religious level to the political level, grounding the political in a divine and unquestionable authority, becomes simply another form of the will to power, only this time in the name of God for the purpose of controlling others.[91] This tendency arises because of the enormous energy required of groups and individuals, "given the multiple mediations involved, given the time and energy needed to shift cultures towards some normatively perceived political goal."[92]

In the case of Egyptian society post-1919, it could be argued that the effects of imperialism and colonialism, poverty, and economic stagnation hampered the development of a cultural space for dialogue. Instead, this space was filled by multiple narratives often antagonistic to each other: the violent Islamist perspective of some members of the Muslim Brotherhood, governments who exercised brutal suppression, an ideology of liberal nationalism and secularism, and the glorification of pre-Islamic society.[93] Qutb's call to the purity and superior way of Islam partially disguised his hatred for the political authorities of his day and his desire for the power to determine the religious, moral, and political direction of Islamic Egypt. While rightly fearing secularism and its ability to diminish the full meaning of the good life,[94] Qutb's confrontational attitude toward the West precluded him from engaging in a cultural transformation grounded in reasonable argument. What this vision positively captures is the importance of not negating the relationship between religious and cultural values. What this vision overlooks is that religious revelation cannot offer answers to all economic, technological, and political issues that emerge throughout history. Such an approach to political and economic issues does not sufficiently distinguish the process of mediation within Lonergan's scale of values from the religious to the personal, from the personal to the cultural, and from the cultural to social values.

91. Ormerod and Clifton, *Globalization*, 112.

92. Ibid.

93. Moaddel, *Islamic Modernism*, 210–14.

94. See Charles Taylor's account of secular humanism presented in chapter 2 of this book.

## Victims and Perpetrators: A Cautionary Note

These insights into moral outrage, retribution, revenge, and *ressentiment* lead me to conclude that, while the categories of victim and perpetrator are helpful in naming evil, the affective, moral, and religious horizon of the subject, together with conversion, are important for any healing to occur. Crysdale argues very convincingly that dividing our concrete historical existence into victims and perpetrators of sin is inaccurate and misleading.[95] She asserts that each person at some level is both a victim and a perpetrator of self-destruction. At some point in the process of conflict, perpetrators of destruction may easily become victims of self-destruction or self-harm. Conversely, without help, victims of violence can be become perpetrators of violence against themselves or others. With an insight that warns against demonization, Volf notes "the world may appear neatly divided into guilty perpetrators and innocent victims. The closer we get, however, the more the line between the guilty and innocent blurs and we see an intractable maze of small and large hatreds, dishonesties, manipulations and brutalities, each reinforcing the other."[96]

## Retrieving Transformative Symbols

I have argued that it is important to distinguish between demonization and a heuristic account of evil. Naming the demonic may help distinguish the evil we suffer from the evil we do. The fact of moral evil raises the question as to how we might collaborate in a redeeming process. I argue that we need religious symbols of love to heal our affective disorders. Symbols of love provide an alternative pathway for dealing with moral outrage and may even prevent demonizing processes from emerging and surviving. I noted in chapter 3 that feelings always enter human consciousness through their connection to some image such that affective responses are a preapprehension of values. Kelly asserts that symbols are more "real" to people than what they symbolize, having a profound affective influence on our perceptions.[97] Symbols enter into the personal and communal identity of groups, motivating social behavior, affecting the tone of interpersonal communication, and

---

95. Crysdale, *Embracing Travail*, 20. See also Brass, "Victims, Heroes or Martyrs?." Brass argues that the distinction between victim and perpetrator is simplistic and misleading in the context of Sikh Muslim clashes in the Punjab during 1947.

96. Volf, *Exclusion and Embrace*, 79.

97. Kelly, *Eschatology and Hope*, 149; Dunne, *Doing Better*, 28–32. Dunne explains the "symbolizing exigency" within the subject.

passing into the deepest meaning of human existence.[98] Again, without the distinction between irresponsible demonization and the legitimate naming of something as demonic, we can easily be socialized and enculturated into distorted meanings and values. Yet it also must be said that genuine anagogic symbols of good and evil heighten the tension between body and spirit and release the psyche for cooperation with the divinely originated solution to the problem of evil.

## The Cross: Symbol of Love

Lonergan was fully committed to the Catholic Christian tradition in which the Cross is the paramount symbol signifying the importance of God's grace in human history through the coming of Christ as a practical solution to evil and its accompanying trauma. The Cross is a symbol of Christian hope to address the problem of evil not through the power of violence or returning evil with evil but through an offering of one's suffering and self-sacrificing love to God. The symbol of the Cross cannot be separated from the symbol of the resurrection and together these symbols tell the story of Jesus, his absolute faith in the Father, his love for enemies, and our hope that the bondage of sin would be broken in human history.[99]

In my account of Lonergan, I noted the contribution he makes to a theology of redemption through the law of the Cross. Doran summarizes Lonergan's law of the Cross in three steps: from basic sin to moral evil; the loving absorption of the evil due to sin and the elevation of human response in grace to a level that transcends the cycle of violence even as that response takes the form of resistance; and the transformation of evil into a supreme good.[100] Basic sin is the willful refusal to accept the creative tension between limitation and transcendence in the dialectic of the subject. Basic sin issues forth into a social surd where the moral evils of the human race include "the deterioration of human relations, the systematization of injustice, the elevation of various forms of bias to the determining principles of human affairs," miring us into ever greater cycles of violence.[101] The supreme good of the human race involves the transformation of all evil within a social context

98. Kelly, *Eschatology and Hope*, 150. Kearney, *Strangers*, 73–76. Kearney gives a good example of artistic symbols that depicts evil by way of Giotto's thirteenth-century mosaics, found in Florence, Pisa, Padua, and San Gimignano.

99. Dunne, *Lonergan and Spirituality*, 166.

100. Doran, "Non-Violent Cross," 51.

101. Ibid., 57.

that gives rise to a new community based on self-sacrificing love, reflected in all the concrete determinations and relations of that community.

As we saw in chapter 6, the church is called to be the new community of the Suffering Servant grounded in the love of God, absorbing evil, and changing the whole way that human relationships are constructed. The Suffering Servant represents the voluntary power to transcend the role of victim and to allow one's own suffering and the evil that is endured to become a response capable of redeeming evil that is committed. Fidelity to the law of the Cross and living out of the vision of the Suffering Servant is identified with "integral fidelity to the normative scale of values."[102] To respond to the problem of evil requires a global network of communities that are intent on living this way of life together.[103] Processes of exclusion as well as humiliating and vengeful acts represent reactions marked by an ethic of control that facilitates more demonization by seeking to cancel out coercively what is perceived as evil in a determined way.

In terms of Lonergan's dialectic of the subject, the ethic of control seeks a resolution to suffering and the crisis of evil through a recovery *within* the tension of the dialectic by either too much transcendence (self-assertion) or too much limitation (self-denigration), rather than by a recovery from *beyond* the dialectic.[104] Inasmuch as transformative grace is effective in our lives the dialectic of body and spirit are contrary poles, not contradictories. Redemption "involves the higher integration of embodied spirit, not the *dissolution* of this reality."[105] Therefore, while demonization lies in the distortion of simply presuming that the right response should be to wrest power from the powerful and make them the powerless, transformative grace can make sense of human alienation only to the extent that "such righting of imbalances *emerges from* or is *the occasion for* the higher viewpoint of love. They are not true to the extent that they are the *means by which* integral balance is established."[106] Grace as a higher synthesis beyond the dialectic provides the possibility of healing, leaving human freedom intact, with the proviso that "healing and forgiveness occur as a matter of probability and not as a matter of direct causality."[107]

This account helps us again to understand why accentuating the oppressor and oppressed dichotomy as a motivation for religious martyrdom

---

102. Doran, *Dialectics of History*, 113.

103. Ibid., 114.

104. Crysdale, *Embracing Travail*, 150.

105. Ibid., 146.

106. Ibid., 147.

107. Ibid., 149.

is dangerous, as we saw in chapter 7. Further, Crysdale makes two points. First, while the desire for retribution and right relations may flow from redemptive love or *be its catalyst*, these kinds of justice alone are not fully redemptive.[108] She states that while the Christian tradition is able to name what is evil and identify its consequences, "making sense of evil cannot be found in acts and their consequences but in the higher viewpoint that emerges from conversion. Such a higher viewpoint arises precisely as an insight that comes with an other-worldly falling in love."[109] The redemption by the Cross is God's response to the traumatized victim as victim and his or her cry for justice, as well as a response to the perpetrator as perpetrator. Second, Crysdale, reflecting on the victimhood of Christ, states that "sooner or later one must discover oneself as both crucifier and victim."[110] The path to transformation is a humble discovery of one's own sin and a healing of one's own wounds through grace. In this assessment, Crysdale highlights that we are never free of the propensity to basic sin, even as the grace of God heals and elevates nature.

## Satanization and Demonization

The symbol of the Cross further helps us retrieve an authentic understanding of another symbol often employed uncritically in the process of demonization: the symbol of Satan. The word "Satan" in Hebrew means "adversary" or "accuser".[111] In chapter 2, we saw that Girard understands the fundamental role of Satan as a force for both division in chaos and union in hatred.[112] Satan is the scandal that prevents subjects from getting what they desire from model/rivals and that leads to a buildup of tension that is released on a scapegoat-victim. Satan fuels the mimetic cycle and as a principle of order coaxes the community to scapegoat innocent others who are blamed for causing conflict. In terms of a Girardian understanding, Alison notes that Satan in the Christian Scriptures is the father of lies, who leads his children to lie and kill.[113] Through the voice of Peter (Mark 3:23–26), Jesus' future suffering must not happen, so that by being spared from suffering, the social order that gives way to scapegoating may be preserved. Further, Jesus links Satan to the murder of Abel by Cain (John 8:44), an act in opposition to

108. Ibid., 147.
109. Ibid., 149.
110. Ibid., 20–25.
111. Lyonnet, "Satan."
112. Girard, *Scapegoat*, 196. See also Alison, *Joy of Being Wrong*, 156–60.
113. Alison, *Raising Abel*, 63.

Jesus' central message, namely, that God who has revealed Godself to Israel is not a god of violence.

Two kinds of paternity are set before humanity. The first kind is a paternity borne of the symbol of Satan, which kills and persecutes in order to serve a distorted image of god.[114] Such a paternity brings forth a multiplicity of victims. The second kind of paternity is demonstrated in self-giving love, witnessing that, for God, there is no death. The paternity of God is revealed in the Cross and resurrection. The Cross of Christ exposes the scapegoat mechanism by which Satan was given the title of "prince of this world." According to Alison, the Cross of Christ reveals that there is no place for distorted sacrifice, which uses the scapegoat mechanism and expulsion as a means of purification.[115]

Ormerod argues for an understanding of the satanic from the realm of interiority. He argues that one's own self-evaluation, self-feeling, or self-esteem is the prism through which the values of the world are refracted so that "human self-esteem is the basic determining principle of the subject's horizon."[116] Satan is the voice within each person continually accusing them, undermining their self-esteem, and loading people with false guilt that then feeds into a false conscience.[117] Ormerod asserts that the voice of Satan in the Garden of Eden (Gen 3:5) is not only a temptation but also an implied criticism that taunts Adam and Eve with human finitude by means of an untruth, leading to a fundamental lie that "there is something wrong with us, that we are not loveable, that God wants nothing to do with us, that God is angry with us before we have done anything. Yet these are the lies that Satan tells us and we believe him."[118]

Satan as the accuser promotes a false conscience, which is manifested in processes of rationalization that condones something objectively wrong or, alternatively, undermines us so that when we have done something good, we feel it is not good enough, leading us to doubt our own moral judgment and our ability to stand up against future evil.[119] Whereas Satan promotes the accusation, the Holy Spirit stands in total opposition to Satan, pleading our cause and quietening the accusations of a false conscience (1 John 3:19–21).[120]

---

114. Ibid., 64.

115. Alison, *Joy of Being Wrong*, 159.

116. Ormerod, *Grace and Disgrace*, 24.

117. Ibid., 157.

118. Ibid.

119. Ibid., 159.

120. Ibid., 158.

## Conclusion

In this chapter I have argued that, first, we must distinguish between demonization as a process and naming the demonic. Juergensmeyer rightly
identifies the process of demonization but he does not explore the notion of
good and evil. Second, the social processes of exclusion and humiliation give
us some understanding as to how we reinforce the process of demonization
and provide the conditions for the demonic to emerge, the dehumanization
of the subject. Third, I have demonstrated that while there is a need to identify good and reject evil, there may also be a need to understand that evil as
something that is done to us profoundly affects us interiorly, eliciting moral
outrage. Juergensmeyer identifies the process of increasing delegitimation
through satanization but he does not identify how people might move
beyond violence and be healed. We can come to understanding and work
through the trauma of evil only by the power of transcendent love, expressing our moral outrage and seeking restoration, in a spirit of mourning and
allowing passive lament to give way to responsible active complaint and,
ultimately, forgiveness, rightly understood. Alternatively victims may turn
to violence through revenge and *ressentiment*. The reactions of revenge and
the psychic distortions of *ressentiment* however require religious and moral
conversion. If these reactions are left unchecked it is likely that cycles of
revenge and *ressentiment* will feed into what Lonergan calls a shorter cycle
of decline. Fourth, in authentic religious cultures, symbols of good and evil
raise awareness within the psyche of the divinely originated solution to evil.
For Christians, the criterion for understanding the difference between good
and evil is to be found in the symbol of the Cross of Christ. Only through a
religious appropriation of the Cross can we gain an authentic appropriation
of religious symbols such as the symbol of Satan.

    In the next chapter, we will explore the fourth of Juergensmeyer's four
symbols for understanding the link between violence and religion, namely,
warrior empowerment.

# 9

# A Dialectical Engagement with Warrior Empowerment

JUERGENSMEYER'S FOURTH SYMBOL FOR understanding the link between violence and religion is warrior empowerment, which joins two interrelated aspects: the practice and code of the warrior, and the empowering of the warrior. Although Juergensmeyer's title chapter uses the term "warrior" to structure his analysis, he does not use the term in the body of his writings, preferring to refer to "fighters" and "soldiers."[1] However, there is evidence that the term "warrior" has been used in communities, for example, the *mujahid* or holy warrior is a key figure in Islamic warfare. Holy warriors are called to *inghimas* or to throwing themselves recklessly at the enemy.[2] For example, in the days following the death of Osama bin Laden in early May 2011, Ismail Haniyeh, head of the Hamas Government in the Gaza Strip condemned the killing of bin Laden and described him as a "holy warrior" for Islam.[3] The term is also used in Western military academic institutions.[4] Alternatively, from a very academic setting, Professor Shannon E. French, who teaches ethics and law at the US Naval Academy, includes a course unit on "The Code of the Warrior."[5]

---

1. Juergensmeyer, *Terror*, 190–218. On the modern reluctance for not equating professional soldering with the term "warriorhood," see Kraugerud, "Shields of Humanity," 266.

2. In May 2011, a senior member of Hamas, Ismail Haniyeh, commenting on the death of Osama bin Laden, referred to bin Laden as a "holy warrior."

3. See "Gaza Hamas Leader Condemns bin Laden Killing."

4. See "Warrior Transition Command."

5. See the bibliography for publication details.

Juergensmeyer grounds his understanding of warriorhood on the premise that "a society provides an accepted, even heroic social role for its citizens who participate in great struggles and have been given the moral license to kill. They are soldiers."[6] His primary focus is the soldier of radical religious movements, whose preparedness to die or be imprisoned in the process of killing the enemy communicates a self-assertive mindset, for example, respectively: the suicide bomber, or the person who kills a doctor working in an abortion clinic. This kind of soldier is likened to a warrior imbued with an honor code and a set of cultural values, who defends his personal dignity. The commitment of such a religiously motivated soldier is empowered through believing that he or she is taking on a project greater than him- or herself individually, indeed a project of cosmic importance. Such actions are connected more specifically to a performative violence in which the goal is not so much concerned to accomplish a major conquest as to demonstrate a determination for their cause in reaching for a new religious, social, and political reality.

Such "militant religious activists"[7] have often been marginalized from political power, and their radical violent acts are a way of claiming back power. Juergensmeyer explores some of the psychological, social, and cultural factors exercising an influence upon people who are attracted to being soldiers. In chapter 8, I considered the importance of humiliation. People become humiliated when an occupying foreign force or the dominant social policies of the state limit the personal power of whole groups of people, especially when this affects their employment and housing, for example, in Israel, Gaza, and Algeria.[8] Juergensmeyer asserts that, for some of these soldiers, "religion and violence are seen as an antidote to humiliation."[9]

Juergensmeyer notes elements of difference among the Christian militia in the United States, where other factors, such as the perceived failure of democratically elected government policies, are more relevant.[10] Timothy McVeigh, the Oklahoma City bomber, for example, was a veteran of Operation Desert Storm who, upon returning to the United States, continued to wear army clothes and carry weapons in private; it seemed that he still imagined himself to be a soldier. While such individuals as McVeigh had been unemployed and drifting in their careers, others such as the Rever-

6. Juergensmeyer, *Terror*, 191–92.

7. Ibid., 9. Juergensmeyer prefers to use the term "militant" for this type of agent rather than "terrorist."

8. Ibid., 194.

9. Ibid., 191.

10. Ibid., 195, 227.

end Paul Hill were more established. But both McVeigh and Hill could be characterized as "white Protestant males and currently members of a privileged class [who] perceive American society to be moving in a direction that would make their class increasingly peripheral."[11]

Similarly, social marginality can become the chosen condition of some activists, leading them to forgo allegiance to any one country or people and to adopt "email ethnicities"[12] tied together by a transnational network of people through cyberspace, or through covert groups acting outside the mainstream of society. The conflicts to which such militant and marginalized individuals are drawn "impart a sense of importance and destiny to men who find the modern world to be stifling, chaotic and dangerously out of control."[13] Soldier allegiance is also influenced by the relationship between attitudes arising from a patriarchal religious culture and personal sexual identity. For example, all Muslim men are taught by their Muslim beliefs to observe sexual control and in some Muslim societies they are also taught a particular understanding of gender roles. Therefore, "sexual aberrations" in the form of "misplaced gender roles," such as where women assume dominant positions in the public arena or where there is an open display of homosexuality, provide the conditions in which men feel the need to rise up and fight.[14] For Juergensmeyer, all these factors lead men to become violent soldiers since, due to these sexual aberrations, they feel a "loss of identity," or "loss of control," and a conviction of a "sinister hand controlling and disrupting the world."[15]

In such a social environment, men are empowered to become violent soldiers by joining a movement that provides belonging through male bonding and friendship joined to religious ideology.[16] For some groups, violent acts deliver a sense of restored power for the purposes of establishing an alternative political rule to secular rule; for other groups, the acts are mainly symbolic, with little thought about an alternative view of the long-term political outcome, should they be victorious.[17] Either way, the sanctioning of killing breaks the state's monopoly over the license to kill and places the

---

11. Ibid., 195.

12. Ibid., 197.

13. Ibid., 193.

14. Ibid., 201–2.

15. Ibid., 204.

16. Ibid., 204–10. I acknowledge that both men and women fighters are taking up an armed struggle in the wider Muslim world. But, predominantly, this is understood by most groups to be the role of men.

17. Ibid., 218.

"claim of power on behalf of the powerless, a basis of legitimacy for public order other than that on which the secular state relies."[18]

Juergensmeyer has identified factors governing the particular political, social, and cultural landscape of those people who become soldiers. His focus is the radical religious soldiers who are prepared to die for a religious cause. Juergensmeyer names such believers' felt loss of control as a contributing factor to their preparedness to die. In response, I considered the difference between an ethic of control and an ethic of risk, as outlined in chapter 3, arguing that only an ethic of risk in the face of suffering and crisis can bring about authentic human development.

Juergensmeyer links warfare, religion, and the desire for social order, and there is no doubt that religiously justified warfare can be found in the sacred texts of monotheistic religions. However, in chapter 5, on warfare, I argued the importance of dialectically engaging with distorted religious and political traditions that might provide a justification for using violence as a means for addressing disempowerment. Following on from this, in chapter 6, I explored a constructive approach to conflict grounded in genuine religion that could ethically guide decision makers and soldiers, and I explored how religious experience and traditions based on self-sacrificing love sublate ethical decision making.

Juergensmeyer demonstrates that distorted religious and cultural dimensions inform citizens' and fighters' acts of violent self-immolation and self-assertion by citizens and fighters, for example the acts of the soldier become suicide bomber. I argue that true religious martyrdom is never about choosing death but rather upholding the dignity of each person even at the cost of one's own life. Juergensmeyer also notes the process of demonization as a key to maintaining anger against the enemy. In chapter 8, I argued that the process of demonization can easily distort the minds and hearts of authorities and their followers, especially when such appeals lack a distinction between demonizing the other and naming the demonic. I also proposed that symbols such as the Cross and Satan, when accurately appropriated, may act as a source of spiritual motivation for right conduct and of a truthful understanding of the demonic.

Juergensmeyer seeks to establish that disempowered people turn to religious movements, with their ideologies and modes of operating, even when these involve symbolic violent acts so that they may be once again empowered. His sociological perspective provides a descriptive and partial understanding of the social and religious attitudes that shape the judgment and performance of the warrior. I argue that it is better to view warrior

18. Ibid.

empowerment through the categories of authentic and inauthentic development. Inauthentic development is not confined to the religious imagination, though it may be manifest in that context joined with a political ideology. Yet within the religious imagination there is also present an alternative understanding of warrior empowerment consistent with authenticity, justice, and the good. Just cause becomes the driver for authentic empowerment for soldiering. For soldiers to be empowered it is not enough that they be handed a "heroic social role" with the "moral license to kill."[19] My aim below will be to demonstrate that authentic empowerment comes about when the soldier is fully exercising the norm of consciousness so as to discern a just cause, enabling a critique of the social and cultural factors that influence the soldier's decision making and actions.

## The Judgment and Performance of the Warrior

First, I will begin by demonstrating the kinds of motivations that influence the performance of the warrior and how our understanding of these motivations has developed in the West. I will present an understanding of authentic warrior empowerment that would prioritize moral and religious conversion. As an alternative, I argue that a values-based ethic is central to the moral agency of the soldier in all societies. I will show that the Christian community can help shape the conscience of the soldier and, through the soldier's participation in the community of faith, a process of discernment can be enacted that might more fruitfully sustain practical military decisions. Second, since soldiering is usually enacted through a military organization by means of political mandate, the soldier looks to the leadership of military superiors for an understanding of what constitutes a good soldier. The leadership of the military mentors the soldier authentically or inauthentically. I will argue that military leadership needs to be critiqued since such leadership has a profound influence on the authentic empowerment of the soldier. As an example of this I will critique the leadership of the current leader of al-Qaeda, Ayman Al-Zawahiri.

### The Homeric Warrior and Achilles

Western society has been shaped by ancient Greek ideas surrounding the warrior ethic and has suggested aspects that are important in the warrior's judgment and performance. According to Moses Finlay, Homeric literature

19. Ibid., 191–92.

correlates warrior and hero such that "warrior" and "hero" are "synonymous and the main theme of the warrior culture is constructed on two notes— prowess and honor. The one is the hero's essential attribute, the other his essential aim. Every value, every judgment, every action, all skills and talents have the function of either defining honour or realizing it. Life itself may not stand in the way. The Homeric heroes loved life fiercely, as they did and felt everything with passion, and no less martyr characters could be imagined; but even life must surrender to honor."[20]

Stefanson argues that the Homeric warrior is held up as an example of manhood. The great deeds of such warriors are memorialized in story and song, and duly recognized with undying fame (*kleos*) and glory.[21] These deeds present particular men as the *telos* and guiding light of humanity.[22] These warriors serve as models, while stretching the limits of what is achievable and reaching heights of excellence that are improbable to reach but not impossible, being motivated by the desire for respect by mortals and the gods.

Homeric man considers earthly human life as the locus for achieving perfection. Achieving glory is a far higher goal than simply rendering retribution against the enemy. The ideal of Homeric epics is one that confines superlative human achievement to male aristocrats, indicating that some are better than others by birthright.[23] No one can simply rise to the ranks of nobility or heroism through merit. In the Homeric world the warrior does not question his motives or suppress his emotions but simply follows them. The great deeds of such warriors can be achieved only in the fullness of battle by means of decisive action that is unqualified, unguarded, and unequivocal. Such warriors become grief-stricken or angry, articulate their desire, and are empowered to act. People of such a character impelled by affectivity can never be helpless or indecisive but are always empowered.[24]

Homeric man finds himself in a society strongly influenced by cosmologically constituted meanings and values. In such societies, the soldier understands the earthly realm of conflict to mirror the heavenly conflict between the gods. No less important is the individual's social position. The warrior is embedded in the key structures of kinship and household with clear boundaries concerning duties and the requirement to be honorable in the face

20. Finlay, *World of Odysseus*, 34.

21. Stefanson, "Man as Hero," 22; Hook and Reno, *Heroism*, 18. "[The warrior with] *kleos* . . . is one whose acts and [whose] achievements attract[s] attention and command[s] the memory of all who come after."

22. Stefanson, "Man as Hero," 26.

23. Ibid., 35–36.

24. Ibid., 47.

of death, which, in its observance, then entitles him to be honored by his kin-ship.[25] He seeks honor and a noble death through the exercise of his fighting skills and his courage in the face of danger.[26] The community by honoring the warrior accumulates a debt, which it collects on the battlefield. The warrior has a privileged social rank and the many benefits that come to him bestow a positive value on war. He considers himself to be part of an infinite and cha-otic world where warcraft is valued, since the existence of every community depends upon its cultivation. Since life is brief in duration and the afterlife a bleak and unknown prospect, war endows life with meaning, ennobling and glorifying the warrior through courage in battle. There is, however, a cost to this glory: one goes into battle without any hope of survival.

This assessment of Homer's portrayal of the warrior concurs with that of Patrick Clark. Clark argues that the dialectical tension between the war-rior's honor and the warrior's longevity begins to be questioned by Achilles in the Homeric poems.[27] When Agamemnon returns the war concubine, Chryseis, to her father, Agamemnon demands Briseis, the wife of Achilles, in compensation. Due to this trade-off, Achilles, who has been dispossessed and disrespected, begins to question the social economy of honor and its ability to pass on the full measure of glory, especially among equals.[28] It is not enough that the warrior be glorified by his kinsmen. Through Achilles's grief, Homer begins to question the preeminence of war as the chosen arena to display acts of enduring excellence.[29] Homer further evaluates Achilles's acts of vengeful anger on his enemies as stripping him of his humanity and rendering him incapable of identifying with the humanity of others.[30] Achilles, who is thus fully alienated by war, cannot find a language with which to express his sorrow apart from the language of violence.[31] He has two choices: either to continue to pursue a socially dependent legacy built on the destruction of sociality (the trade-off of his wife and the death of his friend), or he must accept without consolation death's ultimate annihilation of his own identity and accomplishments.[32]

25. MacIntyre, *After Virtue*, 122. MacIntyre describes kinship groups where a per-son knows who he or she is by knowing his or her role.

26. Clark, "Greater Glory."

27. Ibid., 12.

28. Ibid., 13.

29. Ibid.

30. Ibid., 14.

31. Ibid., 18.

32. Ibid., 22.

In chapter 5, on warfare, we saw that people respond to the experience of crisis and suffering with either an ethic of control or an ethic of risk. Achilles's actions signify a futile rage against mortality, and his moral challenge is that of accepting his own vulnerability with humility. Hook and Reno argue that subsequent actions by Achilles begin to reveal a warrior who is growing disillusioned by the accepted standards of achievement held up by Greek communities.[33] The return of Hector's tortured body to Priam, out of view of the Greeks and in secret, points to Achilles's search for a greater honor than society can provide.[34]

## Socrates, Plato, and Human Excellence

According to Stefanson, a next major development of reflection on the warrior ethic is found in the thought of Socrates. By Socrates's time, Greek political thinking upheld the preeminence of the polis[35] over the household or kinship, and adherence to the values of the polis as the measure for the warrior hero. While the warrior is necessary to political life, he can also be a source of instability and a threat to the polis. Michael Gillespie argues that the preeminence of the polis in Greece meant that the "political realm can only come into existence if the warrior uses violence in the service of his friends, family, and fellow citizens, and it is only through his continued support that it can be sustained. The ferocious warrior who turns against the community . . . destroys the political."[36] By the time of Socrates, the veneration of the warrior was based on the warrior's capacity to be a representative of the virtues of the city of Athens.[37] The lasting glory of warriors was predicated on their capacity to put the polis first.

According to Clark, the Socratic insights provide a new standard for human excellence: one should pursue what is good and honorable even at the risk of one's life and even when that evaluation does not square with the deliberations of the polis.[38] Socrates represents an anthropological breakthrough in consciousness: the measure of an individual's integrity is reason. What makes one's actions good is conformity to justice itself and not to the demands of the polis. Through philosophy the person comes to

33. Hook and Reno, *Heroism*, 29, 32.

34. Ibid., 39.

35. Stefanson, "Man as Hero," 68. The polis is a civil administration of men and women under the rule of law, where the law considers the common good.

36. Gillespie, "New Aristocracy," 5.

37. MacIntyre, *After Virtue*, 132.

38. Clark, "Greater Glory," 37.

know the nature of justice, by which the citizen pursues the true nature and demands of the good. Knowledge will give people the ability to correctly evaluate moral dilemmas, while wrongdoing has more to do with incorrect knowledge than with moral depravity.[39] Therefore, instead of the warrior's honor and glory being decisive, Socrates radically posits the act of philosophy—the love and pursuit of wisdom—as paramount so that the warrior no less than the leader can understand what is true and good amidst the changing opinions of his time.[40] This invitation implicitly sought to restrain the warrior's penchant to use violence to obtain power over others. The human body, at its best, is a source of conflicted emotions to be kept under control and, at its worst, is an insurmountable obstacle in the search for truth. It is the fear of a dishonorable death that must be overcome, according to Socrates, and one's pursuit of excellence rests on the approval of an inner authority that stands apart from concrete relations.[41] This inner authority is a world-transcendent reason characteristic of anthropologically oriented cultures. In this way, the practice of philosophy appears as a subversion of the polis, whose justification for practical governance is based on being internally consistent with its own static self-understanding.[42] Death is a reality that confronts us and its nature cannot be fully understood, yet it remains a happy culmination to a life examined and well lived by pursuing wisdom.[43]

Further, according to Eric Voegelin, Plato as a political philosopher recognizes in the *Gorgias* a central moral question that has implications for the citizen become warrior: Is it better to suffer the evil of injustice or to do the evil of injustice?[44] According to Voegelin, in the *Gorgias* Polus maintains that nobody prefers the suffering of injustice to the doing of injustice, while Socrates maintains that "the price of safety against injustice may be too high."[45] Callicles joins the conversation with Socrates, at first identifying just and good with the self-assertive expression of the stronger man, but then he modifies his position and maintains that the strongest man must be the most wise and courageous.[46] Socrates is highlighting the importance of moral integrity, the difference between mere power and moral power, and the detrimental effects of committing evil so that some good may come of it.

39. Stefanson, "Man as Hero," 105.

40. Clark, "Greater Glory," 38.

41. Ibid., 42.

42. Ibid., 48.

43. Ibid., 81.

44. Voegelin, *Plato and Aristotle*, 24–45; Plato, *Gorgias, Menexenus, Protagoras*.

45. Voegelin, *Plato and Aristotle*, 32, 37.

46. Ibid., 34–35.

This brief exposition of Socrates and Plato moves away from the earlier insights of Homer. For Socrates, the love and pursuit of wisdom by the warrior is important if the warrior is to understand the difference between concrete acts of justice, the universal meaning of justice, mere power, and the right use of power. For Plato, the warrior caste in the service of the republic was needed to repel outside enemies and to prevent the degradation of democracy into tyranny. The warrior was thus set apart by means of a formation, education, and set of pleasurable social goods different from those of the rest of the citizens.

## Aristotle, *Telos*, and Virtues

Aristotle inherited both Socrates and Plato's understanding of human excellence in contrast to the more traditional models of martial excellence evident in Homer. Aristotle's ethics progresses the anthropological breakthrough in culture. According to Clark, Aristotle argues that the highest achievable human excellence is intellectual, so that happiness or *eudaimonia* consists primarily in the exercise of the soul in regard to intelligible objects.[47] Yet closely related to intellectual happiness is happiness that comes from the cultivation of the moral and practical virtues or excellence of character, which are important in political and martial affairs when reason is applied to practical living.[48] The practical and moral virtues are important because of our bodily and affective existence and are legitimate realms of human excellence in as much as higher intellectual activity is dependent on the equilibrium secured by stable passions and social relationships.[49]

Aristotle's moral theory is based on the insight that human beings have a specific nature and that human nature has certain goals, such that persons move by nature toward a specific end or *telos*.[50] If the *telos* represents the full realization of definitive human goods, virtues enable us to achieve and enjoy these goods. If the condition of happiness represents human flourishing, then, according to MacIntyre, virtues are "those qualities the possession of which will enable an individual to achieve *eudaimonia* and the lack of which

---

47. Stefanson, "Man as Hero," 84; Aristotle, *Nichomachean Ethics*, chap. X, 7. In this chapter Aristotle argues that intellectual activity brings with it pleasures amazing in purity and stability (1177a26).

48. Aristotle, *Nichomachean Ethics*, chap. X, 8, 1178b3–7.

49. Ibid., chap. X, 8, 1178b33–35.

50. MacIntyre, *After Virtue*, 148.

will frustrate his movement towards that *telos*."[51] Virtues are dispositions not only to act in a particular way but also to feel in a particular way.[52]

As I indicated in chapter 7 while exploring the nature of heroism, there may be a significant difference between the well-trained soldier and the genuinely courageous soldier. The well-trained one may do what courage demands not because he or she is courageous but because he or she trusts in his or her capacities and skills or even because he or she is more frightened of his or her superiors than of the enemy.[53] The courageous soldier acts on the basis of true and rational judgments. Such a soldier is not immune to the unpredictability of the battlefield, no matter how well he or she is trained in character, yet the courageous person brings the greatest amount of excellence out of any situation despite the danger that befalls him or her.[54]

In the case of warriors, the virtue of courage is of primary importance since warriors put themselves into difficult and dangerous situations on the field of battle. The virtue of courage is an exception to the rule that pleasure always attends virtue. This action goes against the ordinary purpose for performing an act, namely, enjoying some pleasure arising from that act.[55] Courageous persons are set apart by persevering in their pursuit of what is fine in spite of their concealment of fear and uncertainty in their actions.[56] Warriors are placed into conflict situations and therefore must decide between many goods: either saving their own lives or dying with courage, with neither option appearing to offer the prospect of full happiness insofar as happiness requires a nobility of action over the course of one's life.[57] Aristotle grounds the warrior's nobility in achieving a good end and concludes that the warrior in war is the most exalted embodiment of human excellence, at least for those in the civic setting.[58]

The exposition from Homer to Socrates reveals that acting out of passion, in pursuit of glory and social honor is not a sufficient ethical foundation for the warrior's practice. The warrior is also a human person who must guard against descending into brutality, who needs friendship, and who best understands the right reasons for his or her actions by pursuing wisdom and

---

51. Ibid.

52. Ibid., 149.

53. Ibid., 150.

54. Clark, "Greater Glory," 93–94. Aristotle, *Nichomachean Ethics*, chap. I, 9, 1100a5–10.

55. Aristotle, *Nichomachean Ethics*, chap. I, 9, 1099a5–12.

56. Ibid., chap. III, 9.

57. Ibid., chap. III, 9, 1117b14–16.

58. Ibid., chap. III, 8.

the good end. For Plato, warriors would best be able to defend the democratic republic from internal and external enemies if they were set apart into
a warrior class. For Aristotle the practice of the warrior, similar to that of
other citizens of the polis, must be directed toward happiness, an intelligible
end, and virtuous actions. Therefore, we observe in Socrates, Plato, and Aristotle a move toward a more anthropological culture and the importance of
reasoning so as to ascertain the meaning of justice and a just society.

## Soteriological Meanings and Values

The Christian tradition represents an encounter with soteriological meanings and values. The Gospels present Jesus both as distinguishing the providence of God and the political power of Caesar (Luke 20:20–26) and as
responding to soldiers who manifest faith without providing a particularly
extended teaching on soldiering (Luke 7:1–10). The disciple who is also a
soldier believes that the centrality of Jesus' commandment of love is inter-
woven with the mission to right all wrongs by means of God's justice.[59] For
the disciples of the risen Jesus, excellence is to be found in worshipping their
Lord and in living the Beatitudes (Matt 5:1–12), which are central to the
Sermon on the Mount. Slattery argues that Christian discipleship necessi-
tates "a clear election for walking with the economically poor and oppressed
in the struggle to overcome everything that encompasses the enslavement
of humanity under sin."[60] To be a disciple, one must believe in the eschaton
and hope in a future by working for human development grounded in the
love of God and neighbor.

As indicated in chapter 6, discipline for Jesus' followers is grounded
in suffering self-sacrificing love and service, sometimes to the point of one's
own death for the redemption and justice of others, especially the oppressed
(martyrdom).[61] Slattery notes that with respect to those who are antagonistic or hostile enough to act as a lethal enemy toward Christians, Jesus commands the very difficult option of loving one's enemy and praying for those
who persecute them and others (Matt 5:39).[62] Slattery concludes that the
"follower of Jesus is expected to take violence encumbered upon oneself, but
at the same time to be shrewd as serpents and guileless as doves in dealing

---

59. Sagovsky, *Christian Tradition*; see 55–82. See also Fuellenbach, *Kingdom of
God*, 157–66.

60. Slattery, *Jesus the Warrior?*, 55.

61. Ibid., 56.

62. Ibid., 58–59.

with one's enemies in a nonviolent and nonthreatening manner and not go out of one's way to become the recipient of violence."[63]

The Christian tradition has reflected over the centuries on the moral life of those who are both soldiers and Christian, beginning with an ethos that opposed the involvement of the baptized in warfare.[64] From the perspective of the early church fathers, J. Daryl Charles notes that Tertullian warned against idolatry by Christian soldiers since soldiers were expected to swear allegiance to the emperor and wear badges that bore the effigy of the emperor.[65] According to Charles, Cyprian laments the savagery of his day but also speaks about Christian acquaintances who were serving as soldiers.[66] Ambrose, Bishop of Milan, and former Roman governor in the northern military outpost of Milan, acknowledged the need for Christians not to retreat from their civic duties while awaiting the next life.[67] In a set of writings that give direction to clergy shepherding their people, Ambrose emphasizes the importance of the cardinal virtues—prudence, justice, temperance, and courage—and of wisdom integrated into the Christian life while mindful that God is the *telos* of our action.[68] In Ambrose, we find the beginnings of the just war tradition, which we considered in chapter 6.[69] He opposes excessive cruelty toward one's enemy, distinguishing between just retribution and vengeance.[70]

According to Charles, Augustine also presents the case for being both a devout Christian and a good citizen, arguing that reasonable people can have the purpose, however imperfectly, of doing what is just and good for others.[71] Charles asserts that, due to evil, "humans may justify going to war; however they do so only reluctantly. Augustine serves to remind us that political judgments are at bottom moral judgments. Christian justification for coercive force is neighbor love that must be willing on occasion to protect

---

63. Ibid., 74. The adversary or enemy must always be held accountable but never hated, dehumanized, or killed. See also Myers and Enns, *New Testament Reflections*, 50–56.

64. Himes, "War," 977.

65. Charles, *Pacifism and Jihad*, 34.

66. Ibid., 36.

67. Ibid., 38.

68. Charles and Demy, *War, Peace and Christianity*, 124. Charles and Demy quote from Ambrose's letter to his clergy, *On the Duties of the Clergy*, 2.6, 2.7 (32–39). Ambrose firmly believes that it is unjust to gain victory by unjust means such as excessive cruelty.

69. Charles, *Pacifism and Jihad*, 39.

70. Ibid.

71. Ibid., 43.

the innocent third party. The law of love obliges us to use force in the aid of others."[72] In chapter 6, I argued that the Christian tradition recognizes the protection and defense of the common good through the use of force to repel enemies, especially when enemies are intent on killing the innocent and destroying a social and cultural way of life. To engage in soldiering can be a good and noble office and even an act of charity on behalf of the defenseless when carrying out such obligations with a good conscience.

In systematizing Augustine's approach, Aquinas argues for a set of criteria to guide decisions as to the relative rightness for initiating war.[73] He also argues that it is not right to kill or suppress life simply for the sake of any good, for example, as in the case of killing hostages of war as a means of dissuasion and persuasion.[74] His argument is that, in war, while the intention of the soldier to stop the attack of the enemy is permissible, killing is not always defensible. What is excluded is the general "take no prisoners" policy, whose aim is to terrorize enemy soldiers and teach enemy leaders a lesson, killing hostages who are retrained, and shaping one's actions with emotions that exalt killing.[75]

For Socrates, excellence is linked especially to the pursuit of wisdom even to the point of subverting the polis. For Plato, developing a warrior class so as to resist tyranny from within or from outside the polis is highly desirable. For Aristotle, to be excellent is to exercise one's intellectual capacity and focus on developing the virtues, especially the virtue of courage in the case of the soldier. For Christianity, while virtues can be acquired, God's love and our love for God and neighbor bring all the activities of our lives to a different goal, so that the ultimate goal for the cultivating of virtues is God, who heals, elevates, and transforms our human virtues through the gifts of faith, hope, and love.[76] In Christian tradition, the soldier has been able to be both a just citizen and a disciple of Christ as long as the soldier acted from a right intention, treated the enemy humanely, and fought for defenseless victims of aggression. To do evil so that good may come from one's evil acts strikes at the root of human fulfillment: to be who God created us to be and to answer God's call.

From my account of Lonergan in chapter 3, human living is always a movement away from inauthenticity to authenticity, from an inattentive, unintelligent, unreasonable, and irresponsible consciousness to one that is

---

72. Ibid., 44.

73. *Summa Theologiae* II–II, q.40.

74. Ibid., q.64.

75. Finnis, *Aquinas*, 286–87.

76. Lamoureux and Wadell, *Christian Moral Life*, 124–41.

marked by attentiveness, intelligence, reasonableness, and responsibility. Achieving authenticity is ever precarious. Since this is the case, then the warrior must be capable of detachment and wary of the danger of an instrumentalization of reason that underpins a technical approach to warfare. In the field of battle, the warrior is in a practical and dramatic context of meaning, assessing morally what to do so as to avoid death and defeat the enemy. The existential commitment of warriors to the intrinsic value of the human person and their openness to God must not be lost if they are to strive for authenticity. Since biases can derail their pursuit of authenticity in this affectively and morally demanding arena, soldiers require divine grace to maintain the direction of self-transcendence. Outside the battlefield the authentic warrior cultivates a life of affective, intellectual, moral, and religious virtues through a restorative justice that seeks to rebuild the defeated country devastated by war.

## Three Examples of Warriorhood

We have seen the kinds of motivations that influence the performance of the warrior and how our understanding of these motivations has developed in the West. I will now present two examples of authentic, and one of inauthentic, warrior empowerment. Juergensmeyer's focus has been the cause of the religiously motivated soldier whose fighting seeks to bring about the "rule of God" in the political arena.[77] Just cause is part of the moral tradition of all three monotheistic religions as they reflect on war, although each of the traditions approaches these criteria in similar as well as diverse ways.[78] In the Christian tradition we find a fully theoretical exploration of these criteria. While Juergensmeyer notes the importance of the solider fighting for a cause, Juergensmeyer's specific foci are soldiers who show "religious conviction, a hatred of secular society and demonstrations of power through acts of violence."[79] However, he does not explore the relationship between authentic empowerment, just cause, and the religious faith of the soldier. I argue that empowerment is enhanced when reasoning around just cause is grounded in intelligent and responsible reflection, and gives rise to different moral decisions when grounded in transcendent love.

77. Juergensmeyer, *Terror*, 210.

78. Kelsay, "Resistance in Contemporary Islam," 61–88; Kelsay, *Just War in Islam*, 97–124. Kelsay outlines the Koranic texts that shape the formation of Sharia law concerning warfare. Solomon, "Ethics of War," 61–88, examines various Jewish sources that guide conduct in war and the right to self-defense.

79. Juergensmeyer, *Terror*, 61.

## Religious Conversion and Just Cause

Christian discipleship witnesses to moral conversion sublated by religious conversion. In societies influenced by a soteriological culture, a very different set of meanings and values emerge. Grace helps us to appreciate and achieve moral integrity, to render our reasoning authentic, and enables us to be sensitive to the biological rhythms of body, and to develop the life of feelings. For the Christian, moral formation goes beyond simply obeying a code. Formation requires a relationship with God, prayer, a commitment to the moral principles of the Christian community, and education into a process of interior moral discernment. In the Christian moral context, just cause encompasses the protection of the weak, disadvantaged, and vulnerable through meeting human need.[80] One objective of justice is to protect the defenseless and repair harm done to victims of aggression.

My first example of authentic warrior empowerment demonstrates how the soteriological shift can transform the decision-making process. It comes from a person forced to weigh up just cause in the light of his Christian faith when faced with conscription and active service. The Austrian farmer and Catholic, Franz Jägerstätter, was executed in 1943 for refusing to be drafted into the German Army in any role whatsoever after Hitler invaded Austria in 1938.[81] Jägerstätter's firm conviction was that he could not be drafted into a war that did not have a just cause and that had been sponsored by a government determined on imperialistic expansion and the slaughter of the innocent. Jägerstätter's writings prior to—and, secretly, during—his imprisonment reflect a number of responses to contrary arguments used by his fellow countrymen to defend or rationalize their decision to join forces with the Nazi occupiers. He wrote:

> One can always hear Catholics as saying that this war Germany is fighting is probably not so unjust, after all, because it will bring about the destruction of Bolshevism. [His response was that] . . . whenever anyone has taken up arms to wipe out Christianity . . . the blood of their victims has always become the new seed and shoots from which Christianity flowed anew with more vitality than before. Now, could this not happen again, if one spills Bolshevist blood? Could not this too become new seed? Are we Christians today perhaps wiser than Christ himself? Does anyone really think that this massive bloodletting

---

80. Sagovsky, *Christian Tradition*, 182–84.
81. Jägerstätter, *Writings from Prison*, xxiv.

can possibly save European Christianity from defeat or bring it to a new flowering?[82]

A central aspect of Jägerstätter's life was religious conversion, nurtured by daily Mass, and fasting and prayer. In response to his wife and mother, who prayed that he reconsider his decision not to allow himself to be drafted into the German Army, Jägerstätter wrote on the day of his execution: "Dearest wife and mother, it was not possible for me to free both of you from the sorrows that you have suffered for me. How hard it must have been for our dear Lord that he had given his dear mother such great sorrow through his suffering and death! And he suffered everything out of love for us sinners. I thank our Savior that I could suffer for him and may die for him. I trust in his infinite compassion. I trust that God forgives me everything and will not abandon me in the last hour."[83]

## Empowerment and Proper Conduct in War

My second example of authentic warrior empowerment, which focuses on proper conduct in war, is the case of Hugh Thompson, the helicopter pilot who stopped the unfolding massacre of My Lai in Vietnam on March 16, 1968.[84] After Thompson observed soldiers shooting at and in fact killing unarmed civilians, he landed his craft between the soldiers and a group of civilians who were their immediate target, and ordered the soldiers to stop under threat of retaliatory force. He acted with a personal power that came from a responsible conscience. In the period following the events of My Lai, the attempts by Major General Koster to cover up the atrocities, the ensuing cover-ups in the investigation, the harsh treatment toward Thompson by the house Armed Services Committee, and the subsequent years of the harsh judgment of his peers, Thompson proved himself to be a man of integrity.[85]

Authentic power creates people who are intelligent and responsible, who refuse immoral orders, and who stop those who act immorally. As we saw in chapter 6, societies influenced by anthropologically constituted meanings and values have constructed rules of engagement and codes of conduct to guide and bring honor to the actions of soldiers or warriors, often in the face of mistaken perceptions of hostile intentions, and as a way of limiting unvirtuous actions by soldiers that often result in immoral

82. Ibid., 181–83.
83. Ibid., 129–30.
84. Flynn, *War on Terror*, 38.
85. Bilton and Sim, *Four Hours in My Lai*, 185, 195, 237, 285.

consequences.[86] The case of Hugh Thompson is a good example of anthropological reasoning at its best. The rules of engagement represent the directions given to military personnel on how they are to carry out their duties in
particular contexts, on how they are to retaliate, on how they are to treat and
capture targets, on which geographical area they are bound to fight in, and
on what kind of force they are permitted to use during operations.[87] Such
rules follow a basic principle: the soldier is justified in using force out of
self-defense, thus allowing the soldier to judge the difference between mere
harassing actions and threatening hostile acts by the enemy.[88]

Codes of conduct also shape true warrior empowerment. The international conventions agreed to between nations include: the Geneva Convention of 1863,[89] the Hague Convention of 1907,[90] the Geneva Convention
of 1929,[91] the Nuremberg Principles of 1948,[92] the Universal Declaration
of Human Rights of 1948,[93] the Geneva Convention of 1948,[94] the Protocols to the Geneva Convention of 1977,[95] and the International Criminal
Tribunals for the Former Yugoslavia and for Rwanda of 1993 and 1994.[96] In
the case of Hugh Thompson, we observe a soldier who internalized military
codes of conduct regarding innocent civilians and obeyed military rules of
engagement.

## Warriorhood and False Transcendence

My example of inauthentic warrior empowerment concerns the Prussian
Army's "Totenkopf" (dead man's head) battalion. It used the insignia of
skull and crossbones initially as a way of remembering their fallen dead but
in time as a way of overcoming the fear of death. Convinced that they would
die, the soldiers in this way projected a kind of self-assertion over death. The
insignia was also used by the "SS-Totenkopfverbande" (Death's Head Unit),
the military unit assigned by Hitler to administer the SS Nazi concentration

86. French, "Code of the Warrior," 5–16.

87. Flynn, *War on Terror*, 51.

88. Ibid., 52–53.

89. Ibid., 14.

90. Ibid., 14–15.

91. Ibid., 15.

92. Ibid., 15–16.

93. Ibid., 16–17.

94. Ibid., 17–18.

95. Ibid., 18–19.

96. Ibid., 19.

camps for the Third Reich. This unit developed a reputation for ferocity and fanaticism.

According to Taylor, lacking any hope in the power of God, these soldiers manifested a state of "dead men on leave" or the "walking dead." They assumed the moral horizon of "kill or be killed" and became "killing machines."[97] They betrayed a lack of acceptance of human frailty and vulnerability. Taylor gives an interior glimpse of such soldiers, as one marked by false transcendence. He imagines them saying "We live in the element of violence, but like kings unafraid, as agents of pure action, dealing death; we are rulers of death. What was terrifying before is now exciting, exhilarating; we're on a high. It gives us a sense to our lives. This is what it means to transcend."[98] Such inauthentic warriors do not face the fear of death and are unable to humbly accept death within the context of God's providence. Rather, such warriors become exhilarated by the prospect of death, acquire a lust for blood, and lapse into a distorted and excessive transcendence in the dialectic of the subject. Such soldiers are sometimes justified by a distorted religious heritage and other times not, with no hope of receiving or of being willing to receive, and ultimately choose death through acts of self-assertion.[99]

## Soldier Empowerment, Authority, and Authorities

Central to Juergensmeyer's warrior symbol is the relationship between soldiers and their leaders. Juergensmeyer points to the pivotal role that leadership plays for soldiers in religious movements.[100] I argued in chapter 6 that militant religious leaders and leaders of nation-states can use distorted religious ideas to justify their political ideologies and actions. There is no doubt that while a soldier may enlist for personal and patriotic motives, nevertheless the soldier looks to leadership for direction. However, Juergensmeyer's analysis does not go beyond describing how military leaders make themselves attractive and credible to their eventual followers.[101]

Lonergan's analysis of power, authenticity, and authority provides us with a number of important insights. Lonergan asserts that the source of power for any group is its ability to act cooperatively, while the carrier or exercise of power is the community or the word of authority that brings the best

97. Taylor, *Secular Age*, 647.

98. Ibid.

99. Dunne, *Way of All the Earth*, 22.

100. Juergensmeyer, *Terror*, 210.

101. Ibid., 213.

achievements of the past to the present, facilitating cooperation around shared understandings and judgments, and removing barriers to cooperation.[102] This word of authority is the heritage of the community, enshrined in the gains of the past, making sense of human living, and organized into specific tasks.[103] However, this heritage may also contain unhelpful elements and a body of insights that do not resolve the new questions of a particular context.

Within this community of shared and accepted understanding, Lonergan further distinguishes authority and authorities. The authorities are those persons to whom certain offices have been entrusted; they have power delegated to them to perform assigned tasks. However, it is the community who carries valid meanings and values possesses the authority.[104] The meanings and values can be either authentic or inauthentic: authentic in the measure that they are the cumulative result of attentiveness, intelligence, reasonableness, and responsibility, and inauthentic to the measure that they are inattentive, unintelligent, unreasonable, and irresponsible. Authenticity makes power legitimate, while inauthenticity "reveals power as mere power."[105] Authenticity legitimates authorities and authority, while inauthenticity takes away their legitimation. Similarly subjects of authority may be authentic persons, who accept the claims of legitimate authorities and resist the claims of those who are illegitimate; or inauthentic persons, who resist legitimate claims and support illegitimate claims.

Dialectic occurs between the three different carriers (those who exercise power): the community, authorities, and subjects to authority. Lonergan, aware of the difficulties of achieving authenticity, declares that authenticity is reached only by long and sustained fidelity to the transcendental precepts, which we considered in chapter 3.[106] Dunne states that authority "is the moral power arising from authenticity."[107] The fruit of authenticity is progress: the result of inauthenticity is decline and an unintelligible situation, "a stony ground [where] to apply intelligence to it yields nothing."[108] As we saw also in chapter 3, beyond progress and decline there is redemption, which comes from falling in love, and which gives rise to a set of principles that might wipe out grievances and correct absurdities.[109]

---

102. Lonergan, *Third Collection*, 5–6.

103. Dunne, *Doing Better*, 247.

104. Lonergan, *Third Collection*, 6.

105. Ibid., 8.

106. Ibid., 8.

107. Dunne, *Doing Better*, 248.

108. Lonergan, *Third Collection*, 9.

109. Ibid., 10.

## An Example of Political Authority

We have seen that one of the givens of military life is that soldiers are to follow the orders of their military authorities. A good soldier, in commonsense
terms, is one who obeys his or her leader. Such obedience is based on trust in
one's commanding officers. Taking orders is demanded and justified on the
basis that doing so alone will protect the lives of soldiers in the theater of war.
Their moral empowerment is influenced by the religious, moral, and intellectual conversion of their authorities. We have also seen that authenticity makes
power legitimate and inauthenticity takes away authorities' legitimation. Let
us turn now to an analysis of a key figure in the organization, al-Qaeda, who
illustrates an authority figure who lacks legitimation in the Islamic community, Egyptian-born Ayman Al-Zawahiri, and who is now al-Qaeda's first in
command, following the death of Osama bin Laden in May 2011.

Following the London bombings of July 7, 2005, Al-Zawahiri offered
a statement commenting on those events, justifying the violent struggle of
al-Qaeda, and framing his comments by historical allusions to "the land of
Mohammad" and "the lands of Islam."[110] According to Kelsay, these state-
ments link the actions of al-Qaeda to the story of Mohammad and his early
companions, the notion of Islam as the natural religion of humanity, and the
growth of Islam as a civilization.[111] Al-Zawahiri grounded his judgments
and actions on the Islamic belief that the endowment of land for Muslims
is not a question primarily of owning or possessing property. Rather, both
the land entrusted to God's people and its good stewardship involve establishing and maintaining Islamic government. On this view, Islam from its
origins became a power to free people from oppression, and lands depicted
as Islamic conquests were territories where people received freedom from
tyranny so that they could follow the path of God as found in the Koran and
Sharia law.[112] The call of the oppressed was reframed as a call to all Muslims
to end tyranny by establishing governance according to Sharia law. This law
would be enacted and preserved by the development of a political system
with divine guidance.

This religious belief is further grounded in a creation story that states
that, from the beginning, God challenged humans to bear witness to God's
Lordship and, through various prophets, offered humankind both a gift and
a task. The gift is life and freedom, as discovered in the moral precepts of
Sharia, given to humans so that all may know the blessings of God. The task

---

110. Al-Zawahiri, "Speech," 8–9.

111. Kelsay, *Just War in Islam*, 156–57.

112. Ibid., 158; Lapidus, "Islamic Revival," 445.

for Muslim activists and militants is to present the gift of Islamic government to all humanity, a goal that will not be accomplished in a day and
that will require struggle.[113] In this new order, Muslims will take the lead
in setting policies for a new society. The assumption is that the commands
of God are mirrored in the precepts of Sharia, which can be read accurately
and followed responsibly only if one is a Muslim. Therefore, government
guided by God's law will require Muslim leadership and Muslim adherence
to the faith. Al-Qaeda's or the World Islamic Front's *Declaration on Armed
Struggle Against Jews and Crusaders* states the importance of proper Islamic
governance and pronounces harsh judgment on all groups and individuals
who depart from this norm, for example, the Saudi Royal Family, who have
failed Muslim people by allowing US troops to be stationed on Saudi soil.[114]

According to John Calvert, Al-Zawahiri's authority rests primarily on
a radical view of Islam that posits the global community of Muslims, known
as the *umma*, to be a superior historical and spiritual reality to any other
moral society since it is governed by Koranic principles, which reflect the
divine laws of the universe (*namus*).[115] On this view the community first
established by the Prophet at Medina reflected a harmony with God and
all creation, symbolizing a unique generation whose example in matters of
faith and practice were worthy of imitation. Before this time, there was only
the time of ignorance (*jahiliyya*) among the Quraysh people, and after this
revelation there was the possibility of adherence to the sovereignty of God,
who alone is qualified to fashion principles for the proper functioning of the
social, political, and economic order. Further, these principles are constant
and unchangeable, despite historical and cultural variations, and are comprehensive, making no distinction between *ibadat* (devotional duties) and
the world of political affairs. For Al-Zawahiri and the followers of al-Qaeda,
this exclusivist view of Islam is specifically melded to a Wahhabi-oriented
tradition of intolerance to difference, departing from a more classical
discourse that accepted and accommodated differences among people of
faith. It provides a justification for confronting the forces of *jahili* (ignorant

113. This theopolitical view of government is echoed also in the writings of the
Sunni thinker, Sayyid Qutb. See Eickelman and Piscatori, *Muslim Politics*, 48–51.

114. Al-Zawahiri and bin Laden, *Declaration*. This document is believed to have
been authored by Al-Zawahiri and Osama bin Laden. For a more complex discussion
of the Saudi Royal Family and the politics of Saudi Arabia, see Robinson, "Islam and
the West," 77–89.

115. John Calvert, "Mythic Foundations," 1–14. Calvert is associate professor of
history at Creighton University. He is a foremost authority on the writings of Sayyid
Qutb, which, in turn, have influenced the thoughts of Al-Zawahiri.

people and their laws), if necessary by violent force, until true Islam is once
again revived.

The lack of authenticity of Al-Zawahiri's position can be evidenced
on a number of different levels. First, Abou El Fadl argues that the religious faith of al-Qaeda, and by extension Al-Zawahiri, marries traditional
Islamic theology to Wahhabism and Salafism[116] to establish a new hybrid
that El Fadl calls "Salafabism."[117] Wabbabism brings a stance of opposition to all forms of historical scholarship, intellectualism, mysticism, and
sectarianism within Islam. Salafism maintains that all Muslim issues ought
to return to the original texts without being slavishly bound to interpretative precedents.[118] According to El Fadl, the combination of these two
movements, Salafabism, could be characterized as a "supremacist puritanism that compensates for feelings of disempowerment with a distinct sense
of self-righteous arrogance . . . (responding) to feelings of powerlessness
and defeat with uncompromising and arrogant displays of power, not only
against non-Muslims, but even more so against fellow Muslims."[119] The end
result is a religious practice that is exclusivist, intolerant, and isolationist. It
raises a number of questions around whether presumed legitimate rights of
non-Muslim people who live in these territories, and of Muslims who differ
from them, "Salafabists", will be protected.

A second indication that Al-Zawahiri's position is inauthentic concerns how the commitment to establish Sharia and a Muslim government
by violent means goes against the central thrust of the Koran, which places
love of God and neighbor at the heart of being a good Muslim.[120] While
the Koran provides a firm foundation for ethical reasoning for Muslims,
I have argued that methods used to spread fear among enemies, such as
suicide bombing, are not grounded in an authentic Koranic heritage and
are in fact counterproductive to building a just society. The lack of a strict
religious adherence and a broader understanding of moral positions may
contribute to a breakdown of social cohesion. However, there are also other
factors that contribute to this, such as massive urbanization and its associated problems, a population explosion, the increasing gap between rich and
poor, widespread corruption, rampant materialism, and the low premium
being placed on scholarship—all of these occur in a Muslim world that is

116. For a complete analysis of Salafism, see Cooper, *New Political Religions*, 95,
105, 109.

117. Abou El Fadl, "Orphans of Modernity," 179–88.

118. Ibid., 184–86.

119. Ibid., 186–87.

120. See chapter 5 of this book.

"young, dangerously illiterate, mostly jobless, and therefore easily mobilized for radical change."[121]

Third, the idea of a single form of theopolitical connection between government and Muslim faith has never existed historically. Historians judge that the political map of Islam from Spain to northwestern India took on more of the moral character of a patchwork quilt, with various divisions within Islam itself (Sunni, Shia, and Sufi) and differences in political arrangements between caliphates and sultanates. The notion of a resurrected global Islam with one Islamic system of governance is therefore a falsehood, and the notion of a seamless integration between religion and politics is an historical myth used for ideological purposes. The best one can hope for across the globe is a wide variety of blends and interrelationships between political forms and religious institutions.

A fourth indication that al-Zawahiri's position is inauthentic is reflected in the fact that the theological, philosophical, and practical challenges of modern Islam and its revivalist response have been assessed by some authors as being a counterreaction to secularization, the rise of modernity, and the failures of the state to meet the socioeconomic needs of people.[122] Some of the anti-Western and anti-American sentiment is a reaction to the changes wrought by modernity and the manner in which people have been marginalized politically by such changes, admittedly because of an attitude of superiority by the West and its cultural impositions. The ideas of Al-Zawahiri represent a crisis approach toward the complex challenges facing Muslim countries. At best, such a vision addresses the importance of religious and personal transformation, while collapsing the social and the religious levels in the scale of values, not allowing space for the cultural dimension to develop.

Fifth, Al-Zawahiri provides a reading of history that posits a pristine period at the beginning of Islam to which believers need to return. Islam is presented as a haven, especially for those who feel themselves marginalized, while offering a militant means of meeting the challenge of oppression toward Muslims through a return to a Golden Age, adherence to the fundamentals of Islam, and the use of violence. It does not recognize that a less selective reading of history would identify periods of progress, decline and recovery. God acts in history and, as we saw in chapter 3, God provides a new good to communities through a human willingness transformed by charity.

Sixth, far from representing the voice of the traditional *ulama* (learned ones) on matters of faith, Al-Zawahiri could be described as part of a new

---

121. Ahmed, "Islam and the West," 103–18.

122. Ali, *Islamic Revivalism*, 38–55.

intelligentsia of preachers, community organizers, intellectuals, and missionaries whose position on a number of issues departs significantly from the *ulama*.[123] For example, his thoughts on the Saudi Royal Family and the governance of Saudi Arabia make him assume the role of a rebel. There is a right enshrined in Sharia for Muslims to revolt and to become rebels in the name of fulfilling the obligation to establish a just social and political order. However, according to Kelsay, this right is reserved for those situations where the ruler becomes an unbeliever or committed apostate, or thwarts the legitimate right of Muslims to practice their faith.[124] This would be difficult to argue in the case of the whole Saudi Government.[125] Therefore, according to this reading, Al-Zawahiri's call to violent rebellion goes beyond the prescriptions of Sharia.

## Conclusion

Juergensmeyer's social analysis of warriorhood and empowerment does not go far enough. What is needed is a social analysis that enters into conversation with religious and moral conversion. The symbol of warriorhood in the West is founded in premodern narratives that tell stories of mythic heroes who seek glory and honor and become paradigms of excellence for others. I have demonstrated a development in the Western understanding of the warrior and his or her relationship to the polis by examining these narratives when brought into conversation with Christian texts.

But it is possible to engage in soldiering either authentically or inauthentically. A distorted warrior tradition promotes the image of a soldier based on a will to power, or on using others, or on being used by others. The primary axioms are "kill or be killed" and "take no prisoners." If the latter is applied, then a distorted attitude toward death will most likely emerge and the actions of war will become simply a theater of brute force. An authentic

123. Almond et al., *Strong Religion*, 82. Research by these authors has concluded that Sunni radical leaders tend to emerge from the religious laity and, among these activists, shaykhs tend to be rare. Osama bin Laden was considered a shaykh and theologian by only his followers. Al-Zawahiri was originally a physician and surgeon in the Egyptian Army and subsequently was recognized as a theologian by his followers.

124. Kelsay, *Islam and War*, 93–106. Al-Zawahiri's charge of apostasy against the Saudi Royal Family is based on its relationship with the United States Government and its allowing the United States military onto Muslim soil.

125. Saeed and Saeed, *Freedom of Religion*, 44–50. The four comprehensive "apostasy lists" from premodern to modern Islamic scholars specify what may be included in the offense of apostasy according to classical texts in the first list and more modern interpretations in the other three lists, leading to the conclusion that Al-Zawahiri's judgment of apostasy against the whole Saudi Royal Family is problematic.

soldier, on the other hand, takes on the tasks of examining his or her con-science, respecting the conventions of war, and teaching others to do the same. He or she will have to balance the concerns of the state for prosecut-ing a just war over against the lives of combatants and noncombatants who are killed or injured in the field of battle. A soldier's desire for higher status must never be placed above the willingness to allow the suffering of war to touch his or her conscience. Therefore, the empowered soldier or warrior is a person of conscience and possesses a detachment that is not ruled by the instrumentalization of reason and the technologism of war. Such detach-ment is very difficult to realize without the grace of God.

However, as I have argued, the task of critically examining what is a just cause is difficult when personal, social, and cultural biases diminish the soldier's ability to exercise fully the norms of consciousness. The role of the Christian community is neither to reject the duty of the soldier "to stop the strongman" nor to allow governments to forget their duty to work for the avoidance of war and the promotion of the common good.[126] The Christian community can provide a process of discernment for the soldier so that through prayer, fellowship, and reasonable moral principles he or she might be guided to practical and prudential decisions.

126. Charles and Demy, *War, Peace and Christianity*, 164.

# 10

# Conclusions

My aim in this book has been to explore the link between religion and violence, which I have done through four key symbols employed by commentators and academics convinced that religion often promotes violence. These symbols were: cosmic war, martyrdom, demonization, and warrior empowerment. I engaged dialectically with each of these symbols, using the insights of Bernard Lonergan, and through that engagement, I addressed a number of questions: What are the truthful and mistaken assertions made by authors through the lenses of these symbols around the link between religion and violence? Are there better categories to understand religiously motivated violence? If violence is a mark of not living as we should toward the other, can we construct an account of authentic religious living that may help us pastorally discern a path beyond violence and that contributes to better human living? How can we speak about religion in a normative manner so as to better distinguish genuine religion from distorted religion? How can religion help to shape human history toward progress and away from decline?

In chapter 1, and more extensively in chapter 3, I explained why I chose to explore such questions using the insights of Bernard Lonergan and those who have built on his work. These provided several foundational categories for this exploration. For example, Lonergan's foundations helped us to understand that a common ground can be found by the turn to the subject. The common ground is a method founded in the invariant and normative operations of human consciousness that constitute all people as knowers, valuers, choosers, and lovers. Indeed, Lonergan states that "genuine objectivity is the fruit of authentic subjectivity."[1] From this common ground we were able to postulate how religious aberration emerges and feeds the cycle of violence in history. Conversely, we were able to give an account

1. Lonergan, *Method*, 265.

of genuine religion and its part in the *healing* of aberration. The notions of historical consciousness and dialectic, too, are crucial to Lonergan. Any *historical* community is a dialectical mixture of authenticity and inauthenticity and it is through a mutual discourse between people's feelings, questions, thinking, valuing, and choosing that differences between people can be identified. Moreover, the horizons of persons, both as individuals and as members of traditions, change through the dynamic of conversion.

In chapter 2, we worked through a selective literature review around the link between religion and violence, focusing especially on the writings of Mark Juergensmeyer and James Jones, who frame the debate in terms of the four key symbols. The insights of René Girard and Charles Taylor also contributed to the discussion around the link between religion and violence. Girard explores violence from the perspective of mimetic desire, the place of religion in archaic religious communities, the scapegoat mechanism, and the unique revelation of Christianity, namely, that God is on the side of the victim. Taylor explores and critiques the three principal narratives within Western secular societies that try to address violence: secular humanism, immanent counter-Enlightenment humanism, and Christianity.

In chapter 4, we began dialectically engaging the symbol of cosmic war through an examination of "cosmos." Inasmuch as Juergensmeyer asserts that religious agents motivated by violence mirror on earth some struggle by God against evil in heaven, I argued that Juergensmeyer frames their self-understanding in terms of cosmologically oriented symbols. Against Juergensmeyer, I argued that such agents can better be understood as operating out of an implicit dialectic of grace and sin that accepts the distinction between transcendence and immanence. Such religious agents have already judged who is good and who is evil and see their cause as fighting what they have judged to be evil as doing God's will. However, such an understanding presents a grave danger for religious agents: the misunderstanding of cosmic dualism and, consequently, the lack of an appreciation of cosmos in all its richness as a potentially emerging set of processes.

In contrast, Lonergan's approach argues that genuine religious tradition is grounded in religious conversion: an unrestricted and dynamic being in love with God, sublating moral and intellectual conversion. These transformations open the believer to different virtues and different understandings of what constitutes the cosmos. Lonergan affirms the important distinction between the natural and the supernatural. He grasps an understanding of world processes grounded in recurrent schemes and how by understanding the processes of the natural world we may more intelligently understand processes for development in the human world. In the human world we are both conditioned by processes and are the conditioners of world processes. Human development does not happen by forceful control but rather by creating the conditions that would make possible the development of virtuous persons, cultures of integrity, and new social institutions so that they may recurrently deliver basic goods. Lonergan's insights around the relationship between sacralization and secularization, moreover, help to address many of the concerns that may implicitly motivate the minds and hearts of religious agents motivated to violence as well the minds and hearts of those who mistakenly privilege a wall of separation between the sacred and the secular.

In chapter 5, we explored the notion of cosmic war by examining warfare. I argued against Juergensmeyer's claim that warfare is the business of religion and for the assertion that genuine religion is concerned to form the consciences of people in the paths of justice and love. Again, Lonergan's concerns for the horizon of the subject and for conversion within the subject are particularly relevant. Rather than use the category of warfare to understand the horizon of religious agents motivated to violence, I chose the images of pragmatism, militarism, pacifism, apocalyptic consciousness, and just war. Coates's pragmatist type forms the horizon of subjects who promote the primacy of power relationships and national interest that might be found in the minds of leaders of either secular states or terrorist groups—a horizon that tends toward militarism. When these horizons of understanding are married to distorted religious traditions, there emerges the potential for violence underpinned by a religious justification. I focused on the distorted religious traditions that justified the Second Iraq War, demonstrating the way in which secular states can clothe their decisions for war in religious meaning. I also explored the distorted Islamic tradition of jihad as a justification for war, arguing that there is an alternative and more authentic tradition of jihad that is concerned to advance peace. To move beyond distorted thinking requires a new cultural understanding of justice and new social institutions that deliver stability and economic progress. What is needed is a promotion of conditions that make possible peace, not victory; community, not empire; loving mutuality, not division; legitimate plurality, not a monocultural attitude; and leadership achieved through an appeal to freedom, not domination.

In chapter 6, I argued that Christianity privileges suffering through self-sacrificing love, founded on religious conversion, as the integrating principle within religion that informs a just war tradition. This is an example of what Lonergan calls the healing vector within human history. A careful investigation demonstrates that rather than justifying war or violence, the just war tradition is a means to control violence in the period of deliberation before war, to guide the conduct of war, and to guide the reconstruction stages after battles have ceased. The just war tradition stands in contrast to a dualistic view of the cosmos that understands human communities through the dialectic of friend and enemy, good and evil, grace and sin. Drawing on the just war theory, grounded in religious conversion, people can arrive at a set of principles to guide their deliberations toward what is just. However, I also demonstrated that there are complex methodological issues around the natural law basis of the just war tradition that present problems for those who would argue that only a natural law basis can provide a cross-cultural or global ethic of war. There are also issues emerging from a dialectical engagement with the three key criteria for deliberating about war: legitimate leadership, right intention, and just cause.

In chapter 7, we examined the symbol of martyrdom and its practice within both Christianity and Islam. I demonstrated that martyrdom goes beyond Juergensmeyer's idea of sacrifice, which equates it with a rite of destruction. I argued that true heroism is a necessary, but not a sufficient, condition for true martyrdom. The challenge to true heroism is potentially put before us all when we face suffering, crisis, and dread. The hero or heroine who is informed by courage and strengthened by hope allows suffering to destructure and restructure his or her horizon, even to the point of giving up his or her status as hero. The true hero's or heroine's horizon is morally structured in an ethic of risk, in which no matter how accurate one's judgments of value and decisions may be, in the end they are based on probable averages from which concrete instances diverge. Religious conversion sublates true heroism into an ethic of gratitude and love. An ethic of gratitude postulates that we are discoverers of values before we are creators of them. There is a possibility of discovering authentic values from religious traditions. The ethic of love asserts that we live in a universe in which the love of God invites us to become co-creators with God and not to usurp the role of Creator.

Authentic Christian martyrdom is the outcome of true heroism founded in a love of God and neighbor, seeking to overcome victimization and taking a courageous stance on matters of justice. We also examined Islamic martyrdom and saw both problematic issues that emerge when martyrdom is linked with killing and the need within Islam to control meaning when speaking about martyrdom. Within Islam, one extreme form of killing is suicide martyrdom, which seeks to kill combatants and noncombatants through a form of false heroism. It portrays martyrdom as an overspiritualized reality often fueled by rage and mediated though reactive anger, lacking in charity as its commanding virtue, and contributing to the cycle of violence and further victimization.

In chapter 8, we explored the symbol of demonization and I argued that demonization is a psychological mechanism that stereotypes people and effectively prevents a full understanding of what are the facts and what might be worthwhile. Demonization should not be confused with the process of naming what is evil. Lonergan's account of evil helps us understand the nature of demonization. I explored the social and psychological processes of exclusion and humiliation that provide the conditions for the continuation of demonization that ultimately lead to dehumanization. I also explored the processes of revenge and *ressentiment* that might underpin the kind of stereotyping found in demonizing practices. Further, since the narratives of demonization rely on the powerful use of symbols, I examined the religious symbol of the Cross as a countersymbol to demonization. Lonergan's understanding of redemption in terms of the law of the Cross helps us grasp the link between redemptive love and the emergence of new insights, and provides the means by which a transformation from sin to new cycles of forgiveness can take place. In authentic religious cultures, symbols of good and evil function in such a way as to sensitize the psyche to the divinely originated solution to evil. For Christians, the criteria for understanding the difference between good and evil are to be found in the symbol of the Cross of Christ. Only through a religious appropriation of the Cross can we gain an authentic appropriation of religious symbols such as the symbol of Satan.

In chapter 9, we explored the symbol of warrior empowerment. I dialectically engaged with this symbol and its relevance for twentieth- and twenty-first-century soldiering in Western societies. We saw a development in the Western understanding of the warrior and of his or her relationship to the polis by examining the Homeric traditions, the insights of Socrates, and the virtue ethics of Aristotle. This development can be understood as reflecting a shift from cosmological oriented societies to more anthropologically oriented ones. There is the possibility of both authentic and inauthentic empowerment in soldiery and therefore of different responses to being a soldier, depending on the soldier's religious, moral, and intellectual conversion. A true soldier takes on the task of examining his or her conscience, respecting the conventions of war, and teaching others to do the same. He or she will have to balance the concerns of the state for prosecuting a just war over against the lives of combatants and noncombatants who are killed or injured in the field of battle. The morally empowered soldier is willing to possess a form of detachment that is not ruled by the instrumentalization of reason and the technologism of war.

To conclude, we can see that the work of Juergensmeyer and of Jones is simply inadequate in their analysis of religiously motivated violence and provide no real solutions to the problem. Juergensmeyer's analysis of cosmic war does not fit the self-understanding of religious agents. His understanding of martyrdom, demonization, and warrior empowerment are empirical and lack a normative framework. Though Jones introduces us to the importance of conversion, again his understanding is empirical. In terms of the religious agent's horizon, the grace–sin dialectic and the inadequate understanding of the cosmos that it proposes more accurately describe the religious agent's self-understanding.

By contrast, Lonergan's understanding of the cosmos; his distinction between supernatural and natural; his emphasis on authenticity; his understanding of progress, decline, and redemption in human history; and his exploration of the relationship between the sacred and the secular provide a more complete framework for seeking a solution to the problem of religious violence. What is needed to bring about peace and a just social order is not simply meeting violence with violence but a higher integration in human living personally, culturally, and socially. Lonergan's understanding of conversion is normative, showing us what must happen to human consciousness if a higher integration is to be achieved. Such higher integration helps us distinguish genuine religion from false religion, distorted religious traditions from authentic religious traditions. Genuine religion grounded in transcendent love is the key to conversion and the lens through which we understand authentic martyrdom, the truly demonic, and authentic warriorhood.

# Bibliography

Abou El Fadl, Khaled. "The Orphans of Modernity and the Clash of Civilizations." In *Islam and Global Dialogue: Religious Pluralism and the Pursuit of Peace*, edited by Roger Boase, 179–88. Farnham, UK: Ashgate, 2005.

Accattoli, Luigi. *When a Pope Asks Forgiveness: Mea Culpas of John Paul II.* Translated by Jordan Aumann. New York: Alba House, 2005.

Ahmed, Akbar S. "Islam and the West: Clash or Dialogue of Civilizations?" In *Islam and Global Dialogue: Religious Pluralism and the Pursuit of Peace*, edited by Roger Boase, 103–18. Farnham, UK: Ashgate, 2005.

Ali, Jan A. *Islamic Revivalism Encounters the World: A Study of the Tabligh Jamaat.* New Delhi: Sterling, 2012.

Alison, James. *The Joy of Being Wrong: Original Sin through Easter Eyes.* New York: Crossroad, 1998.

————. *Knowing Jesus.* Springfield, IL: Templegate, 1993.

————. *Raising Abel: The Recovery of the Eschatological Imagination.* New York: Crossroad, 1996.

Allman, Mark. *Who Would Jesus Kill? War, Peace and the Christian Tradition.* Winona, MN: St Mary's, 2008.

Allman, Mark, and Tobias L. Winright. *After the Smoke: The Just War Tradition and Post War Justice.* Maryknoll, NY: Orbis, 2012.

Almond, Gabriel, et al. *Strong Religion: The Rise of Fundamentalisms Around the World.* Chicago: University of Chicago Press, 2003.

Al-Zawahiri, Ayman. "Ayman Al-Zawahiri's Speech." http://www.intelcenter.com/AZAVRA-PUB-vl-l-pdf.

Al-Zawahiri, Ayman, and Osama bin Laden. *Declaration on Armed Struggle Against Jews and Crusaders.* February 23, 1998. http://www.fas.org/irp/wporld.para.docs/980223-fatwa.htm.

Ambrose. *On the Duties of the Clergy.* In vol. 10 of *Nicene and Post-Nicene Fathers of the Christian Church*, edited by Philip Schaff and Henry Wace. Grand Rapids: Eerdmans, 1955.

"America the Beautiful." http://www.scoutsongs.com/lyrics/americathebeautiful.html.

Appleby, R. Scott. *The Ambivalence of the Sacred: Religion, Violence and Reconciliation.* Lanham, MD: Rowman and Littlefield, 2000.

————. "The Unholy Uses of the Apocalyptic Imagination: Twentieth Century Patterns." http://128.36.236.77/workpaper/pdfs/MESV6-4.pdf.

Arendt, Hannah. *The Human Condition: A Study of the Central Dilemmas Facing Modern Man*. Garden City, NY: Doubleday, 1959.

Aristotle. *Nicomachean Ethics*. Translated by Sarah Broadie and Christopher Rowe. Oxford: Oxford University Press, 2002.

Aslan, Reza. *How to Win a Cosmic War: God, Globalization and the End of the War on Terror*. London: Random House, 2009.

Bailie, Gil. *Violence Unveiled: Humanity at the Crossroads*. New York: Crossroad, 1995.

Baum, Gregory. "Remarks of a Theologian in Dialogue with Sociology." In *Theology and the Social Sciences*, edited by Michael Barnes, 3–11. Maryknoll, NY: Orbis, 2001.

Baur, Michael. "What Is Distinctive About Terrorism?" In *Philosophy 9/11: Thinking About the War on Terrorism*, edited by Timothy Shanahan, 3–22. Chicago: Open Court, 2005.

Becker, Ernest. *The Denial of Death*. New York: Free Press, 1973.

Bellinger, Charles K. "Religion and Violence: A Bibliography." http://www.wabashcenter. wabash.edu/resources/article2.aspx/id=10516.

Benedict XVI. *Caritas in Veritate*. http://www.vatican.va/holy_father/benedict_xvi/ encyclicials/document/hf_ben-xvi_enc.

Bergen, Wesley J. "The New Apocalyptic: Modern American Apocalyptic Fiction and Its Ancient and Modern Cousins." http://www.usak.ca/relst/jrpc/art20-newapocalyptic-print.html.

Bilton, Michael, and Kevin Sim. *Four Hours in My Lai: A War Crime and Its Aftermath*. London: Viking, 1992.

Bloch, Maurice. *Prey into Hunter: The Politics of Religious Experience*. Cambridge: Cambridge University Press, 1992.

Bobbit, Philip. *Terror and Consent: The Wars for the 21st Century*. London: Allen Lane, 2008.

Borradori, Giovanni. *Philosophy in a Time of Terror: Dialogues with Jurgen Habermas and Jacques Derrida*. Chicago: University of Chicago Press, 2003.

Bourbonnais, Gaetan. *Behold My Servant: A Study in Reading the Bible Thematically*. Collegeville, MN: Liturgical, 1974.

Boyer, Charlotte. "If You Can, Kill, and If You Cannot, Die: The Development of the Concept of Martyrdom in Islam." http://www.researcharchive.vuw.ac.n2/ handle/10063/1756.

Brass, Paul R. "Victims, Heroes or Martyrs? Partition and the Problem of Memorialization in Contemporary Sikh History." *Sikh Formations* 2 (2006) 17–31.

Brown, Raymond. *Introduction to the New Testament*. New York: Doubleday, 1996.

Burke, Kevin F. "The Crucified People as 'Light to the Nations': A Reflection on Ignacio Ellacuria." In *Rethinking Martyrdom*, edited by Teresa Okure et al., 123–30. London: SCM, 2003.

Burrell, David B. *Towards a Jewish-Christian-Muslim Theology*. West Sussex, UK: Wiley-Blackwell, 2011.

Bush, George. "Address by the President to the Joint Session of Congress: 27 February 2001." http://www.presidency.ucsb.edu/ws/index.php?pid=29643.

————. "Inaugural Address, January 20, 2001." http://www.whitehouse.gov/news/ inaugural-address.html.

————. "State of the Union Address, January 29, 2002." http://www.whitehouse.gov/news/2002/01/20020129-11.html.

Byrne, Patrick H. "Lonergan, Evolutionary Science and Intelligent Design." *Revista Portuguesa de Filosofia* 63 (2007) 893–918.

————. "*Ressentiment* and the Preferential Option for the Poor." *Theological Studies* 54 (1993) 213–41.

Calvert, John. "The Mythic Foundation of Radical Islam." *Orbis* 48 (2004) 29–41.

————. "Sayyid Qutb in America." *International Institute for the Study of Islam Newsletter* 7 (2001) 8.

*Catechism of the Catholic Church.* 2nd ed. Strathfield, NSW: St Pauls, 2003.

Cavanaugh, William. *The Myth of Religious Violence: Secular Ideology and the Roots of Modern Conflict.* Oxford: Oxford University Press, 2009.

Charles, J. Daryl. *Between Pacifism and Jihad: Just War and Christian Tradition.* Downers Grove, IL: InterVarsity, 2005.

Charles, J. Daryl, and Timothy J. Demy. *War, Peace and Christianity: Questions and Answers from a Just War Perspective.* Wheaton, IL: Crossway, 2012.

Choueiri, Youssef M. *Islamic Fundamentalism: The Story of Islamist Movements.* London: Continuum, 2010.

Clark, Patrick Mahaney. "For the Greater Glory: Courage, Death and Virtue in Aquinas and His Philosophical Inheritance." PhD diss., University of Notre Dame. http://etd.nd.edu/ETD-db/theses/available/etd-07152009-101823/unrestricted/ClarkP072010D.pdf.

Clausewitz, Carl von. *On War.* Translated by Michael Howard and Peter Paret. Oxford: Oxford University Press, 2007.

Cliff, Amanda. "Disinhibition and Terrorism." http://ir.canterbury.ac.nz/bitstream/10092/896/1/thesis_fulltext.pdf.

Coates, Anthony Joseph. *The Ethics of War.* Manchester: Manchester University Press, 1997.

Cohn, Norman. *Cosmos, Chaos and the World to Come: The Ancient Roots of Apocalyptic Faith.* New Haven: Yale University Press, 1993.

*A Common Word Between Us.* http://acommonword.com/lib/downloads/CW-Total-Final-v-12g-Eng-9-10-07.pdf.

Cook, David. "The Implications of 'Martyrdom Operations' for Contemporary Islam." *Journal of Religious Ethics* 32 (2004) 129–51.

————. *Martyrdom in Islam.* Cambridge: Cambridge University Press, 2007.

Cooper, Barry. *New Political Religions or An Analysis of Modern Terrorism.* Columbia: University of Missouri Press, 2004.

Cronin, Brian. "Value Ethics: A Lonergan Perspective." http://www.lonergan.org/wp-content/uploads/2010/12/Total-Book.pdf.

Crowe, Frederick. *Lonergan and the Level of Our Time.* Edited by Michael Vertin. Toronto: University of Toronto Press, 2010.

Crysdale, Cynthia. *Embracing Travail: Retrieving the Cross Today.* New York: Continuum, 2001.

————. "The Law of the Cross and Emergent Probability." In *Finding Salvation in Christ: Essays on Christology and Soteriology in Honor of William P. Loewe,* edited by Christopher Denny and Christopher McMahon, 193–214. Eugene, OR: Pickwick, 2011.

――――. "Playing God? Moral Agency in an Emergent World." *Journal of the Society of Christian Ethics* 23 (2003) 243–59.

――――. "Risk, Gratitude, and Love: Grounding Authentic Moral Deliberation." In *The Importance of Insight: Essays in Honour of Michael Vertin*, edited by John Liptay and David Liptay, 151–71. Toronto: University of Toronto Press, 2007.

Crysdale, Cynthia, and Neil Ormerod. *Creator God, Evolving World.* Minneapolis: Fortress, 2013.

Cunningham, Agnes. "Martyr." In *The New Dictionary of Theology*, edited by Joseph Komonchak et al., 628–30. London: Gill and Macmillan, 1987.

Cunningham, Lawrence. "Martyrs Named and Nameless." *America* 195 (2006) 10–13.

Dadosky, John. "Naming the Demon: The 'Structure' of Evil in Lonergan and Girard." *Irish Theological Quarterly* 75 (2010) 355–72.

――――. "Sacralization, Secularization and Religious Fundamentalism." *Studies in Religion* 36 (2007) 513–29.

Daly, Robert. *Sacrifice Unveiled: The True Meaning of Christian Sacrifice.* New York: T. & T. Clark, 2009.

Danner, Mark. "The Horrors of a Camp Called Omarska." http://www.markdanner. com/articles/show/the_horrors_of_a_camp_called_omarska.

Daponte, Paul. *Hope in an Age of Terror.* Maryknoll, NY: Orbis, 2009.

Dawkins, Richard. *The God Delusion.* Sydney: Bantam, 2006.

Denton-Borhaug, Kelly. "The Language of 'Sacrifice' in the Buildup to War: A Feminist Rhetorical and Theological Analysis." http://www.usask.ca/relst/jrpc/art/art15-langsacrifice.html.

Diba, Bahman Aghai. "Role of Hidden Imam in History and the Islamic Republic." http://www.com/main/blog/diba/role-hidden-iman-history-islamic-republic.

Doorley, Mark. "Nonviolence, Creation and Healing." In *Method: Journal of Lonergan Studies* 17 (1999) 97–110.

Doran, Robert. "The Analogy of Dialectics and the Systematics of History." In *Religion in Context: Recent Studies in Lonergan*, edited by Timothy P. Fallon and Philip Boo Riley, 35–57. Lanham, MD: University of America Press, 1988.

――――. "Essays in Systematic Theology 20: Imitating the Divine Relations: A Theological Contribution to Mimetic Theory." http://www.lonerganresource.com/ pdf/books/1/20520%-%Imitating520the%20Divine520Relations.pdf.

――――. "Essays in Systematic Theology 24: Lonergan and Girard on Sacralization and Desacralization." http://www.lonerganresource.com/pdf/books/1/24%20 %-%20Lonergan%20and%20Girard%20on%20Sacralization%20and%20 Desacralization.pdf.

――――. *Intentionality and Psyche.* Vol. 1 of *Theological Foundations.* Milwaukee: Marquette University Press, 1995.

――――. "Introductory Lecture: Lonergan's *Insight*." http://robertmdoran.com/Design/ Assets/Text/Insight%20Notes%20WHOLE.pdf.

――――. "Mimesis." http://www.robertmdoran.com/The%20Trinity%20in%20 History%204%20Mimesis.pdf.

――――. "The Non-Violent Cross: Lonergan and Girard on Redemption." *Theological Studies* 71 (2010) 46–61.

――――. "Suffering Servant and the Scale of Values." *Lonergan Workshop Journal* 4 (1983) 41–68.

————. "System and History: The Challenge to Catholic Systematic Theology." *Theological Studies* 60 (1999) 652–78.

————. "Theological Grounds for a World-Cultural Humanity." In *Creativity and Method: Essays in Honor of Bernard Lonergan*, edited by Matthew Lamb, 105–22. Milwaukee: Marquette University Press, 1981.

————. *Theology and the Dialectics of History*. Toronto: Toronto University Press, 1990.

————. "The Two Ways of Being Conscious: The Notion of Psychic Conversion." http://www.lonerganresourses.com/pdf/lectures/2011-12-10_Doran_-_Two_Ways_of_Being_Conscious.pdf.

Dunne, John. *The Way of All the Earth: Experiments in Truth and Religion*. Notre Dame: University of Notre Dame Press, 1978.

Dunne, Tad. *Doing Better: The Next Revolution in Ethics*. Milwaukee: Marquette University Press, 2010.

————. "Faith, Hope and Charity." *Lonergan Workshop Journal* 5 (1985) 49–70.

————. *Lonergan and Spirituality: Towards a Spiritual Integration*. Chicago: Loyola University Press, 1985.

Durkheim, Emile. *The Elementary Forms of the Religious Life*. New York: Free Press, 1965.

Eickelman, Dale F., and James Piscatori. *Muslim Politics*. Princeton: Princeton University Press, 1996.

Eliade, Mircea. *Cosmos and History: The Myth of Eternal Return*. New York: Harper and Row, 1954.

Esposito, John L. *The Future of Islam*. Oxford: Oxford University Press, 2010.

Farzaneh, Mateo Mohammad. "Shia Ideology, Iranian Secular Nationalism and the Iran-Iraq War (1980–1988)." *Studies in Ethnicity and Nationalism* 7 (2007) 86–103.

Finlay, Moses. *The World of Odysseus*. 2nd ed. London: Penguin, 1979.

Finnis, John. *Aquinas: Moral, Political and Legal Theory*. Cambridge: Cambridge University Press, 1998.

Flanagan, Joseph. *Quest for Self-Knowledge: An Essay in Lonergan's Philosophy*. Toronto: Toronto University Press, 1997.

Flynn, Eileen P. *How Just Is the War on Terror?* New York: Paulist, 2007.

French, Shannon E. "The Code of the Warrior: Why Warriors Need a Code." *Pacem* 6 (2003) 5–16.

Freud, Sigmund. *Totem and Taboo*. Edited by James Strachey. New York: Norton, 1990.

Fuchs, Josef. "Natural Law." In *The New Dictionary of Catholic Social Thought*, edited by Judith Dwyer, 669–75. Collegeville, MN: Liturgical, 1994.

Fuellenbach, John. *The Kingdom of God: The Message of Jesus Today*. Maryknoll, NY: Orbis, 1999.

"Gaza Hamas Leader Condemns bin Laden Killing." http://www.news.yahoo.com/s/afp/20110502/wl_mideast_afp/usattacksbinleadenpalestiniansh.

German Bishops Conference. "Statement of the German Bishops on the 50th Anniversary of the Liberation of the Extermination Camp of Auschwitz on 27 January, 1945." http://www.bc.edu/dam/files/research_sites/cjl/texts/cjrelations/resources/documents/catholic/german_bishops_statement.html.

Gillespie, Michael Allan. "Towards a New Aristocracy: Nietzsche Contra Plato on the Role of the Warrior Elite." http://www.users.polisci.wisc.edu/polphil/GilespieNietzscheWarriors.pdf.

Girard, René. *Deceit, Desire, and the Novel.* Baltimore: Johns Hopkins University Press, 1966.

———. *The Girard Reader.* Edited by James G. Williams. New York: Crossroad, 1996.

———. *I See Satan Fall Like Lightning.* Translated by James G. Williams. Maryknoll, NY: Orbis, 2004.

———. "On War and Apocalypse." http://www.firstthings.com/article/2009/07/apocalypse-now/.

———. *The Scapegoat.* London: Athlone, 1986.

———. "Violence and Religion: Cause or Effect?" http://www.mimetictheory.net/bios/articles/Girard_Violence_and_religion.pdf.

———. *Violence and the Sacred.* Baltimore: Johns Hopkins University Press, 1977.

Girard, René, et al. *Things Hidden Since the Foundation of the World.* London: Continuum, 2003.

Goldziher, Ignaz. *Muslim Studies.* Vol. 2. London: Allen and Unwin, 1971.

Gregson, Vernon. "'The Faces of Evil and Our Response: Ricoeur, Lonergan and Moore." In *Religion in Context: Recent Studies in Lonergan*, edited by Timothy P. Fallon and Philip Boo Riley, 125–39. Lanham, MD: University of America Press, 1988.

———. *Lonergan, Spirituality and the Meeting of Religions.* New York: University Press of America, 1985.

Griffith, Lee. *The War on Terrorism and the Terror of God.* Grand Rapids: Eerdmans, 2002.

Gulen, Fethullah. "Lesser and Greater Jihad." http://www.fethullahgulen.org/fethullah-gulens-works/toward-a-global-civilization-of-love-and-tolerance/jihad-terrorism-human-rights/25257-lesser-and-greater-jihad.

Harris, Sam. *The End of Faith: Religion, Terror and the Future of Religion.* New York: Norton, 2005.

Herbert, T. Walter. *Faith-Based War: From 9/11 to Catastrophic Success in Iraq.* London: Equinox, 2009.

Hicks, Madelyn Hsiao-Rei, et al. "Casualties in Civilians and Coalition Soldiers from Suicide Bombings in Iraq, 2003–2010: A Descriptive Study," *Lancet* 378 (2011) 906–14.

Himes, Kenneth R. "War." In *The New Dictionary of Catholic Social Thought*, edited by Judith A. Dwyer, 977–82. Collegeville, MN: Liturgical, 1994.

Hitchens, Christopher. *God Is Not Great: How Religion Poisons Everything.* Crows Nest, NSW: Allen and Unwin, 2007.

Hook, Reno, and R. R. Reno. *Heroism and the Christian Life: Reclaiming Excellence.* Louisville: Westminster John Knox, 2000.

Howard, Damian. "Differently Crucified: Understanding the Islamic Martyrs." *The Way* 48 (2009) 79–94.

Hughes, Glenn. *Transcendence and History: The Search for Ultimacy from Ancient Societies to Postmodernity.* Columbia: University of Missouri Press, 2003.

Ibrahim, Fouad. "Al Shahada: A Centre of the Shiite System of Belief." In *Dying for Faith: Religiously Motivated Violence in the Contemporary World*, edited by Madawi Al-Rasheed and Marat Shterin, 111–22. London: I. B. Taurus, 2009.

International Theological Commission. *Memory and Reconciliation: The Church and the Faults of the Past.* http://www.vatican.va/roman_curia/congregations/cfaith/cti_documents/rc_con_cfaith_doc_20000307_memory-reconc-itc_en.html.

Jägerstätter, Franz. *Letters and Writings from Prison*. Edited by Erna Putz. Translated by Robert Krieg. Maryknoll, NY: Orbis, 2010.

Jaspers, Karl. *The Origin and Goal of History*. New Haven: Yale University Press, 1953.

John Paul II. Homily from the Day of Pardon, March 12, 2000. http://www.vatican.va/holy_father/john_paul?ii/homilies/documnets/hf_jp-ii_hom_20000312_pardon_en.html.

Johnston, David L. "Chandra Muzaffar's Islamic Critique of Globalisation: A Malaysian Contribution to a Global Ethic." http://www.latrobe.edu.au/dialogue/assets/downloads/WP2006-3.pdf.

Johnston, William M. "Whatever Happened to Doctrine? Ninian Smart's Scheme of Seven Dimensions of Religion and the 'Spirituality Revolution' in the West." In *Wisdom for Life*, edited by Michael Kelly and Mark O'Brien, 169–82. Adelaide: ATF, 2005.

Jones, James W. *Blood that Cries Out from the Earth: The Psychology of Religious Terrorism*. Oxford: Oxford University Press, 2003.

———. *Converting to Terrorism: What the Psychology of Religion Tells Us about Religiously Motivated Terrorism*. http://www.bloodthatciresout.com/sitbuildercontent/sitbuilderfiles/terrorismconversionpaper2.pdf.

———. "Eternal Warfare: Violence on the Mind of American Christianity." In *The Fundamentalist Mindset: Psychological Perspectives on Religion, Violence and History*, edited by Charles B. Strozier et al., 91–103. Oxford: Oxford University Press, 2010.

———. "Why Does Religion Turn Violent? A Psychoanalytic Exploration of Religious Terrorism," *Psychoanalytic Review* 93 (2006) 167–90.

Juergensmeyer, Mark. "From Bhindranwale to bin Laden: The Rise of Religious Violence." http://escholarship.org/uc/item/7322q2p5.

———. "Gandhi vs. Terrorism," *Daedalus: Journal of the American Academy of Arts and Science* 136 (2007) 30–39.

———. "Is Religion the Problem?" http://juergensmeyer.com/files/hedgehog.doc.

———. "Religious Violence." In *The Oxford Handbook of the Sociology of Religion*, edited by Peter B. Clarke, 890–908. Oxford: Oxford University Press, 2009.

———. *Terror in the Mind of God: The Global Rise of Religious Violence*. Berkeley: University of California Press, 2003.

Karawan, Ibrahim. "The Islamist Impasse." International Institute for Strategic Studies, Adelphi Paper 314, 1–80. Oxford: Oxford University Press, 1997.

Kearney, Richard. *Strangers, Gods and Monsters: Interpreting Otherness*. London: Routledge, 2003.

Kelly, Anthony J. *Eschatology and Hope*. Maryknoll, NY: Orbis, 2006.

———. "The Global Significance of Natural Law: Opportunities, Quandaries and Directions." http://acu.edu.au/_data/assests/phf_file/0004/107527/Kelly_Natural_Law.pdf.

Kelsay, John. *Arguing the Just War in Islam*. Cambridge, MA: Harvard University Press, 2007.

———. "Arguments Concerning Resistance in Contemporary Islam." In *The Ethics of War: Shared Problems in Different Traditions*, edited by Richard Sorabji and David Rodin, 61–88. Farnham, UK: Ashgate, 2006.

———. *Islam and War: The Gulf War and Beyond*. Louisville: Westminster John Knox, 1993.

Kereszty, Roch A. *Jesus Christ: Fundamentals of Christology*. New York: Alba House, 2002.

Kimball, Charles. *When Religion Becomes Evil*. New York: HarperCollins, 2002.

Kirwan, Michael. *Discovering Girard*. London: Darton, Longman and Todd, 2004.

———. *Girard and Theology*. London: T. & T. Clark, 2009.

———. "Girard, Religion, Violence and Martyrdom." In *The Oxford Handbook of the Sociology of Religion*, edited by Peter Clark, 909–23. Oxford: Oxford University Press, 2009.

Kleiderer, John, et al. *Just War, Lasting Peace: What Christian Traditions Can Teach Us*. Maryknoll, NY: Orbis, 2006.

Kraugerud, Hanne A. "Shields of Humanity: The Ethical Constraints of Professional Combatants." *Journal of Military Ethics* 10 (2011) 263–73.

Kristeva, Julia. *Strangers to Ourselves*. London: Harvester, 1991.

Kung, Hans. *Islam: Past, Present and Future*. Oxford: Oneworld, 2007.

LaHaye, T, and John B. Jenkins. "Left Behind." http://www.leftbehind.com.

Lamb, Matthew. "Christianity within the Political Dialectics of Community and Empire." In *Cities of Gods: Faith, Politics and Pluralism in Judaism, Christianity and Islam*, edited by Nigel Biggar et al., 73–100. Westport, CT: Greenwood, 1986.

———. "The Social and Political Dimensions of Lonergan's Theology." In *The Desires of the Human Heart: An Introduction to the Theology of Bernard Lonergan*, edited by Vernon Gregson, 255–84. Metcalfe, ON: LWS, 2004.

Lamoureux, Patricia, and Paul Wadell. *The Christian Moral Life: Faithful Discipleship for a Global Society*. Maryknoll, NY: Orbis, 2010.

Lapidus, Ira M. "Islamic Revival and Modernity: The Contemporary Movements and the Historical Paradigms." *Journal of the Economic and Social History of the Orient* 40 (1997) 444–60.

Lee, Steven P. *Ethics and War: An Introduction*. Cambridge: Cambridge University Press, 2012.

Lerner, Michael. *Healing Israel/Palestine: A Path to Peace and Reconciliation*. San Francisco: Tikkun, 2003.

Lewinstein, Keith. "The Revaluation of Martyrdom in Early Islam." In *Sacrificing the Self: Perspectives on Martyrdom and Religion*, edited by Margaret Cormack, 78–91. Oxford: Oxford University Press, 2002.

Lewis, Scott M. "Is Apocalyptic Imagination Killing Us?" http://www.baylor.edu/content/services/document.php/106710.pdf.

Lieven, Anatol. *America Right or Wrong: An Anatomy of American Nationalism*. Oxford: Oxford University Press, 2004.

Lind, Millard C. *Yahweh Is a Warrior: The Theology of Warfare in Ancient Israel*. Ontario: Herald, 1980.

Loboda, Luke. "The Thought of Sayyid Qutb." http://wwwashbrook.org/publicat/thesis/loboda/home.html.

Loewe, William P. *Introduction to Christology*. Collegeville, MN: Liturgical, 1996.

Lonergan, Bernard. *Collection*. Edited by Fredrick E. Crowe and Robert M. Doran. 2nd ed. Vol. 4 of *Collected Works of Bernard Lonergan*. Toronto: University of Toronto Press, 1988.

———. *Grace and Freedom: Operative Grace in the Thought of St Thomas Aquinas*. Edited by Frederick E. Crowe and Robert M. Doran. Vol. 1 of *Collected Works of Bernard Lonergan*. Toronto: Toronto University Press, 2000.

———. *Insight: A Study in Human Understanding*. Edited by Fredrick E. Crowe and Robert M. Doran. Vol. 3 of *Collected Works of Bernard Lonergan*. Toronto: Toronto University Press, 1997.

———. *The Lonergan Reader*. Edited by Mark D. Morelli and Elizabeth A. Morelli. Toronto: University of Toronto Press, 1997.

———. *Method in Theology*. Toronto: University of Toronto Press, 1996.

———. *Phenomenology and Logic: The Boston College Lectures on Mathematical Logic and Existentialism*. Edited by Philip McShane. Vol. 18 of *Collected Works of Bernard Lonergan*. Toronto: University of Toronto Press, 2001.

———. *Philosophical and Theological Papers, 1958–1964*. Edited by Robert C. Croken and Robert Doran. Vol. 6 of *Collected Works of Bernard Lonergan*. Toronto: University of Toronto Press, 1996.

———. *Philosophical and Theological Papers, 1965–1980*. Edited by Robert C. Croken and Robert Doran. Vol. 17 of *Collected Works of Bernard Lonergan*. Toronto: University of Toronto Press, 2004.

———. *Philosophy of God and Theology*. London: Darton, Longman and Todd, 1973.

———. *A Second Collection*. Edited by William F. J. Ryan and Bernard J. Tyrrell. London: Darton, Longman and Todd, 1974.

———. *A Third Collection*. Edited by Frederick Crowe. New York: Paulist, 1985.

———. *Topics in Education*. Edited by Frederick E. Crowe and Robert M. Doran. Vol. 10 of *Collected Works of Bernard Lonergan*. Toronto: Toronto University Press, 1993.

———. *Understanding and Being*. Edited by Frederick E. Crowe and Robert M. Doran. Vol. 5 of *Collected Works of Bernard Lonergan*. Toronto: Lonergan Research Institute, 1990.

Long, D. Stephen, and Geoffrey Holdsclaw. "Is There Anything Worth Dying For? Martyrdom, Exteriority, Politics after Bare Life." In *Witness of the Body: The Past, Present and Future of Christian Martyrdom*, edited by Michael L. Budde and Karen Scott, 171–91. Grand Rapids: Eerdmans, 2011.

Lovett, Brendan. *A Dragon Not for the Killing*. Quezon City, Philippines: Claretian, 1996.

Lyonnet, Stanislas. "Satan." In *The Dictionary of Biblical Theology*, edited by Xavier Leon-Dufour, 522–23. London: Geoffrey Chapman, 1973.

MacIntyre, Alasdair. *After Virtue: A Study in Moral Theory*. 2nd ed. Notre Dame: University of Notre Dame Press, 1984.

Malka, Haim. "Must the Innocent Die? The Islamic Debate over Suicide Attacks." http://www.meforum.org/530/must-innocents-die-the-islamic-debate-over.html.

Marranci, Gabriele. *Jihad Beyond Islam*. New York: Berg, 2006.

McCarthy, Michael. *The Crisis of Philosophy*. Albany: State University of New York Press, 1990.

McEvenue, Sean. *Interpretation and the Bible: Essays on Truth in Literature*. Collegeville, MN: Liturgical, 1994.

McInerney, Patrick J. "Religion and Violence." In *Religion and Violence*, edited by Jonathan Inkpin, 1–16. Adelaide: ATF, 2007.

McPartland, Thomas. *Lonergan and the Philosophy of Historical Existence*. Columbia: University of Missouri Press, 2001.

Melchin, Kenneth R. *Living with Other People: An Introduction to Christian Ethics Based on Bernard Lonergan*. Collegeville, MN: Liturgical, 1998.

————. "Moral Knowledge and the Structure of Cooperative Living." *Theological Studies* 52 (1991) 495–523.

Melchin, Kenneth, and Cheryl Picard. *Transforming Conflict through Insight*. Toronto: University of Toronto Press, 2008.

Miller, Jerome A. "All Love Is Self-Surrender." *Method: Journal of Lonergan Studies* 13 (1995) 53–81.

————. *In the Throes of Wonder: Intimations of the Sacred in a Post-Modern World*. Albany: State University of New York Press, 1992.

————. "The Trauma of Evil and the Traumatological Conception of Forgiveness." *Continental Philosophy Review* 42 (2009) 401–19.

————. *The Way of Suffering: A Geography Crisis*. Washington, DC: Georgetown University Press, 1988.

————. "Wound Made Fountain: Toward a Theology of Redemption." *Theological Studies* 70 (2009) 525–54.

Moaddel, Manoora. *Islamic Modernism, Nationalism and Fundamentalism: Episode and Discourse*. Chicago: University of Chicago Press, 2005.

Moghadam, Assaf. "Motives for Martyrdom: Al Qaida, Salafi Jihad and the Spread of Suicide Attacks." *International Security* 33 (2008–09) 46–78.

Mooney, T. Brian. "Old Wine in New Skins: Aquinas, Just War and Terrorism." *Pacifica* 20 (2007) 204–18.

Moore, Sebastian. *The Contagion of Jesus: Doing Theology as If It Mattered*. London: Darton, Longman and Todd, 2009.

Morelli, Elizabeth A. "The Appropriation of Existential Consciousness." *Method: Journal of Lonergan Studies* 6 (1988) 50–62.

Morelli, Elizabeth M. "Reflections on the Appropriation of Moral Consciousness." *Lonergan Workshop Journal* 13 (1997) 161–89.

————. "*Ressentiment* and Rationality." http://bu,edu/wcp/Papers/Anth/AnthMore.htm.

————. "*Ressentiment* and Redemption." *Lonergan Workshop Journal* 14 (1998) 197–228.

Moussalli, Ahmed. *Radical Islamic Fundamentalism: The Ideological and Political Discourse of Sayyid Qutb*. Beirut: American Beirut University Press, 1992.

Myers, Ched, and Elaine Enns. *New Testament Reflections on Restorative Justice and Peacemaking*. Vol. 1 of *Ambassadors of Reconciliation*. Maryknoll, NY: Orbis, 2009.

Nasr, Vali. *The Shia Revival*. New York: Norton, 2006.

Niditch, Susan. *War in the Hebrew Bible*. New York: Oxford University Press, 1993.

Noor, Farish A. "Islam and/in the West: The Revenge of a Distorted History." In *Terrorizing the Truth: The Shape of Contemporary Images of Islam and Muslims in Media*, edited by Farish A. Noor, 37–57. Penang, Malaysia: Juta Print, 1997.

Northcott, Michael. *An Angel Directs the Storm: Apocalyptic Religion and American Empire*. London: SCM, 2007.

————. "An Angel Directs the Storm: The Religious Politics of American Neo-Conservatism." *Political Theology* 5 (2004) 137–58.

Olkovich, Nick. "Conceptualism, Classicism and Bernard Lonergan's Retrieval of Aquinas." *Pacifica* 26 (2013) 37–58.

Omar, A. Rashied. "Islam and Violence: Revisited." http://www.ocw.nd.edu/peace-studies/islamic-ethics-of-war-and-peace/readins-1/islam-and-violence-revisted.

"Onward, Christian Soldiers." http://www.hymnsite.com/lyrics/umh575.sht.

Ormerod, Neil. *Creation, Grace and Redemption.* Maryknoll, NY: Orbis, 2007.

————. "A Dialectical Engagement with the Social Sciences in an Ecclesiological Context." *Theological Studies* 66 (2005) 815–40.

————. "The Eucharist as Sacrifice." In *The Eucharist: Faith and Worship*, edited by Margaret Press, 42–55. Strathfield, NSW: St Pauls, 2001.

————. *Grace and Disgrace: A Theology of Self-Esteem, Society and History.* Sydney: E. J. Dwyer, 1994.

Ormerod, Neil, and Shane Clifton. *Globalization and the Mission of the Church.* London: T. & T. Clark, 2009.

Otto, Rudolf. *The Idea of the Holy.* Translated by John W. Harvey. New York: Oxford University Press, 1958.

Plato. *Gorgias, Menexenus, Protagoras.* Edited by Malcolm Schofield. Translated by Tom Griffith. Cambridge Texts in the History of Political Thought. Cambridge: Cambridge University Press, 2010.

Qutb, Sayyid. *Milestones.* http://www.majalla.org/books/2005/qutb-milestones.pdf.

Rahimi, Barak. "Dying a Martyr's Death: The Political Culture of Self-Sacrifice in Contemporary Islamists." http://hirr.hartsem.edu/sociology/rahimi.html.

Ramadan, Tariq. *Western Muslims and the Future of Islam.* Oxford: Oxford University Press, 2005.

Rapoport, David C. "Messianic Sanctions for Terror." *Comparative Politics* 20 (1988) 195–213.

Renard, John. *Islam and Christianity: Theological Themes in Comparative Perspective.* Berkeley: University of California Press, 2011.

Reuter, Christopher. *My Life Is a Weapon: A Modern History of Suicide Bombing.* Princeton: Princeton University Press, 2004.

Reuther, Rosemary. "American Empire and the War against Evil." http://www.r1911truth.org/index.php?option=com_content&view=article7id=54:reuther-ros.

Ricoeur, Paul. *The Symbolism of Evil.* New York: Harper and Row, 1967.

Riley, Philip Boo. "Theology and/or Religious Studies: Bernard Lonergan's Option." *Lonergan Workshop Journal* 4 (1983) 115–40.

Robinson, Francis. "Islam and the West: Clash of Civilisation?" In *Islam and Global Dialogue: Religious Pluralism and the Pursuit of Peace*, edited by Roger Boase, 77–89. Farnham, UK: Ashgate, 2005.

Sachedina, Abdulaziz. "The Development of *Jihad* in Islamic Revelation and History." In *Cross, Crescent and Sword: The Justification and Limitation of War in Western and Islamic Tradition*, edited by James Turner Johnson and John Kelsay, 35–51. Westport, CT: Greenwood, 1990.

Saeed, Abdullah, and Hassan Saeed. *Freedom of Religion, Apostasy and Islam.* Farnham, UK: Ashgate, 2004.

Sagovsky, Nicholas. *Christian Tradition and the Practice of Justice.* London: SPCK, 2008.

Said, Jawdat. *The Way of Adam's Son: The Problem of Violence in Muslim Activism.* Beirut: Dar al-Fikr al-Mu'asir, 1993.

Scarry, Elaine. *The Body in Pain.* New York: Oxford University Press, 1985.

Schubeck, Thomas L. "Salvadoran Martyrs: A Love that Dares Justice." *Horizons* 28 (2001) 7–29.

Schweitzer, Yoram. "Suicide Bombing: Development and Characteristics." http://www.ict.org.il.

Segev, Tom. *Soldiers of Evil: The Commandments of the Nazi Concentration Camps.* New York: Berkeley, 1987.

Shah-Kazemi, Reza. "God, the Loving." In *A Common Word: Muslims and Christians on Loving God and Neighbor,* edited by Miroslav Volf et al., 88–109. Grand Rapids: Eerdmans, 2010.

Shriver, Donald W., Jr. "Bridging the Abyss of Revenge." http://www.religion-online.org/showarticle.asp?title=1523.

———. *An Ethic For Enemies: Forgiveness in Politics.* Oxford: Oxford University Press, 1995.

Shute, Michael, and William Zanardi. *Improving Moral Decision Making.* Halifax, NS: Axial, 2003.

Singer, Peter. *The President of Good and Evil: Taking George W. Bush Seriously.* London: Granta, 2004.

Sivan, Emmanuel. *Radical Islam: Medieval Theology and Modern Politics.* New Haven: Yale University Press, 1985.

Slattery, William M. *Jesus the Warrior? Historical Christian Perspectives and Problems on the Morality of War and the Waging of Peace.* Milwaukee: Marquette University Press, 2007.

Smart, Ninian. *The World's Religions: Old Traditions and Modern Transformations.* Cambridge: Cambridge University Press, 1989.

Solomon, Norman. "The Ethics of War: Judaism." In *The Ethics of War: Shared Problems in Different Traditions,* edited by Richard Sorabji and David Rodin, 108–30. Farnham, UK: Ashgate, 2006.

Sonn, Tamara. "Irregular Warfare and Terrorism in Islam: Asking the Right Question." In *Cross, Crescent and Sword: The Justification and Limitation of War in Western and Islamic Tradition,* edited by James Turner Johnson and John Kelsay, 55–71. Westport, CT: Greenwood, 1990.

Squire, Aelred. *Asking the Fathers: The Art of Meditation and Prayer.* 2nd ed. New York: Paulist, 1994.

Stefanson, Dominic. "Man as Hero—Hero as Citizen: Models of Heroic Thought and Action in Homer, Plato and Rousseau" PhD diss., University of Adelaide, 2004. http://www.digital.library.adelaide.edu.au/dspace/bitstream/2440/37731/1/02whole.pdf.

Stein, Ruth. "Evil as Love and as Liberation: The Mind of a Suicidal Religious Terrorist." *Psychoanalytic Dialogues* 12 (2002) 393–420.

———. "Fundamentalism, Father and Son and Vertical Desire." *Psychoanalytic Review* 96 (2009) 201–29.

Strozier, Charles. "The Apocalyptic Other." In *The Fundamentalist Mindset: Psychological Perspectives on Religion, Violence and History,* edited by Charles B. Strozier et al., 62–70. Oxford: Oxford University Press, 2010.

———. "Opening the Seven Seals of Fundamentalism." In *The Fundamentalist Mindset: Psychological Perspectives on Religion, Violence and History,* edited by Charles B. Strozier et al., 104–19. Oxford: Oxford University Press, 2010.

Strozier, Charles, and Katharine Boyd. "The Apocalyptic." In *The Fundamentalist Mindset: Psychological Perspectives on Religion, Violence and History,* edited by Charles B. Strozier et al., 29–37. Oxford: Oxford University Press, 2010.

Sullivan, Anthony T. "Conservative Ecumenism: Politically Incorrect Meditations on Islam and the West." In *Islam and Global Dialogue: Religious Pluralism and the Pursuit of Peace*, edited by Roger Boase, 139–58. Farnham, UK: Ashgate, 2005.

Tamini, Azam. "The Islamic Debate over Self-Inflicted Martyrdom." In *Dying for Faith: Religiously Motivated Violence in the Contemporary World*, edited by Madawi Al-Rasheed and Marat Shterin, 91–104. New York: I. B.Taurus, 2009.

Taylor, Charles. "Notes on the Sources of Violence: Perennial and Modern." In *Beyond Violence: Religious Sources of Social Transformation in Judaism, Christianity and Islam*, edited by James L. Heft, 15–42. New York: Fordham University Press, 2004.

———. *A Secular Age*. Cambridge, MA: Belknap Press of Harvard University Press, 2007.

———. "Spirituality of Life and Its Shadow." *Compass* 14 (1996) 10–13.

Treverton, Gregory F., et al. "Exploring Religious Conflict." http://www.rand.org/pubs/conf_proceedings/2005/RAND_CF211.sum.pdf.

Tuman, Joseph S. *Communicating Terror: The Rhetorical Dimensions of Terrorism*. London: Sage, 2010.

Voegelin, Eric. *The Ecumenic Age*. Vol. 4 of *Order and History*. Edited by Michael Franz. Columbia: University of Missouri Press, 2000.

———. *Israel and Revelation*. Vol. 1 of *Order and History*. Baton Rouge: Louisiana State University Press, 1956.

———. *Plato and Aristotle*. Vol. 3 of *Order and History*. Baton Rouge: Louisiana State University Press, 1957.

Volf, Miroslav. *The End of Memory: Remembering Rightly in a Violent World*. Grand Rapids: Eerdmans, 2006.

———. *Exclusion and Embrace: A Theological Exploration of Identity, Otherness and Reconciliation*. Nashville: Abingdon, 1996.

Wagner, Walter H. *Opening the Qur'an: Introducing Islam's Holy Book*. Notre Dame: University of Notre Dame Press, 2008.

Waller, James. *Becoming Evil*. Oxford: Oxford University Press, 2002.

"Warrior Transition Command." http://wtc.army.mil/about_us/command_staff.html.

Webb, Eugene. *The Self Between: From Freud to the New Social Psychology of France*. Seattle: University of Washington Press, 1993.

———. *Worldviews and Mind: Religious Thought and Psychological Development*. Columbia: University of Missouri Press, 2009.

Wilkins, Jeremy D. "Grace and Growth: Aquinas, Lonergan, and the Problematic of Habitual Grace." *Theological Studies* 72 (2011) 723–48.

Wink, Walter. *Engaging the Powers: Discernment and Resistance in a World of Domination*. Minneapolis: Fortress, 1992.

———. "The Myth of Redemptive Violence." In *The Destructive Power of Religion: Violence in Judaism, Christianity and Islam*, vol. 3, edited by J. Harold Ellens, 265–86. London: Praeger, 2004.

Wittgenstein, Ludwig. *Philosophical Investigations*. Oxford: Blackwell, 1953.

Wright, N. T. "The Servant and Jesus." In *Jesus and the Suffering Servant: Isaiah 53 and Christian Origins*, edited by William H. Bellinger and William R. Farmer, 281–97. Harrisburg, PA: Trinity, 1998.

Yearley, H. *Menius and Aquinas: Theories of Virtues and Conceptions of Courage*. Albany: State University of New York Press, 1990.

# Index

Lonergan's *Insight* and *Method in Theology* are not listed in this index, but topics from those books are.

Suffering Servant
   in New Testament, 144
   in Old Testament, 143
Sufism, 187–88
suicide and martyrdom, 177
suicide bombers and Islamic
     martyrdom, 182–86
suicide bombings, 183
Sullivan, Anthony T.
   on *hirabah*, 135
Sunni martyrdom, 177, 180
Sunnis and Shiites, 178
supernatural, the
   natural and, 99–100
surd, social, 111
symbols
   death and, 157
   feelings and, 54
   genuine, 210–11
   God and, 98
   idolatry, 94

*tawhid*, 136
Taylor, Charles
   on Christianity and transcendence,
     24–27
   on immanent counter-Enligtenment
     humanism, 23–24
   on inauthentic warriorhood, 234
   "maximal demand," 24
   *Secular Age, A*, 19–27
   on secular humanism, 20–23
*telos*, 225–26
terror, 160
*Terror in the Mind of God*
   (Juergensmeyer), 32–40
terrorism, 37, 130
   guerilla warfare and, 130
   religion and, 131
   social conditions and, 154
Tertullian on soldiering, 228
theological virtues, 169n66
theory, realm of, 51–52
Thomas Aquinas, St.
   on charity and martyrdom, 169
   on courage, 162
   on courage and hope, 170
   criteria for a just war, 147

   on martyrdom and the Christian
     faith, 171
   on war, 229
Thompson, Hugh
   proper conduct in war and, 232–33
totalitarianism, 109
   religious, 97
"Totenkopf" battalion and inauthentic
     warriorhood, 233–34
tragic set. *See* humanism, immanent
   counter-Enlightenment
transcendence
   Christianity and, 24–27
   divine, 79
   false, 233–34
   immanence and, 68–69
   realm of, 53
   religion and, 34
transcendence and limitation and
     human development, 64–65
transformation, personal
   jihad as, 136
tribalism, 57
Truth and Reconciliation Commission
   (South Africa), 106
Tylor, E. B.
   on cosmological culture, 92

Umayyad dynasty, 133
understanding, 4, 49–50
   *See also* insights
unintelligibility and evil, 193–94
United States of America and
     justification of war, 125–30

values
   deliberating on, 47
   dialectic and, 11
   feelings and, 53
   formative influences on, 55–56
   hierarchy or scale of, 63–73
   moral conversion and, 59
   mutual conditioning between,
     72–73
   self-transcendence and, 53
vectors, 55
*via negativa*, 77